SSD

◇ LIFE LINES ◇

ex libris

When you have read
this book please return
it immediately to the
Ship's Library — another
reader may be waiting
for it. It will help greatly
if books are returned in
good time prior to your
leaving the ship.

◊ LIFE LINES ◊

Politics and Health 1986–1988

EDWINA CURRIE

Look to your health: and if you have it, praise God, and value it next to a good conscience; for health is the second blessing that we mortals are capable of; a blessing that money cannot buy.

Izaak Walton, *The Compleat Angler*

SIDGWICK & JACKSON
LONDON

First published in Great Britain in 1989 by
Sidgwick & Jackson Limited

The Author and Publishers would like to extend their thanks to
the following for permission to reproduce and/or quote: The
Agriculture Committee for the salmonella chart on p. 256; The
Coronary Prevention/British Heart Foundation for the map on
p. 15; the *Daily Mail* for the cartoon by Mac on p. 263 (6 December
1988); Mirror Group Newspapers for the cartoon by Reg Smythe
on p. 37; the *Evening Standard* for the bill board on p. 137; Express
Newspapers for the cartoon by Giles reproduced on p. 98
(15 February 1987) and for the cartoon by Bill Caldwell on p. 51
(12 March 1987); The Health Education Authority for the cartoon
on p. 49 taken from *The People Say How They Gave Up Smoking*;
Independent Television News Limited for the interview on pp.
259–61 (3 December 1988); London Weekend Television Limited
for *First Aids* on p. 82 (February 1987); The *Northumberland
Gazette* for the extract on pp. 17–18; Solo for the cartoon by Mac
on p. 209; The Royal Norwegian Embassy for the illustration
on p. 81.

ISBN 0-283-99920-9

Photoset by Rowland Phototypesetting Limited
Bury St Edmunds, Suffolk
Printed and bound in Great Britain by
Mackays of Chatham plc, Chatham, Kent
for Sidgwick & Jackson Limited
1 Tavistock Chambers
Bloomsbury Way
London WC1A 2SG

This book is for those,
including Jeanette Smith,
who died too young;
and for the civil servants,
who did all the work

Contents

Foreword

This book does not attempt to be a comprehensive account of Conservative health policy in the 1980s, nor, I hope, is it simply a piece of self-justification. My academic background is in economic and social history and I hope this contribution can be seen in that light.

I wrote it because I was there, from 1986 to 1988, under three different Secretaries of State for Health, and because there were issues which seemed important to me and to many others in our country during those years. They were times of tremendous change and development and of considerable shifts of attitude to health. The book cannot be comprehensive: I have therefore concentrated on those areas of work which were my particular responsibility and, within that, mainly topics to do with the promotion of better health. That means the omission of many other items – transplantation and our work on donor cards, community care, mental illness, the reforms of the NHS which dominated our thinking in 1988 and onward.

To what extent all this effort will produce an improvement in general health remains to be seen. One result may well be that no one will ever believe again that life-style has no effect on health. Instead, the links, albeit complex, between health and diet, smoking, alcohol, exercise and other patterns of culture and behaviour will be better understood. Individuals will expect far more information from ministers to help them make changes and so improve their own health rather than turning, helpless and dependent, to medicine and to the state. Independence and choice are the essence of the Conservative philosophy in my view. Others will judge in years to come whether the campaigns worked, but I am satisfied that the effort was worthwhile.

Acknowledgements

Many people contributed to the work described in the book, but my thanks are especially due to: Terry Banks of the Office of Population and Census Surveys; Jinty Blanckenhagen of the Breast Care & Mastectomy Association; Lady Ewart-Biggs; Michael Fallon, MP; Drs Spencer Hagard and Donald Reid and staff of the Health Education Authority; Sammy Harari of TBWA; Evangeline Hunter-Jones of the Women's National Cancer Control Campaign; Professor Bernard Isaacs and the 'Thousand Elders' of Birmingham University; Robin N. Maddy, MHCIHMA; Norma Major; Dorothy Moriarty and Tom Riley at Help the Aged; Renee Myers; Mike O'Connor of the Coronary Prevention Group; Esther Rantzen and Valerie Howarth of Childline; Gillian Shephard, MP; Peter Thompson of the Advertising Standards Authority.

Thanks also to Hilary Rubinstein, William Armstrong, Alan Gordon Walker, Brian MacArthur who encouraged me to write; to Clare Whelan who did so much more than typing the script, and Christine Heald and Jane Lea who kept my other work going meantime; to my husband, Ray, and to many more who offered support, friendship and advice.

1

Moving the Goalposts

Fain would I climb, yet fear I to fall
scratched on a window pane by Sir Walter Ralegh
If thy heart fails thee, climb not at all
underneath, reputedly by Elizabeth I

The telephone rang. And rang again.

It was 3 p.m. on Wednesday 10 September 1986. I had never really expected it to ring; these things only happen in dreams – other people's dreams usually. There had been endless press speculation but no wise politician takes any notice of that. Outside, in the early autumn sunlight, there was a flurry of activity. A TV cameraman was scrambling to his feet and hauling equipment on to his shoulder. Someone else switched on a spotlight and played it through the window. They had been out there all day. There was not much I could do about them as a public footpath goes close to my house. Anyway, I wasn't paying them any attention.

The telephone was still ringing, a bit impatiently now.

I picked the receiver up, and was surprised to hear not the expected familiar female tones, but a man's voice, someone I didn't know.

'Mrs Currie? Ah yes, good. Are you busy this afternoon? Nothing important? The Prime Minister would like a word with you, and she was wondering if you could come down to Number 10. How long would it take you?'

'Must allow four hours from Derbyshire,' I whispered. 'Could get there by 7 p.m.'

'Excellent, that will do. There's no hurry, mind. If it is more convenient, tomorrow will do.'

'No, I'll come now.'

1

I put the phone down, a little puzzled. This was not the way it was supposed to happen, quite. Doubt suddenly spawned. It would not be the first time I had been the victim of a practical joke. On one occasion I had had an odd request, apparently from the constituency, to go up midweek for an obscure function, and had politely refused. A few days later, someone else phoned and asked if I was free that day to address a big London lunch for a fee of £1,000 and I had (naturally!) said I was interested. A certain satirical magazine then printed a story that I wouldn't go near my constituency but was available in London for money. Some bright spark could just be behind that voice, and what a story: Mrs Currie went haring off down to London on a wild-goose chase and knocked on the door at Downing Street, only to be told to get lost.

I phoned a friend in the Whips' Office. 'If someone with a name like X phoned you and told you the Prime Minister wanted you to come to London, what would you do?' I asked him. He chuckled.

'Get on my bike and go,' he said. 'That's her Private Secretary. And good luck. I hope you get what you want.'

And so into my battered Maestro, through the lanes of Derbyshire and on to the M1, suffering then, as always, from endless road-works and contraflows. I was still puzzled, as no particular job had been mentioned. Maybe I wasn't part of the main ministerial reshuffle; perhaps she had something else for me to do; or wanted to see me about some other question entirely? Why didn't it matter if I couldn't get there till tomorrow? Reshuffles were usually all announced together. Never mind, I told myself, you will do whatever it might be, and be proud to do it. It is an extraordinary honour even to be considered.

By 5 p.m. I was stuck in traffic near Luton and turned on the radio for the *PM* programme and the latest news. 'We are expecting the government reshuffle to be announced from Downing Street at 5.30 p.m.,' came the gravelly voice of the newsreader, 'and we'll bring you all the details then.' I felt a bit sad, for it seemed my musings were right; nothing in that for me. I wondered, as we crawled along, what it could be instead.

By 5.30 p.m. there was no news, and no mention. At 6 p.m., as I came off the motorway at Brent Cross, the radio was apologizing. 'We understand the reshuffle announcement has been held up because Downing Street is having trouble contacting all the people involved,' it intoned. 'We are informed now that the announcement is likely to be around seven o'clock.'

Seven o'clock. I should be there soon after so I'll hear it first hand. How exciting. Seven o'clock! Heavens above, they can't be waiting for *me*, can they?

They could. It was 6.30 and I was still stuck – at Swiss Cottage. The cars ahead were jammed nose-to-tail in the London rush-hour. At the other end I had still to park – my intention had been to leave the car in the House of Commons underground car-park – and at this rate I was going to be very late indeed. That would never do! So I ditched the car at a friendly garage behind the cinema and ran for the Underground. It was equally crowded but much faster and by ten to seven. I was emerging, blinking and breathing hard, on to the pavement by Embankment tube station.

Now it would not do to run along Whitehall, either – I had to retain some vestige of dignity. So even if it meant I was going to be a few minutes late, I was going to walk, steadily. There were not going to be any photographs of me looking scatty in the following day's newspapers; I would make sure of that. And so I nodded to the policemen, who smiled knowingly, swept past the pressmen, and strolled up to the door.

It opened as I arrived and there she was, smart in blue, of course. 'Ah! Edwina. I'm glad you've arrived. Now we can get on.' And then the offer – the Department of Health, the one job I had hoped I might get, after years of working in the Health Service.

Another door opened and we came into one of the drawing-rooms, chandeliers now twinkling as the lights were turned on and staff brought drinks in huge tumblers. The door into government had opened wide for several of us. There were half a dozen of my colleagues, some erstwhile back-benchers like myself, others taken from the Whips' Office, all in a slight daze and unsure of the etiquette for a moment like this. My whip, former Guardsman Archie Hamilton, had also been appointed to the job he wanted, at the Ministry of Defence. He was standing there, all six-foot-seven of him, grinning from ear to ear. I was delighted for him. Apart from anything else, it would mean a new whip, someone smaller, so I would not have to stand on a chair to argue. One person was missing, uncontactable on a walking holiday in Greece, and his job announcement had to wait several days. So why the mystery? Because, at least at junior minister level, that is the way it is done.

*   *   *

Into the fire, no doubt. The hottest kitchen of all. The Department of Health and Social Security had the largest budget in Whitehall by a streak and was responsible for more employees than any other business in the country. The National Health Service is one of the nation's biggest landholders with billions of pounds worth of assets – no one knows how much, really.

The Department of Health is the focus of constant attention both inside and outside Parliament. In my time there I met dozens of delegations and travelled literally thousands of miles on visits around the country. Junior ministers are the departments' letter-writers and I would every week regularly sign 300 letters – just in reply to MPs, since officials deal with queries from the general public. I would respond to, on average, 100 written parliamentary questions, before I started on my own constituency work. By the time I left, twenty-seven months later, I had answered some fifty-eight adjournment debates, mostly in the dead of night, and umpteen other debates on subjects from European pharmaceutical pricing policy to health warnings on cigarette packets. A ninety-hour week was normal and it is surprising how easily one can get used to it.

Although we did not run the health authorities, we answered for them in Parliament and were drawn into day-to-day management, both publicly and behind the scenes: with decisions to be made about matters as detailed as the use of four beds in a children's ward in a hospital in Lancashire, or the placing of twelve mentally-handicapped children in Northampton. We were also heading for a General Election, probably within eighteen months or sooner, when health matters loom large and are always a problem for the government of the day. Just keeping things steady is a monumental job for all the Department of Health ministers and I was proud to be part of a first-class team.

It would have been quite easy, therefore, simply to have accepted the Department's agenda. Doing no more than was expected of me would have kept me very busy and made me a national figure in no time. But I didn't want to do it that way. I wanted my own agenda, and, in an action somewhat reminiscent of another Tory woman junior minister long ago, who turned up to her department on her first day with a list of seventeen items she wanted doing, written in an exercise book, so I sat down and wrote a paper which I circulated in the Department on 18 September 1986. It was entitled: 'The Conservatives and the NHS – Moving the Goalposts'. It set out the themes I wanted to follow as Junior Minister, and I asked officials to fill in the gaps and then use it for articles, press releases, speeches and the like. In reality I was telling them, arrogant upstart that I was, that I was interested in more than just running the National Health Service (NHS) and answering parliamentary questions. There were new games to play. I could see the opportunities and I wanted to pick up the ball and run.

The objective, the paper said, was to develop themes incorporating the Conservative philosophies of personal responsibility, a diminished role for the State, and an increased attention to outputs (results) over inputs (resources). (To my amusement all this was so new that the Department typist spelled 'Conservative' with a small 'c'.) If we were successful, we should shift the argument from endless hassles over funds and 'cuts' in the NHS – arguments which even generous governments find difficult to win – to the question of whether our nation is enjoying good health.

'Everyone thinks that my job is to look after the Health Service,' I complained. 'But that's only part of it. My interest is the *health of the nation*. Not just its health care, and not just the NHS part of health care, and certainly not just the hospital part. The whole hog: are we a fit and well country? Is this a good place to be well in?'

So to the basic questions which should underlie any health planning in my view, then as now. What do people die from? What do they suffer from? People die from lung cancer, but a far greater drain on the NHS is mental illness, lasting for years, with lifelong medication and care required in thousands of cases. How are the death rates and morbidity rates changing? What's getting better, what worse? The implication is obvious: as health and disease patterns change, our ideas have to as well.

When my father was young, people died of diphtheria, scarlet fever, flu and tuberculosis – which they could catch from milk. There were no antibiotics or penicillin, few blood tests, no scanners, no ultrasound, no lasers. The elderly were not a problem because there weren't very many of them. The Beveridge Report, the foundation for the welfare state in 1944, hardly mentioned old people. Kidney failure was a certain killer – my grandmother, middle-aged, died of a version of it called Bright's disease before the last war, while cancer was never mentioned, and a 'growth' only ever talked about in hushed whispers.

Now, however, said my little homily, our people are better housed and better fed than ever before. They are taller, heavier and live longer than at any time in our history. Life expectancy for my own daughters

5

is nearly eighty and we have over 2 million people aged between 75 and 84 and half a million – expected to rise to nearly a million by the year 2000 – of our citizens are over eighty-five. Many illnesses have disappeared altogether, most infections are quickly and effectively treated; most accident injuries are efficiently patched up, most pains can be relieved. Psychotropic medicines have released many people from the brutal prisons of those old mental hospitals. In most cases epileptics can drive, asthmatics can live a normal life and diabetics can take it for granted that they will collect their pensions. Health and safety legislation has reduced the dangers of the workplace. More awareness and openness about cancer is bringing earlier detection and improving the chances of cure.

But some things are getting worse. A hundred thousand people die from the effects of smoking every year. Heart disease is the biggest killer of men in the age group 50 to 65. One person in five over eighty is likely to suffer some form of senile dementia and we have no solution yet. We can detect congenital conditions such as Down's syndrome or spina bifida before a baby is born, but the only 'cure' is termination of the pregnancy. Meanwhile new troubles appear: most obviously drug abuse and AIDS.

'Now we suffer from the illnesses of plenty,' I went on, 'and too many of our people have a miserable old age and do not enjoy good health. We must and can make more effort to take charge of our own health as individuals – to take responsibility far more than we do.' Sounds familiar now, but although it wasn't new in health circles it must have sounded crackers then, especially coming from a minister. I declared myself against the term 'preventive medicine' as a title for what I had in mind. 'That implies it is all the province of doctors, that the only way to good health is through hospitals and drugs and operations. Of course that is true for many. But for most of us, most of the time, the way to good health is within our own hands, and thereby lies the potential for much improvement.'

I was nailing my flag to the mast with a vengeance, and the document gets even more didactic and pompous as it goes on for the rest of its sixteen pages! Officials did their best to flesh out my points with data, tables, learned articles and the like. The final version which came back to me had doubled in size. I had in fact forgotten, until I looked at it again recently, that some of the ideas must have sounded quite bizarre. 'The importance of health and fitness amongst the elderly – I mean looking after yourself even if you're eighty-two' must have sounded pretty daft then, as it did to many people two

6

years later when I spoke about woolly hats. Some suggestions were even against the rules as they stood at the time.

For example, I said: 'I don't just mean wise eating or sensible life-style or giving up smoking. I mean getting a check-up even when you feel well, if you haven't seen your doctor for ages.' Well, yes, Minister, they said, but at the moment there is a question as to whether busy doctors looking after the sick have time for that sort of thing. It was also pointed out to me that the British Medical Association, the doctors' trade union, had in fact proposed that doctors should be able to charge their NHS patients for a routine medical check if there were no clinical indications that an examination was needed.

But 'Moving the Goalposts' was not just about prevention of bad health and the promotion of good health, not just the assertion that the sense of individual responsibility for health could be increased. It was also about ministers with responsibility for the NHS getting off the treadmill of endless detail. 'When people think of health care, they immediately think of the NHS,' I wrote. 'But there are many other bodies we can and do look to for health care. There is the private sector – small in this country but important, partly because we Conservatives believe in freedom of choice – remember, it was not that long since Barbara Castle was closing the pay beds, and there are still unnecessary restrictions on the size of private hospitals – partly, also, because of the private sector's pioneering work in how to care for patients, making them feel comfortable and even enjoying their stay. 'We can learn from that "customer service".'

The private sector is widely used and developed in industry, I pointed out, having just spent a year on an industrial scholarship with British Petroleum (BP) and marvelling at their splendid health facilities for employees. The private and voluntary sectors make an excellent job of looking after thousands of elderly people and special groups, as in the Ukrainian old people's home in my constituency, while the hospice movement has shown us new ways of caring for the dying. There are plenty of self-help groups ranging from local branches of Alcoholics Anonymous to the National Schizophrenia Fellowship, Mencap, the Spastics Society and other big national charities. Many of these do more than just raise money and public awareness; they often provide services in highly specialized and competent ways, and bring companionship and mutual support to sufferers and their families, and we should encourage them. Health care is not, in other words, just the NHS and we should not talk or act as if the NHS is the whole story.

Conscious that the NHS was not too competent at ensuring that its facilities were accessible, I also wanted a better approach to people in work. For example, they should not have to wait around in out-patients all day for attention, losing a day's pay. Clinics should be open in the evenings and at weekends, and there should be a shift to day care and day surgery instead of unnecessary time spent in bed in hospital. Only a tiny proportion of the then 24 million people in work could get attention at the work site. I wondered if we could encourage employers to take more interest in their employees' health, developing occupational health services along the lines of those I had seen at BP, though more modestly perhaps, offering such things as antenatal clinics and facilities for smear tests to be done at factories, and paying more attention to conditions such as lifting injuries and back pain. Certainly if the NHS itself did that, we would have less sickness amongst our half a million nurses.

Governments in the past had paid a great deal of attention to industrial disease or injury, and companies often sent their key executives for regular (usually private) check-ups; but what about their secretaries, and what about the cleaning lady? How many companies regarded heavy drinking or smoking with alarm and offered those employees concerned the chance to put things right? Many employers, I said, insist on medicals before offering job appointments (and thereby exclude many fit disabled people). Then they ignore the health of their employees for the rest of their careers. Many employers moan about absenteeism and early retirement through illness but how many take steps to reduce these – by looking after their work-force a little bit better and getting their employees to look after themselves?

Watch, I said. We require the workman to wear a mask when handling dusty materials and dangerous chemicals. That is the legal responsibility of the employer. Then we put an ashtray on the table in the canteen, and we wonder why the workman drops dead at fifty.

Lay off, warned the civil servants. That's not your responsibility. In this country, occupational health services are the fief of the Department of Employment, and that hasn't been their line at all. So I did, but I needn't have worried. Some aspects of government campaigning were already moving that way, as, for example, the campaign against heart disease, 'Look After Your Heart!' (LAYH), which was being developed elsewhere in the Department for launch the following spring. It called for a hefty element of employer involvement and most have taken to it enthusiastically. And once Norman Fowler moved on to the Department of Employment in the summer of 1987, he took with him his own quiet commitment to 'prevention' policies and the promotion of better health, and the frostiness between the Departments disappeared.

* * *

Heaven knows what the officials made of this 'agenda': a mixture of politics and practice, prevention and pragmatism. Still, the document acquired a number, 'PRH/0693p', and a short minute from them on top, 'reference B640'. That, as it happens, was that, for it took almost two months – till 6 November – to come back and I work faster than that. A week after writing it, having heard nothing more, nor received any of their excellent words of wisdom, I was on a cramped plane to Newcastle. We were up and running and we didn't stop until December 1988. The game was changing, and the goalposts were moving all by themselves.

2

Look After Your Heart!

The only way to keep your health is to eat what you don't want,
drink what you don't like and do what you'd druther not
Mark Twain, *Pudd'nhead Wilson*

It is a myth that Ministers are cosseted, pampered, ushered in soft efficiency from place to place by discreet minions. At least, if it happened to others it didn't always happen to me and, on the whole, I should not have liked it if it had. But my journey to Newcastle in September 1986, a few days after I had been appointed to the Department of Health, stood ever afterwards in the Department's annals of how not to do it.

It was a grey, cold day with a hint of winter in the air. The car – best of British, a Montego, the loss of which was one of the smallest regrets on my resignation – was waiting at the flat at a horribly early hour and we trundled through heavy traffic, breathing carbon monoxide fumes diluted by London air for the next fifty minutes. That was making good time to Terminal One at Heathrow and not for the first time I wondered how long it would be before the capital jammed up altogether. In the car my driver, Steve, a cheerful young Cockney, handed me an envelope with the ticket in it. Steve was a smashing bloke who looked and sounded like the actor Bob Hoskins. He was fiercely proud of London; I used to tease him about how much more pleasant life is in the East Midlands. One day he met a Nottingham girl and took me at my word, left the civil service, married her – I went to the wedding – and as far as I know is living happily ever after.

Clutching my briefcase, two newspapers, coat, scarf, gloves,

10

briefing papers and ticket I approached the check-in desk for the Newcastle shuttle. The stewardess looked at the ticket and sniffed.

'This ticket is in the name of Mr Ray Whitney,' she said. 'Is that a mistake – should it read Mrs Ray Whitney?'

Oh, Lord. Ray Whitney is the pleasant and distinguished former Foreign Office man who was my predecessor. The travel office had been told to book for the Parliamentary Secretary and clearly didn't read newspapers.

'No,' I said. 'I'm not Ray Whitney. But I do need to catch this plane.'

'Well, you can't do it on this ticket,' she said, and looked at me, appraisingly. 'You can if you say you are his wife,' she offered helpfully. 'Otherwise I'm sorry, Madam, it's full.'

'It can't be full. I've got one of the tickets here in my hand. Mr Ray Whitney is not travelling today. Please will you let me get on that plane?'

The minutes were ticking away. No breakfast and I was desperate for a cup of coffee. People were pushing past, clearing their baggage, starting to run for the boarding gate.

'You'll have to buy another one, then,' she said grudgingly.

Out came the Amex card and then I was running down the long corridor, too. Of course I was the last one on the aircraft, the subject of somewhat malevolent glances from better organized fellow passengers. Worst of all, because I was late, all the seats in the No Smoking section were taken and I found myself at the back jammed tight in a dark little corner between an overweight Geordie, who puffed away throughout the flight, and a morose Scotsman who picked his teeth. It was too crowded to do any work or to relax. By the time the shuttle touched down I was not at my sweetest. The car which came to collect me was too small for the several large local officials who planned to get in it with me, and the journey, during which they briefed me about the new chest wards at the local hospital, the expanded heart programme in Newcastle, the visit to the clinic and the alcoholics' centre in the afternoon, became a miserable test of endurance.

So when, a little later, a reporter asked for a response to yet another book about the north-south divide, written by some middle-class professor from Bristol, I was ready to eat somebody. There was a horrendous amount of ill-health in the area. He was telling us nothing new. I had grown up in Liverpool, had spent a decade as a councillor in Birmingham and on its Health Authority, and I knew something about city problems and patterns of life. Heart disease, lung cancer, strokes, respiratory problems and high levels of perinatal mortality were problems found clustered along the Tyne, as they were along the Mersey.

'Isn't it all caused by the high levels of unemployment round here?' asked the local Granada TV reporter.

I explained that most of the local work-force was in work and their health statistics were pretty rotten too. 'Ill-health is also very high among the senior executives in companies,' I said, so poverty alone couldn't be the whole answer.

'But the Professor says it's all because of deprivation and it's the government's fault. What do you say to that?'

Ah, he would. I knew of the professor in question; his texts had been widely quoted in my university days, when socialism was all the rage. My clothes still stank of cigarettes. I took a deep breath. Not feeling in the least self-righteous, but getting annoyed at the supercilious leer of the reporter, I retorted crossly, 'I honestly don't think the problem has anything to do with poverty. We have problems here. Heavy smoking and drinking, for example. Some of these problems are things we can tackle by impressing on people the need to look after themselves better.'

'And why, Mrs Currie, do you think they don't do that?'

Now there I was stumped. I have never been much good at winkling out the motivation of people who don't share mine; some day I'll be better at it than I was on 24 September 1986.

'I suppose they don't know about it,' I said, not wanting to be negative or critical.

'Ignorance?' said the reporter helpfully.

'Yes, I suppose that's it,' I replied. 'The problem very often for people is just ignorance – failing to realize that they do have some control over their lives. I recognize that is easy for me to say. *My* problem is to encourage all our people here to help get that message across.'

'But why do you think it is so bad here?' he persisted.

I thought of all the money spent in Newcastle and Birmingham and elsewhere trying to improve people's housing conditions. My old Birmingham council ward had contained twenty-nine tower blocks complete with their broken lifts, their leaking roofs, their vandalism, their disillusion. Trying to improve the health of ordinary people by such indirect means was going to take a long time. Meanwhile life-style made a thumping big difference, and I was determined that they should hear the message in Newcastle; it served no purpose if the already healthy heard it yet again and the rest not at all.

'Well, there's no reason,' I said. 'Other people do better. It is something which seems to be taken more seriously down south, and perhaps in the United States. There is no reason why it can't be taken seriously here, and then we will end up with better health for everyone.'

'But they can't afford a proper diet,' he said.

'Oh yes, they can!' I retorted. 'This nation spends £900 million a year on crisps; eating well can be done just as cheaply as eating badly.'

And that was it. The crew went off, the editor cut out all the questions, running my answers together so that it sounded, as the *Guardian* put it next day, like 'a lecture, with a hint of Sir Keith Joseph's comments about the birth rate of the lowest social classes'. Neat technique, that, one I tried thereafter not to forget.

Granada apparently did not regard this interview as particularly revolutionary; it was just what you would expect a health minister to say to a 'blame the government' report in the run up to an election. After it was broadcast on local news they wiped the thirty seconds of tape and kicked themselves ever after.

Granada followed up the interview with a *World in Action* documentary on 6 October. I stuck to my guns, to their evident surprise. They filmed in the Newcastle clinic I had visited, they filmed in a smoke-filled club, they filmed the depressed streets, they interviewed a tubby lady in her early sixties, who looked so much older, and who had lost her husband from heart disease at a relatively early age. Yes, he had been a smoker, but his heart attack was caused by stress and over-hard work, wasn't it? No doubt the producer tried, but they failed to interview anyone in all the north-east who would stand up and say, go look at the research, it is not enough to sneer and shake your fist, nor to blame the government, nor indeed to blame anyone. The question is, how do we get the health of the sicker parts of our country more in line with everywhere else?

It was party conference time, too. The Labour Party gleefully provided a 'graffiti board' on which delegates were invited to write their views on my activities. Journalists flocked to it with delight, but when the innocents on Labour's National Executive realized just how lively – and worse, sexist – the vocabulary of their delegates could be, it was hurriedly withdrawn. Not quite the Neil and Glenys image! The Liberals did even better. They were meeting somewhere down south, Eastbourne I believe, and Mr Arthur Collinge, prospective candidate for Darlington, told the conference: 'We have never seen such a dreadful slander on the people of the north as we have had from Mrs Currie this week.' He added, 'She is the typical southerner come up north to tell us what to do . . .', and the dear souls duly passed a motion to that effect. A solid view was offered by 30-stone Cyril Smith. 'If I was as skinny as her and looked like a banana, I'd keep my mouth shut.' In the subsequent general election Darlington was retained by the Conservatives and Mr Collinge came bottom of the poll.

*   *   *

My target, in Newcastle and everywhere else, was heart disease. Death rates from coronary heart disease (CHD) in the UK are the worst in the world, and worst of all in Scotland and Northern Ireland. Some of the figures quoted about heart disease are, in my view, misleading. You'll hear that there are 160,000 deaths from CHD every year. Yes, that is true. But most of the victims are old. Heart attacks and heart failure are what polish us off. It is far more revealing to look at the damage done to younger people, under retirement age for example. They account for around one fifth of all these deaths, more than 30,000 per year. The key age group is 55 to 64. And here the British lead in the international mortality tables is very large: for every ten men in this age group in Scotland and Ulster who die of CHD, eight will die in England and Wales, six in Belgium, Germany, the Netherlands and Sweden, four in France and Greece and so on. The figures are only marginally better for women.

Most scientists and doctors would regard CHD – with lung cancer – as more preventable than most illnesses. It is, however, foolish to pretend that all heart disease can be prevented, even in younger people. It can't. Genetic factors are implicated in around half of all the CHD deaths in this country. Doctors are now recommended to look at family history, and to advise contacting other close blood-relatives if a heart attack occurs in an unexpected victim, though it is particularly hard in this work to disentangle nature (our genes) from nurture (the family's bad habits). To make life more complicated, the risk factors (smoking, cholesterol, lack of exercise, etc.) in heart disease are a complex mixture and each gives rise to other diseases, too. Thus, research from Scotland published in April 1989 suggested that a low-cholesterol diet caused cancer. A closer look revealed that *smokers* who ate a *high*-cholesterol diet tended to die from heart disease. The smokers who tried a low-cholesterol diet were more likely to die from

14

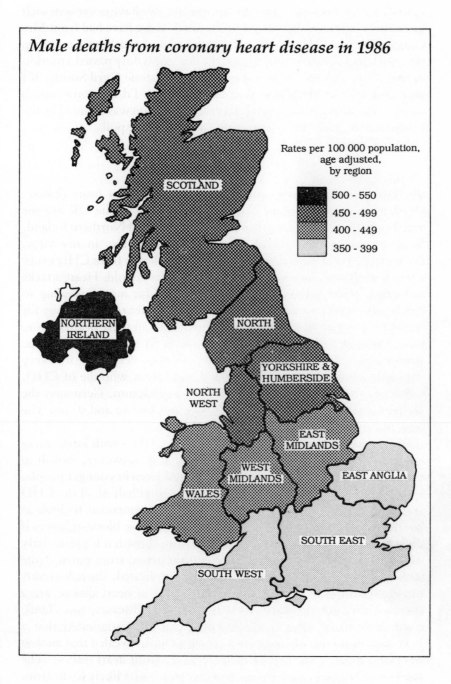

Male deaths from coronary heart disease in 1986

SCOTLAND

Rates per 100 000 population,
age adjusted,
by region

500 - 550
450 - 499
400 - 449
350 - 399

NORTHERN
IRELAND

NORTH

YORKSHIRE &
HUMBERSIDE

NORTH
WEST

EAST
MIDLANDS

WEST
MIDLANDS

EAST ANGLIA

WALES

SOUTH EAST

SOUTH WEST

cancer. To my humble mind, all that proves is that if one thing doesn't get you, something else will. The Scottish smokers have a ghoulish choice, but are likely to discover their fate a lot sooner than their non-smoking brothers and sisters.

The death rate from heart disease in the UK is 50 per cent higher than it was in 1950 when I was a child. Still, it is not all doom and gloom, for it has fallen among the under sixties, by about a quarter, in the last decade. That is probably because people cut down their smoking some years ago, and are now reaping the benefit. Nor are we, generally, an unhealthy nation. On the contrary: the British are healthier now than they have ever been and our health is improving steadily. Life expectancy has increased by thirty years in this country since the turn of the century. We have one of the longest life expectancies in the world. On the other hand, heart disease is getting more common among women, partly because the younger ones smoke more and partly because the Pill increases the risk. A study of over 40,000 women published in the *British Medical Journal* (BMJ) in January 1989 said women on the Pill who smoke are up to twenty times more likely to suffer heart attacks than non-smoking women. The low smoker (fewer than fifteen cigarettes per day) has around twice the risk of the non-smoker, and the risk rises rapidly after that.

People often say to me when the subject of death comes up, that we all have to go some time, and the speedy cleanliness of a heart attack seems appealing. They are usually demonstrating their willingness to take the risks associated with CHD as they talk, and often trying to tempt me with something I don't fancy, like a cigarette or a disgusting hamburger or greasy chips. The trouble is, it doesn't work that way. One third of all men in this country will have a heart attack before they reach state retirement age. Not one of them, I would guess, would welcome it when it happens. They would regard themselves indignantly as too young to leave this life, with so much yet to enjoy and do. Many have no symptoms at all. Challenged the week before, they would have offered themselves as a picture of robust good health, proof positive, if any were needed, that all this talk of cholesterol and high blood pressure is so much nonsense. We all know the type: you'll find them in every pub, in every office, in every street, more of them in the north of England and in Scotland, daring you to argue with them.

Half of those middle-aged men struck by heart attacks are likely to die quite quickly. The other half won't, and the survival rate is rising. But none of them goes home unchanged. Heart attack victims describe the agonizing pain which persists for hours, weeks. Many men, faced with their own mortality, come to terms with it; others never do and are depressed, angry and bitter afterwards. Some face angina, breathlessness, open heart surgery, restricted diet. They will be told to stop smoking and cut down the alcohol, the very things which they claimed gave them so much pleasure before. Nearly all will face a shortened life and the likelihood of further agonizing and terrifying attacks in future. If that's their idea of a 'nice way to go' then I'm afraid it isn't mine – not to speak of their families and those who are dependent on them, who may be financially seriously damaged when the bread-winner has to give up work prematurely through ill health, and who then can't get insurance cover because of a history of 'heart trouble'.

*   *   *

Following the 'ignorance and crisps' comments there began a furious debate in the press, and a huge post-bag, which continued unabated the whole time I was a minister. Some of the northern papers defended my line and had to put up with the same torrents of criticism.

The *Northumberland Gazette* had its own line in invective:

Mrs Edwina Currie, a Junior Health Minister, has blamed many of our health problems on ignorance. She is absolutely right. And the reaction from most of us has been, as usual, chauvinistic, belligerent . . . and in many cases you can add brainless and ignorant. Criticized, our entire aspect changes and we band together in a great welter of self-pity, whimpering of deprivation and a lack of opportunity. It's a grand platform for masochism run rampant.

But let us get our facts right. The woman said we smoke too much, drink too much and don't eat the right food. And with quite a few of us she was spot on. Yet she is somehow accused of not understanding unemployment, failing to appreciate our social background and needs . . . and will doubtless be held responsible for the weather in winter. There really are few more pathetic animals than we Geordies challenged.

It got better; the writer was clearly enjoying himself.

We scream about the north-south divide; we protest about the geography around Watford – and two-bit politicians swarm aboard the howway the laads bandwagon and with sycophantic opportun-

17

ism talk of the heel of the southerner being in the nape of our respective necks pushing our faces deeper into the mire. What so many of us so often need is not the heel but the toe of the boot – applied vigorously to our scrawny, undernourished backsides.

The Thunderer lives. They don't write it like that in Guildford.

I was bewildered by all the fuss. I had issued no statement, made no speech, meant no harm, and said nothing wrong. Clearly, I had put my finger quite inadvertently on an important issue – in fact, on a matter of huge interest to everyone; and it seemed I had a talent, for good or evil, for getting the issue across to every household in the country – particularly to those traditionally totally impervious to any discussion about their health and how to improve it. In that case, I thought ruefully, no point in wasting time analysing it; if you've got it, use it. But the 'prevention' section of the Department of Health was thinly staffed, reflecting the low degree of public interest in it until then, while my own office was maintained at the correctly meagre level for the nation's most junior minister. My staff burned the midnight oil and creaked under the strain.

Early in November I bumped into the most distinguished person in the building, Sir Kenneth Stowe, the Permanent Secretary, in the corridor outside my office. Long after, I reflected that such meetings are not accidental. The real mandarins have a way of being in the right place at precisely the right time, and Sir Kenneth was very much the mandarin's mandarin. A small, slight, dapper man, boyish, with quick neat movements, he looked like Hergé's Tintin. His eyes would light up when there was 'something on'. This was his last year before retirement.

We chatted briefly; there were bits of etiquette flying around of which I was only dimly aware. The 'Perm Secs' acquired their name two centuries ago, to reflect their immovable positions in Whitehall by contrast with politicians, also called Secretaries, who came and went. Parliamentary Under-Secretaries – junior ministers to you and me – were a nineteenth-century invention to assist in answering questions in the increasingly assertive Commons, while the Cabinet Minister, usually then a peer, did his bit elsewhere. Permanent Secretaries had been known to refuse to talk to junior ministers, and could be stuffy about being summoned; so I hadn't. Sir Kenneth, however, was a wise old bird. He put his hand on my arm.

'Are you all right?' he asked, briskly. 'Is there anything you need?'

Offer made, offer accepted.

'Yes, there is,' I said promptly. 'My girls in the office are working all hours and it is not fair on them. It's all right for me, I asked for it but they didn't. It looks like this is not going to peter out either. Can we please have some more staff?'

Sir Kenneth's mouth twitched. Manpower controls in Whitehall were squeezing hard; we both knew that. 'Leave it to me; it will be done,' he said, and within a few days a new desk, a new chair and a new cheerful young man were crammed into the private office, snowed under with papers, with the phones all going like crazy. Not long after, the Department's Press Office decided to allocate one of their number to look after me on a semi-permanent basis. That is how I came to be the only junior minister with my own press officer. Each one lasted about a year and they were great: large youngish men with a journalistic background and a world-weary air, permanently trying to give up smoking or something else, they did their best both to protect me and to help me serve the public, and I am grateful to them.

This was the start of my long-running dialogue with the public about the personal influences which bear on our health, in Newcastle and in many another city, north and south. No one believed it then. Now, even the shuttle is 'No Smoking' and there is fresh fruit for the airborne breakfast.

$$* \quad * \quad *$$

'Welcome! We are here today because of what has rightly been called Britain's Number One Killer – coronary heart disease. Heart disease kills about 150,000 people in England every year. This is thirty times the number who die as a result of road traffic accidents. To put it another way, one person dies from heart disease every three-and-a-half minutes.'

With these words, Secretary of State for Social Services, Norman Fowler, launched the £2.5-million 'Look After Your Heart!' campaign at Lancaster House, at 11 a.m. on Wednesday 22 April 1987. You will read Norman's name in this book on many occasions. He was appointed Secretary of State at the Department of Health and Social Services in 1981 and moved to Employment after the General Election in mid-1987. He was thus my boss for just under a year, from September 1986 to June 1987. Tall, slim, pleasant, by profession a journalist, outwardly smooth but inwardly – almost secretly – a man of compassion and conviction, he was the driving force behind much of the work on prevention and encouraged my efforts.

Ours wasn't the first or only heart disease campaign running in the country at the time. The Welsh had launched a 'Heartbeat Wales' programme in 1985, and one had started in Northern Ireland in 1986. I loved both their approaches. The Welsh garnered Delia Smith, dark-haired, slim and attractive, wearing a suitably sloganned T-shirt, to teach the people how to cook approved dishes other than welshcake. The Ulstermen – leading the world in early deaths from heart attacks – ran TV advertisements showing a despairing housewife trying to wean her husband off the frying pan with the words, 'If Oi froied yer socks, John, ye'd eat them!' The campaigns all attracted a great deal of interest, the television programmes gaining large audiences, to everyone's surprise. Opinion polls showed a high measure of acceptance and approval; the people wanted more. The Scots followed suit soon after us. There was thus nothing new about all this, and however much my name was associated with it afterwards, the credit for the campaign, and the origin of its rather messianic tone (Norman said 'we hope it will turn into a crusade'), lie elsewhere.

The LAYH campaign was planned during early 1986, before I arrived at the Department, and was intended both to draw on the successful work in the other parts of the United Kingdom, and to put to the public in England the information on the links between diet and cardiovascular disease published in 1984 by the Chief Medical Officer's Advisory Committee on the Medical Aspects of Food Policy (known as COMA). COMA now review the available evidence every year to keep Ministers up to date.

The Department of Health is not, of course, the Ministry of Food. That work is the responsibility of the Ministry of Agriculture, Fisheries and Food (MAFF). Health Ministers are responsible only for the health *effects* of food and thus for trying to influence what people eat on *health* grounds. MAFF officials were drawn into the LAYH campaign at a rather late stage, in early October 1986. They sent a young woman official, who made sensible suggestions, pointing out for example that there was no benefit in encouraging a switch from chips to baked potatoes if people just slathered the latter in butter or cream. So in their view – and I will defend it – there are no bad *foods*, only bad *diets*. You can eat whatever you fancy as long as it's not too much. The problem, of course, is to help people understand what for them is 'too much'. As a nation we like firm statements, along with firm leadership. In health, however, there is only one aggressive comment to offer which matches all the research – 'Don't smoke'. The rest is more a plea for moderation and common sense.

The risk factors for CHD are now well known – smoking, excessive drinking, the wrong diet, not enough exercise, high blood pressure, stress. They caused so many other illnesses that awareness of the combinations of risk factors, if tackled well, could have not only a potentially big effect long-term on Britain's 'Number One Killer', but substantial spin-offs for a lot of other painful, debilitating, expensive and lethal disorders, including strokes and cancer.

A campaign against heart disease was certainly worth trying. We knew that improvement in the figures for these conditions would take some time and that we should not expect instant success. Yet – and this consideration weighed powerfully in ministers' and advisers' minds – the fact is that other countries, notably the United States, Finland and Australia, have tackled the problem successfully and vigorously, so it can be done. If they could do it – in both big and little countries – what was to stop us?

* * *

What were we trying to do? First, *raise awareness* of the problem of heart disease and its possible solutions. Second, *change attitudes*. Third, *change behaviour*. I am sure we were very successful with the first, moderately successful with the second. On the whole progress with the third was already on the way, independently of our campaign – and it will be another decade before anyone knows whether heart disease is receding as a result of all these efforts. The LAYH campaign was seen as long-term and is planned to continue in the 1990s.

The attitudes of the public were regarded as very important in this campaign and ministers went to a lot of trouble to find them out. We did not bash on regardless! The Welsh heart campaign, which had been running two years already, showed very clearly that the public did want to know about heart disease. They do not want facts hidden from them and they are not, on the whole, fatalistic about it. In Wales it was found that people would co-operate whole-heartedly in doing something about heart disease, if a lead were provided. The view of virtually everyone polled in the run up to our launch day was to agree with the statement, 'Everyone has a clear responsibility towards his or her own health'.

We learned in 1986, however, that there was a generation gap in attitudes. Younger people did want information, especially on food. Older people, the research said, often found such information intimidating, implying that what they currently ate was wrong. It also showed that they eat less healthily than the younger generation, they eat more, and are less willing to change. Eating well for them means more meat, more cheese, eggs and so on, and fruit doesn't matter. Younger people have a better understanding about fat and fibre and express more interest in improvement.

I wondered if the 1986 wariness in old people was still so strong later, as it became obvious that large numbers of elderly people were very interested in the heart campaign and eager not to be written off. The Southern Derbyshire Health Authority, as part of its contribution to LAYH, had a Health Roadshow which went round the villages and spent a day in Swadlincote, in the old coal-mining area. Some of the Derbyshire doctors were a bit indignant and proclaimed it unnecessary. They gave an excellent service to their patients, didn't they? To everyone's amazement the queues started forming long before the event started, with people standing patiently out in the cold for hours so they could have their health check. Many of them were elderly. *They* thought it was grand, but when asked why they hadn't asked their doctor for help said they didn't like to bother him. I suddenly realized, as a child of the NHS, what lay at the root of this diffidence. The idea abroad amongst our older generation, brought up before the NHS, was that people should only 'bother' the doctor when there's a pain they can't deal with themselves. Asking, say, for a blood-pressure check when there is nothing actually wrong is seen as being a nuisance. Some of these attitudes, brought out into the open, really have begun to change.

A constituent of mine, who moved house and had to change doctor, told me with great amusement that the new chap virtually insisted on checking his blood pressure and wouldn't let him out of the surgery till he had done so. Preventive medicine of this kind is to be an integral part of the new GPs' contract, coming in April 1990. In future they will be contracted for this kind of work and will be expected to do it.

So far, so good. The problem was, that all the research showed that those least receptive to 'healthy life-style' messages were also those at greatest risk of getting heart diseases. They were the C2DE socio-economic groups – semi-skilled and manual workers – men especially, the middle-aged most of all. That meant that the campaign would have to be tailored to this traditionally resistant group: the *Sun* and the *Mirror* readers, rather than the good souls who read the *Guardian*, who already have bean sprouts coming out of their ears.

That explains why the daftest picture of the LAYH campaign launch was me in a track suit on a gigantic exercise bike – for the first time in my life – in the baroque glory of Lancaster House, next door to the Queen Mother's home in the Mall, chandeliers a-twinkling, cameras a-popping and the minister pedalling for dear life. The press loved it. Only one newspaper the next day had a photo of Norman, and none mentioned the presence of Tony Newton, the other minister.

The bike, an 'Ergocycle', was a huge computer-controlled affair, costing thousands, more suited to Alton Towers than a health launch. The manufacturer, Nissen International, was lending six free for use round the country for 'sponsored calorie burns', and just a little free publicity too. Well, why not? When John Moore took over from Norman in June that year as Secretary of State, I remarked to him that I was fed up with being photographed on exercise bikes when I never (then) used one and didn't know anyone who did. 'I do,' he said pointedly, 'every morning.' Exercise bikes are useful and they do work. But they are so boring. I'd rather toddle down a Derbyshire lane any day.

If we were to reach our C2DEs, there wasn't much time to lose, for the Thatcher revolution was reaching their pockets as the 1980s wore on. Amongst smokers, the heaviest-smoking group is the better-off working class. Often, the first happy reaction to an improvement in fortunes is to increase spending on all the risk factors! So it is not surprising that one of the first reactions to the rapid fall in unemployment in 1988, with a concomitant sharp increase in earnings, was an increase in the sale of cigarettes for the first time in many years. Perhaps the surprise is that the increase was not even bigger.

I come from that sort of background. Growing up in Liverpool I have lived most of my life with people who have always believed in a hard life, but a happy one, and are later indignant to find they have to live on, coping with pain and bits missing. These days I represent some of them in my Derbyshire constituency, but there the health figures are bang on the national averages: middle England, my lot. I get furious at the patronizing notion that such people are not capable of understanding risk or acting on the complex information the scientists had to offer. I willingly and frequently crossed swords with those arrogant intellectuals, remote from the tower blocks and the broken street lamps, who would venture out to do research and then scuttle back to Hampstead, writing off millions of people as beyond saving. I do not believe that such information should be withheld. If it means putting it out occasionally in an unministerial way, so be it. At least it will get noticed. And then it will get heard.

I remain quite convinced that ordinary people do take notice. I was invited to a health promotion by Tesco, which took place in their Thornton Heath store, in a nondescript part of south London. We were a little early, so I wandered aound the store, chatting to the manager and, by degrees, made my way over to the fats counter. Broadly speaking the big supermarkets give shelf space to products in proportion to the quantity sold. The shelves were groaning with Flora, St Ivel Gold and the other polyunsaturated and low-fat spreads, with only a small space for butter. I watched fascinated for some minutes as people from every walk of life examined the goodies and selected low-cholesterol products. Eventually I stopped one middle-aged lady, a dead ringer for Pauline from *EastEnders*, and asked why she had chosen the Flora.

'Better for you, innit?' she said, looking at me as if I was daft. 'Better for me ol' man. I wanna keep 'im just a bit longer, I do,' and off she went.

If life-style has such influence, and life-style is another word for culture and behaviour, the concomitant is that there is, in health, not only a north-south divide, but also huge differences in health and disease in electoral wards barely half a mile from each other. The 'health gap' is the result and relic of differences in behaviour over a very long period past and will take decades to eradicate – if ever. In all the fuss about my being rude to my fellow Northerners, only journalist Valerie Grove, writing in the *Evening Standard*, picked this point up: it is a class difference. But the figures speak for themselves.

The average overall death rate from CHD is 313 per 100,000 of the population in England (my area of responsibility). Using the English regional health authority areas, we find that Trent, South East Thames and Wessex are on the national average, while Oxford at 232, North West Thames at 247, North East Thames at 280, South West Thames at 291 and East Anglia at 293 are below it. West Midlands – which includes the smarter areas of Worcester and Shrewsbury as well as Birmingham and the Black Country – stands at 297. Mersey – which includes Cheshire – is at 326, just above the average, and South Western – the West Country – with its luscious dairy pastures is above the average at 338.

Then the figures soar. Northern Region scores 366 deaths per 100,000, Yorkshire 369 and North Western 370. Their death rate is 60 per cent higher than Oxford's, and their people die on average five years younger. Some of these regions have concentrations of Asian and West Indian populations. For obscure reasons, not fully understood, they have strikingly higher levels of heart disease. Their presence can't be the whole story. Here we are a fairly homogeneous nation. We have bigger differences *within* our country than between the United Kingdom and other nations with totally different habits. The figures north of the border are even worse. Suffice to say that the average Scottish *woman* scores almost twice as high as the average French *man*, while her husband has a score nearly off the graph.

The statistics that were thrust under my nose in Newcastle had demonstrated further that life expectancy could be as much as ten years less in one city ward on Teesside than in a neighbouring ward across the river. That was not news to those of us who lived and worked in our cities, and not just in the north. It was a matter I could never wish to ignore. What annoyed me about such surveys was that they went on to measure indices of deprivation, but not of smoking; levels of poverty, but not of heavy drinking and alcoholism; amounts available to spend on food, but not what actually went into the shopping basket (after the cigarettes, of course). They could tell us how many houses had no inside toilet (not many these days, but still concentrated in some areas), but they could not tell us how many heads were empty of the basic information needed to feed the family a sensible diet on that restricted budget.

Of course, unemployment has its effect on people's health, most notably and tragically in mental illness. But low income by itself is not a major cause of strokes or lung cancer or heart disease – health problems which are mainly found in affluent countries. Heavy smoking *is* a cause, horrible fatty diets are implicated, along with lack of exercise in these sedentary days, drinking to excess plays its part. All these habits are common, and may even be part of a *normal* life-style, for millions of British people, concentrated in those areas where ill-health, hopelessness and fatalism go together. How do I know? That's where I come from, that is where my voyage started.

* * *

Oh heavens, Edwina's at it again! There are those who would say, *laissez-faire*, let them stew in it. If people want to drink or smoke themselves to death, why should we try to stop them, provided that they don't hurt or annoy anyone else? What is a Tory government doing, playing nanny to intelligent people like this?

There are several answers to that. First, it is darned expensive to do nothing. On average, in England alone, nearly 6,000 hospital beds are occupied by patients with heart disease each day. Those beds cost nearly £200 million a year and the cost of surgery (which is not always successful) is nearly £50 million per year (and these are 1986 estimates). The cost of GPs' prescriptions for heart drugs and the like for England alone in 1987 was £360 million. It is a good principle not to spend if we don't have to, and at least some of that expenditure, all of which falls on the public purse, is avoidable. (Lung cancer is cheaper than heart disease, because the victims die quite quickly.) Add the costs to industry and the social security budget of an estimated 25 million days off every year through CHD. The sickness benefit for victims runs at over £260 million, while lost industrial production caused by that sickness costs over £1.4 billion every year. As the pressure on the work-force expands in the next few years, we will find it harder to justify this drain on productivity. However seriously or otherwise the nation takes heart disease, employers needing to keep the lathes and computers going in future will have to. In fact, industry, without much prompting, is very well aware of the savings in time and money they can make with a nudge in the direction of healthy life-styles for their employees. That's why British Airways, British Telecom, Kodak, W. H. Smith, the CEGB and Whitbreads the brewers (oh, yes) all lined up with ministers for LAYH that first day, and why many more companies have since declared their support; now over 2 million workers are covered. So the first reason is that *not* to run one costs money and damages the productive part of the economy.

The next argument in favour of campaigning is that the sufferers only want something done when they get to the stage where the illness interferes with their enjoyment of life. But by then it is a bit late. If we want our people to be healthier, then action 'ante-post' is necessary whether we like it or not. The medical model is not enough. We are accustomed to illness which comes out of the blue, which is then treated and which goes away again. The answer to disease, in that scenario, is to spend more money on the NHS – and we do. But that is '*post hoc*' – after the event – and it won't by itself produce healthy people. We can double, treble the amount we spend on the NHS, but if there is no change in life-style then the costs I've just mentioned will increase.

The third reason for LAYH was that such campaigns are popular and very much appreciated by the general public. They are a Good Thing to Do. You might not have thought so from reading the newspapers, but then journalists are amongst both the most cynical and the most self-abusing sectors of the population. Lunches with journalists show them to be divided between those still young enough to be gasping for a fag and those old enough to describe their coronary by-pass operation; there are hardly any in between. I preferred to trust the attitudes in my post-bag, which said: 'We are interested; tell us more.'

To me this ministerial effort was the antithesis of the nanny state. In other countries the law was changed, products were banned, compulsion and enforcement were the rule. In this country – partly through conviction, and partly because it takes so long to get legislation into the programme and so many endless hours through the night to get it through – we have tried mostly to proceed by persuasion. The information about health care is there, and is offered in as attractive and effective a way as possible. If the public won't act on it, then at least we have done our bit and can have a clear conscience as we vote yet another huge increase in the NHS budget.

*   *   *

What exactly is the role of diet in the fight against heart disease? I believe it plays a big part. More than a year after the LAYH launch, on 2 May 1988, the Department of Health invited Richard Peto, a world-renowned epidemiologist, to come and speak to a private seminar on cholesterol and its role in heart disease. A tall, blond, slim and very shy man from a well-known scientific family, Richard was adviser to other governments besides our own. Epidemiologists look at the pattern of illness in a society over a long period of time, or compare geographical variation, hunting for clues as to the causes or risk factors in disease. Most doctors are only trained to diagnose and treat individual patients, so epidemiologists are invaluable people. The other aspect of fighting disease is the painstaking work in laboratories, tracking down the vital physical link between diseases and what caused them: between the bacteria in water and legionaire's disease; between a scrap of retrovirus and AIDS; between the components of cigarette smoke and lung cancer. Healthy lunch eaten, I was to chair the meeting in Room 60, a large, grey-carpeted, air-conditioned room deep in Hannibal House, one of the Department of Health's twenty-seven buildings in the capital. The audience consisted of around 100 civil servants, including our medical and nursing advisers. All had given up their lunch hour to come.

The talk was erudite, detailed, earnest. As cigarette smoking had declined in this country in the 1970s, he said, so diet had become relatively more important as a factor in heart disease. If we wanted to improve our atrocious figures we were going to have to think about tackling cholesterol, and testing for it. Cholesterol is a fat we need for activity and energy: we eat it – mainly in the form of animal fat – and our bodies also make it, so we all have some circulating in our blood stream. If there is too much, it gets deposited on our arteries, blocking them. Hence the link between diet and exercise – which uses up some cholesterol.

The charts and diagrams were flying around on the screen behind my head. Richard had lots of examples to show. In many countries there is precious little choice about life-style: the average African must needs tuck into his meagre fare, or starve. In his country the diet is rough, the work is heavy and his life expectancy is around forty – as it was in Britain at the turn of the century. The Chinese Republic, it transpired, has very little heart disease, about one fortieth of ours. But, yes, they were worried about a slight increase, and there were geographical differences, with one inland area showing a higher level of heart attacks. At question time Richard was asked why. Maybe it is because in that part of the country, so far inland, people have a taste for fish preserved with excessive salt, but he really didn't know.

I was fascinated but I wanted it in simple language. 'Tell me,' I said. 'Apart from that bit of fish, what else do they eat?'

'Oh, rather what you would expect in China,' he answered. 'Rice, rice, rice, more rice and a few vegetables.'

I grimaced. I could not see efforts at persuading the British public to adopt those ways as likely to meet with any success! A thought occurred to me. 'And if they don't die of heart disease, what do they die of?'

'Tuberculosis,' he replied.

On reflection, the shifts in diet that might come as Britain gets deeper into the European Community after 1992 might be more promising. The pattern of heart disease varies dramatically across Europe. Spain, Portugal, Italy, Greece and France are well down in the international tables, though the French, who drink far more than we do, tend to keel over instead from cirrhosis of the liver. Even within those countries there are regional variations, with Normandy, enjoying a diet very rich in animal fats (all that lovely butter and cream), display-ing the same pattern of heart disease as much of the UK, while the sparser areas of the south, closer to the Mediterranean, have less. Now there's a pleasant thought, I mused, thinking of holidays in sunnier climes. Lots of gorgeous fresh fruit, melons and peaches, oranges by the ton, salads, huge tomatoes, dressed with a little olive oil, onion, garlic, some real bread, washed down by a glass of wine, followed by a siesta before a swim or a walk in a balmy evening; oh yes, I could live with that. So I bought some olive oil and tried it in my own kitchen. It certainly tastes better than polyunsaturated margarine. The Department of Health, I note, has recently taken to endorsing pasta. The tragedy may well be, however, that instead of our copying them, the poorer areas of Europe may well choose to adopt our life-style as they get richer, with the average Greek housewife learning to make Yorkshire puddings and worrying about her husband's heart attack in years to come.

*   *   *

Was Richard Peto right – should we be thinking about mass screening for cholesterol? On a different occasion I had heard the view of Professor Geoffrey Rose, Chairman of the World Health Organization's committee on coronary heart disease, which was scathing. There was no point, I heard him say at a lecture, for the British cholesterol score was so high that virtually everyone needed to change their habits. The recommended maximum blood-cholesterol concentration was 5.2 mmol/litre, but two thirds of the British are generally reckoned to be over that figure.

Yet I had seen the little cholesterol testing machines in action and was surprised at the fascination they held for many intelligent ordinary people. The Family Heart Association is a voluntary group composed of people with inherited hyperlipidaemia. Their blood makes too much cholesterol, causing heart attacks among both men and women in their twenties and thirties. Lots of people, perhaps one in 500 of us, they reckon, suffer from this condition in some form and never know it till they have their coronary. They want people to have readier access to blood testing and were sponsored by my Leicestershire neighbour, David Ashby MP, to put on an exhibition and demonstration in the same week as the LAYH launch at the House of Commons, in the Upper Waiting Hall. David is a large, affable barrister, who came to national prominence making a fuss about a huge fire burning in underground coal-seams, so bad that our locals were digging up the potatoes from their allotments ready-roasted.

David had family reasons for his interest and encouraged me to come and be tested. The machine – a Boehringer Reflotron, costing about £2,000 – is desk-top, about the size of a small personal computer. The finger is pricked (the nurses always overdid it on me for the cameras, leaving my finger sore for days), the drop of blood wiped on the reagent strip and stuck into the machine. Whistle a little tune for three minutes and then your score comes up on the screen for all to marvel at. I scored 4.6 that day – comfortably below the national average, to my relief.

What amazed me was the degree of interest shown by the staff of the Palace of Westminster. They were queuing up to be tested all week. Huge great policemen, helmets in hand; door-keepers, who used to be called the Royal Messengers, in white tie and tails, gold badges of office dangling across midriffs; secretaries, clerks, kitchen staff, waiters and a surprising number of peers and MPs. The rotund and jovial Scots MP, George Foulkes, joked at Question Time that he had gone off and eaten lots and *lots* of low calorie food but it had made no difference. A number of people had scores over 10 or 11 and were advised to go and see their doctor, clutching a bit of paper, pronto. For months afterwards burly policemen would sidle up to me in the Commons, demonstrate the handfuls of spare fabric now in their trousers, pat their tummies and tell me how much weight they had lost since adopting a 'proper diet'. All were fascinated by the whole process. We were on to something here. What was it?

The official answer would be that here was another example of how keen people are, given a chance, to look after their own health better, to know more about its mysteries. But there was more to it. I think we all believe in magic. The machine, with its ability to tell you something you don't know about yourself, is magic; and the ability to change its reading, within weeks, shows how rational man can control the unseen forces around him, giving a curiously deeply satisfying feeling. There is a practical side too. The test might help people understand where cholesterol is to be found – not just in butter and cheese, but in avocado pears, pâté, innocent-looking Greek yoghurt. Just because it has a 'healthy' image doesn't make it so. It might also help people distinguish better between one kind of fat or oil and another. That could enable a family to devise their own diet to suit them precisely. It might help doctors to monitor their own success in helping a patient: if his score goes up instead of down, something ain't right, but at least they both know it.

By dint of considerable effort, watching what I ate, taking exercise – especially before being tested! – I got my level down further, and at the stand run by Merck Sharp and Dohme (the pharmaceutical company) at the Conservative Party conference in October 1988 scored a respectable 4.1. Other parliamentary colleagues told me their scores; there was quite an air of competition about it. The company representatives run such a stall every year at the main conferences, and they told me people come back with last year's score and are delighted when they do better. 'And what are the Labour Party like?' I asked roguishly, but they were being careful. Just 'a lot worse than the Tories' was all they would say. But whatever I tried, I could not get my score down any more, or anywhere near the level in China – around 2.5 – and I doubt if it can be done with a Western way of life.

It was suggested to me that cholesterol testing might save the NHS a lot of money, as well as saving lives. In particular, it might cut down the demand, increasing steadily, for anti-cholesterol drugs. These can cost around £800 per person per year at current prices and it is reckoned that around 5 per cent of British adults may have cholesterol levels high enough to justify drug therapy (around 7 per cent get anti-hypertension drugs at present). This medication is hardly used at present in this country so that could cost a great deal of money – easily over a billion pounds every year – and it often has side effects too. On the other hand, testing could be Pandora's box and cost us more, not less.

The American experience, for example, worried ministers and officials. The US government launched a 'Know Your Cholesterol' campaign in the autumn of 1987. It is now estimated that around a third of all Americans know their cholesterol reading. Partly as a result, the drugs bill for anti-cholesterol drugs there is now increasing by 36 per cent a year. So their Department of Health and Human Services has just issued guidance to doctors on detection, evaluation and treatment of excess cholesterol, emphasizing diet and risk re- duction before drugs.

I think cholesterol testing is coming, good thing or not (and on the whole I think it is a good thing). Better therefore to give the matter some careful thought and, as I noted at one meeting with officials, if the government is to consider introducing it, it must be done in an orderly and economical fashion, with proper standards and laboratory facilities – which would cost money. So ministers referred the whole question to the official Standing Medical Advisory Committee, and

31

their report is expected as this book goes to press. It will make interesting reading.

* * *

Better-off people tend to have better health. They know more about it, are more likely to adapt to new ways, have more choice in every aspect of their lives. Is the reverse also true – that poorly-off people can't afford to be healthy? This is an argument I have always rejected, in this country at least. It costs nothing to change cooking methods – to throw out the frying pan. There's very little price difference now between white and brown bread, between skimmed and whole milk; chicken and fish are cheaper than most red meats, and so on. When a 'healthy' food emerges, the manufacturers, sensing a valuable premium, naturally charge more – as currently with low-alcohol lager and as once with brown bread. Make a fuss and they'll stop it. Buy lots and the price differential will disappear. Call for choice and then choose. It's only marketing.

In any case, the average expenditure on food bought for consumption in the home in this country is barely £11 per person a week. Relatively we spend a lower proportion of family income on food than most other countries in Europe.

In my firm view, you don't have to be rich to be healthy. You do, however, according to John Smith, the senior Scottish Labour MP who had a heart attack in October 1988 which put him out of action for months. John is one of the few remaining members of Mr Neil Kinnock's team who has had his feet under the Cabinet table. Owlish in appearance, sharp and quick talking, he was lucky. He was attending the big teaching hospital in Edinburgh and discussing his queasy feelings with a cardiologist when he collapsed. Otherwise he is sure he would have been a dead man. On his return to Parliament, several stones lighter, he complained of a lack of information about healthy eating. Yet his own colleagues had whinged about the whole LAYH campaign, and the London Food Commission, a left-wing group originally funded by the GLC (Greater London Council), had called LAYH a waste of money and called for more spending on welfare benefits instead. John admitted that he found it difficult to adjust to a healthy diet. According to the *Sunday Times* of 19 February 1989: 'I learned to look at the calories on everything I bought, but it's quite hard to find that out,' he said. 'It should be on everything that is sold . . . I have devised my own diet. I went out for lunch yesterday and had melon, salmon as a main course and raspberries without cream.' Salmon and raspberries – in February, forsooth! Now that's some diet to recommend to the poor of Glasgow, is it not? He'd do just as well on porridge and haggis and mashed neeps and an apple. He, like many other fellow Scots who have been through CHD, might reflect what damage it is doing to Scotland and might just like to think a little harder about how to get a more helpful and practical message across.

*   *   *

I had a most enjoyable day learning what the human body *can* do with good food when I went to the Army Catering Corps at Aldershot. Brigadier Maddy and the ACC training centre had co-operated with the Department of Health in the preparation of the *Catering for Health File*, a cookery book of healthier recipes originally designed for NHS hospitals. We tried out the recipes with their help, on the principle that if soldiers would eat it, it would do for the rest of us. We stood in the gymnasium admiring England's finest as they heaved and sweated on the ropes and bars. The Brigadier swelled with pride. 'We have quite a job keeping this lot satisfied,' he said. 'Growing teenagers, on active duty. We aim to feed them 4,000 calories a day.'

'Good grief,' I said. 'That's about twice what the rest of us need, or what they will need later, when they settle in Civvy Street to a desk job.'

'Oh, it's worse than that,' he grinned. 'We reckon that after they have polished off our low-fat hamburgers in their high-fibre buns, and two platefuls of chips done in polyunsaturated oil, followed by apple bran crumble with dollops of semi-skimmed custard, they add a few Mars bars and the like and several pints and push it up to around 6,000. An army marches on its stomach, you know.'

And Warrant-Officer Harold Ash, cook-in-charge, spanking-clean chef's hat on head, plied me with food, as they explained how the Argentinians had tried to hold Goose Green on a diet of biscuits and cigarettes.

The Forces, to their credit, are now taking the whole health business more seriously. The Air Force staff at Aldershot – where they also have their catering training – were noticeably slimmer than their army colleagues and talked knowledgeably about heart disease. Their machines cost *real* money, commented one officer, pointing to a picture of Trident on the wall. The Navy are phasing out 'Blue liners', the duty-free cigarettes and tobacco available even in onshore bases; they will have gone completely by 1991, and the extra money obtained from increasing the price will be used for welfare services. The Minister at the Ministry of Defence responsible for this was Roger Freeman, who is now Junior Minister of Health. The Army is still hesitating a bit over smoking, though heart attacks in a normal year, Falklands apart, kill two or three times as many serving soldiers as those who die on active service. A recent study of soldiers with CHD showed that 95 per cent of them smoke. When I suggested that the Forces should have a serious anti-smoking campaign, the Tobacco Advisory Council (the front for the industry) took full-page ads calling the idea 'barmy'. Oh no, it isn't.

Is our diet improving? The British diet has changed a great deal in a generation. We eat less overall; the calorie content is slowly falling, from around 2,230 calories per person per day in 1980, to 2,000 in 1988. But we eat far less carbohydrate – about half as much bread as we did thirty years ago, for example – and about the same amount of total fat. The average proportion of our total calorie intake which comes from fat is over 40 per cent. The COMA recommendation is to get it down to 35 per cent but there is no evidence that this is happening, though there is a substantial shift from saturated fats to polyunsaturated, which does show some awareness.

Changes in food purchasing for home consumption were happening already, before the LAYH campaign. The MAFF bulletin of 16 March 1987, which gave the latest evidence of the National Food Survey for the last quarter of 1986 (before I got going), showed that, compared with the same period in 1985, low-fat milk consumption was rising fast and was up by 50 per cent, while whole milk fell by 9 per cent; butter consumption had fallen 12 per cent offset by increased purchases of margarine and low-fat spreads; egg consumption (which had been dropping for years as cooked breakfasts disappeared) was 6 per cent lower, at fewer than three per person per week; poultry consumption was up, but bacon, ham and sausages were down; spending on fish was up 5 per cent, and green-vegetable and fruit purchases also increased. Sugar was down 7 per cent. Purchases of wholemeal, brown and other breads rose but standard white loaves (much cheaper) fell. Somebody seemed to know what they were doing long before LAYH started. The results of the nation's shopping basket showed, said Donald Thompson, my opposite number at MAFF, 'a welcome sign that the British people are heeding the Government's advice on healthy eating'–though we hadn't given out too much at the time. The bandwagon was already

rolling. It was being encouraged both by housewives' natural incli-
nation to do what was right for their families, and by the manufacturers'
own advertising campaigns, well aware that they, too, were on to a
Good Thing. And good luck to them.

By late 1988, two years on, some patterns had changed very
considerably. Household consumption of low-fat milk, low-fat
spreads, fresh green and salad vegetables and fruit were well up.
Purchases of whole milk, butter, red meat and white bread were
down again. We drank two-and-a-half times as much fruit juice as in
1980. We were now spending a lot more on meat than we used to,
but had switched from red meat to chicken, with its lower cholesterol
content. At under 2 ounces per person per week, we were buying less
butter than at any time since rationing in the war. Still, the overall
fat intake is too high and has hardly budged.

All very interesting, but the survey itself is too limited; it doesn't
cover snacks or soft drinks or alcohol, as if they didn't count. No
attempt is made to estimate what people eat when out, whether at
the canteen at work or a night out on the tiles. There is a crying need
for a regular, well-publicized and much more comprehensive survey
than this, complete with a regional analysis. Then we would know
far more about the links in Britain between disease and diet and
income and diet.

* * * *

There were some aspects of the LAYH campaign which were not
entirely to my satisfaction. A substantial part of the £2.5 million was
for television and poster advertising, organized on our behalf by the
Health Education Authority. I approved the details of the campaign,
so if it didn't work very well then I take full responsibility. The
resulting posters were muddled, their message unclear. Showing lots
of different plates of food was confusing – were fish fingers with
mashed potatoes or baked beans good or bad? The slogan was awful,
too – 'It doesn't have to be hell to be healthy' – implying, of course,
that it does. You need a big chest to look good in a T-shirt with that
lot on it. The recognition rate of the campaign among the C2DE
target groups was only around 55 per cent; it simply made no impact
on nearly half of them.

Fortunately, the drugs companies, in the shape of the Association
of British Pharmaceutical Industries (ABPI), came to the rescue with
a marvellous couple of posters which pulled no punches. 'The British

Diet', they proclaimed, showing a vast plateful of pie and chips, the pie in the macabre shape of a coffin. The meat traders were furious, and the ensuing public row brought the campaign lots of attention. The ABPI needed courage to do that and deserve a lot of credit. Another of their advertisements showed a vastly overweight man contemplating his dinner, flesh bursting out between the buttons of his shirt. A year later, as we prepared for the first birthday party of LAYH, I asked for any anecdotes of change as a result of the campaign. Yes, said officials, they had just had a letter from that actor, who had never worried about his appearance before and, indeed, had made a good living out of it. He had been struck by the message of the ads and had started taking an interest in his health and had lost several stone. Good for him, but I hope it doesn't lose him his job!

By the autumn of 1988 Kenneth Clarke was our Secretary of State. I had known Ken for many years, for he is a Midlands MP and had lived in Birmingham. He is bouncy, ebullient and brainy, but it might be safer not to describe him physically! He and I approved the new LAYH advertising campaign for the Health Education Authority, which started just after Christmas 1988. That's a good time, for the rates charged by the television companies slump after their pre-Christmas bonanza, and loads of people are watching TV for rather more than the average thirty hours per week. So no sooner had they started on the turkey left-overs than the Department of Health started on them, complete with a rendition of the Supremes' old hit 'Stop – in the name of love, before you break my heart'. I also wanted humour; you can't go on at people for ever, saying 'don't'. So we approved a series of gently comic little advertisements for newspapers and magazines. We had to drop one ad I liked, showing David (an ordinary little man) beating Goliath (a big cigarette), when test marketing showed that too few people in the target groups knew who David and Goliath were. We did go ahead with others, cartoons by Calman (who does the British Heart Foundation, too) and Reg Smythe's Andy Capp. Smythe had quietly removed Andy's ever-present cigarette some time ago, and now the little rogue stood there, clutching his pants, caught at the doctor's and getting some good advice. The campaign was heavily played in the North and Midlands where CHD is worst, and achieved a recognition there of 63 per cent (78 per cent on prompting) by February 1989. In the Tyne-Tees area – Newcastle again – 81 per cent claimed to have seen the TV ad. Now that's more like it. Who says making a fuss doesn't have an effect?

The heart campaign was pursued by the press with alacrity. Even the *Sun* converted its page-3 pictures in the week of the launch into 'Heart-throb beauties', photographed with chest extenders in unusual places and captions such as 'keeping abreast of the news', 'lovely Natalie, 18, is a work of heart'. Clearly someone in the Department of Health approved, for in March 1989 I found that whole week's collection of very healthy-looking ladies carefully cut out and filed away in a bright red folder for posterity. We targeted the tabloids quite deliberately, placing more of the 'No Smoking Day' advertisements with them, for example. They did their bit, with many pages of advice on cutting down smoking and avoiding heart attacks, including 'Twenty ways to avoid heart disease' and the like. Ministers, if occasionally embarrassed, were well pleased with their efforts.

As the programme rolled around the country it was obvious that each neighbourhood would find different problems and solutions to highlight. I visited many of their events – Maidstone's 'Apple-a-Day' campaign, Slough's 'Health Habit' and many many more. I scribbled, 'Oh golly, another one' on one of the dozens of invitations still in the file, and although I was having a whale of a time I don't doubt that the public regarded me as somewhat hyperactive. Those endless blood tests and public aerobic exercises did me some good, though. My pride would not let me score anything but 'excellent' and I was somewhat put out at one event on a Friday morning, when, after I had already worked a sixty-five-hour week, including two late-night debates, I was told I was only 'average for my age'!

The place I came to know best was the town of Dewsbury in Yorkshire, which was believed to have the worst record in England for heart disease deaths in England in middle age – at 422 per 100,000 for men and 379 for women. The Dewsbury team was led by a sincere and thoughtful man, Dr Mohammad (Steve) Ashraff, who was their District Medical Officer. When LAYH started he had the services of half a Health Education Officer. By the time my links with them came to an end, the whole town was engaged in an intensive campaign to do something about the killer in their midst.

Dewsbury was interesting, as we found that many of our assumptions were unfounded. For example, although it had the largest mosque in Yorkshire, Asians made up only 5 per cent of the population; their very high levels of heart disease could not be accounting for the results. (Steve himself promptly went on a diet and lost a stone.) There was a surprisingly low level of reported smoking – under 30 per cent. There was not that much unemployment, either. In 1987, at 13.5 per cent, it was 2 per cent over the national average. So that meant we should also be concerned about the 86.5 per cent of the work-force in work.

The locals were all worried about heart disease and only too well aware of it. A questionnaire in the town in the early part of 1987 produced a response of 85 per cent. One in five had been to hospital within the previous year and over 40 per cent had been to a health centre or clinic, yet only 12 per cent had received any advice – with 'Relax more' as the most common. Some 6 per cent knew they had high blood pressure (a quarter had not had their blood pressure measured within the last five years) but they did not see high blood pressure as a disorder. A quarter were taking pain killers: 18 per cent had bought a headache remedy in the previous week and 10 per cent an indigestion remedy. Thus there appeared to be a generally poor level of health which showed itself in mild but persistent disorders. Then the sufferer would keel over suddenly, unexpectedly to anyone but an informed observer.

Dewsbury people claimed to be eating all the right foods, too, despite the town's fifty-five chip shops, and a third claimed they had made some beneficial changes to their diet in the previous twelve months. So what was going on? Our clue came from articles in the local newspaper by journalist Margaret Watson who had seen several heart-attack deaths in male relatives in their forties. It was the diet, she said. As a long-standing tradition they seemed to eat fat with everything, usually beef fat and lard left over from endless fat roast meat. 'Fat and bread' was the local tasty snack and was eaten at all hours of the day or evening to help 'line the stomach'. Because it was a snack, it wasn't seen, it didn't count. All the attention focused on the plate at table, not what was munched while waiting for breakfast, in the tea-break at work, after dinner, on the way home, with a cup of tea in the evening in front of the telly, with the Horlicks before turning in. Yuk!

The town had a Health Day like virtually everyone else in the summer of 1988. It was opened by the Mayor, who started to make a speech about how all the heart disease in Dewsbury was the Government's fault. Incensed beyond measure, Steve, normally so shy and self-effacing, seized the microphone and told the people that was nonsense and that they carried responsibility, in part, for their own health, and they could do something about it, Mr Mayor included. So there. And he was roundly applauded. Later I talked to one of the nurses who helped out that day. 'It was all very upsetting, really,' she said. 'Everyone came, they were so enthusiastic. We tested over 2,000 people's blood pressure; we worked till we dropped. We found more than 200 of them walking around with very high blood pressure indeed. They had no idea they were in such danger. At the end of the day I was so upset I just sat down and burst into tears. I knew Dewsbury and Yorkshire was bad, but I had no idea it was as bad as this.' Then she brightened. 'Don't worry, Mrs Currie,' she continued. 'This has taught us all a lot, doctors as well. We're all going to tackle this now, together. And we'll beat it.' I hope they do.

*   *   *

Steve Ashraff came with me on the trip to Scandinavia in 1987. My officials and staff had been working horribly hard so, partly as a reward, partly because we all needed refreshing, we agreed to a short trip to Scandinavia in September 1987. Governments in the 1970s would look to the Scandinavians as exemplars, much as their predecessors at the turn of the century had looked to Bismarck and the Germans. Sir Keith Joseph told me that in the inner circles of the Tory party, preparing for the 1979 general election, much mention was made of Swedish success. Lord Hailsham, wise wizard, was heard to mutter that 'the first thing we should put in the manifesto is to abolish Sweden!' We have a natural tendency to run ourselves down in this country and are always convinced someone else can do it better. But a visit to Sweden and Finland *would* pay dividends. The Swedes had been pioneers, along with parts of the United States, in mass screening for breast cancer, the Finns for cervical cancer. Sweden had a system of 'no-fault compensation' which was attracting interest in Britain, and Finland's Northern Karelia province, up near the Arctic Circle, had a remarkable record in reducing its previously staggeringly high levels of heart disease.

The main visit in Sweden was to Kopparberg, where we met the staff involved in the breast-cancer screening programme. Sitting in on one consultation I understood, despite not having a word of Swedish, that the key was the gentle but thorough discussion between the woman patient and her doctor – on what they had found, how serious it was, what could be done about it and what it would mean for her. Golly, the doctors were so nice, so serious, not patronizing or embarrassed. Something in their training taught them a very high order of communication with patients. The Swedes were also introducing cervical-cancer screening all over the country and getting an 80 per cent response from the women.

We ended the Swedish visit with a tour of the extraordinary old copper mines which gave the area its name. Looking at the primitive working conditions one realized why heart disease is only of recent concern. My constituents used to work like that, hauling coal. They crawled out of the pit and expired, and their widows collected the pension. One old Derbyshire lady told me how, before the first war, the mothers would gather at the pit-head and carry their exhausted children – down the mines at twelve and thirteen – home, asleep on their backs. The degenerative diseases of old age were not a matter of concern.

The highlight, however, was the trip to Finland – stranger, more remote, than Sweden. We started off in Helsinki, with the Finnish Cancer Society's Director General, a marvellous, brainy, elegant woman called Dr Liisa Elovaniio. She came to London nine months later, at my invitation, to speak at the Women's Health Conference.

We were puzzled by the Finns' special experience, in which, over ten years, not only had the death rate from cervical cancer dropped very sharply, but so also had the incidence, the number of cases. I could understand detecting cancer early enough to reduce mortality; but how do you make cancer go away, not occur in the first place? 'We don't know yet,' she said, 'but as long as we have been doing this programme, we have found on the slides of the smear test all sorts of conditions, infections, inflammations and the like. The rule in Finland is that we do not send people away and tell them to come back for another test; we treat whatever we find and always have, and we treat the boyfriend or husband too.' Now that does raise interesting questions. Could a persistent infection, or one that only flares up occasionally, lay the groundwork in our cells for cancer at a later date? Or might it be that a weakened immune system, or a person with a proneness to infection, might suffer both the inflammation and the cancer, which we know is linked to a virus? More research needed is the frustrating conclusion.

And so to Northern Karelia, ten miles from the Arctic Circle, close to the Soviet border. We could not fly there from the capital, so we took the overnight sleeper for the long journey. I had never been on a sleeper before and anyway was too keyed up to sleep (sounds of merriment and chinking glasses in the next cabin; dark circles under eyes the next morning . . .). I spent a lot of time looking out of the window, realizing what distance really is as the vast dark wet wastes of Finland sped past. Karelia, apart from giving its name to a nice piece of music, meant nothing to me. It was heavily wooded, with the main occupation being timber work.

When the Finnish death rate for heart disease led the world in the early 1970s at more than 500 deaths per 100,000 for men in their middle years, Northern Karelia led Finland with an average rate of over 800. The widows eventually petitioned the Finnish Parliament to do something about it, and a substantial ten-year programme started, which had succeeded in bringing down the death rate by nearly 20 per cent. It was not as successful as in the United States, where the drop then was over 30 per cent, but it had the advantage for us that the programme had originally been confined to a particular region, where it had involved all the local agencies. including schools, employers, retailers and food producers, as well as the health and local authorities, so maybe it would give us a model we could adapt.

There was also a sauna. My staff decided it wouldn't be Finland without one, so as we arrived in Joensuu in Karelia in the grey light of dawn, we checked into the town's hotel and saunaed first, with breakfast later. It was all most decorous and I saw no huge Finnish maidens or birch twigs. Then into a heavy day's talks and visits. The Finns were lovely to us every step of the way.

They had managed to reduce smoking, they told us, though their women had responded better than their men. Their programme planners had not bothered about exercise, they said, as Finns tend to take a lot of it. I wondered how true that was, as I jogged along the path by the river the following morning, overtaken by dozens of cars and one lone cyclist. There were no other joggers and I got some curious looks. They had a lot to teach us, but it was obvious from the start that they had not convinced everyone.

On the plane going home we had our lunch, nicely packaged, lots of cream, a quarter-bottle of wine for every passenger; not exactly what you would expect from a nation which was supposed to have taken heart disease prevention into its culture. They told us proudly that more Finns were now drinking 'light milk', which I took to mean skimmed milk. In a snatch of conversation I understood that 'light milk' was about 4 per cent fat. 'But that's ordinary milk, whole milk,' I said; skim has virtually none, and semi-skimmed is 1.5 to 2 per cent. 'Golly, what were they drinking before?' The answer was butterfat-enriched milk, so thick you could stand your fork up in it. It was the usual drink of thirsty lumberjacks before they started on the harder stuff. They would put away a couple of litres – four pints – of 'real' milk at one go. No wonder they had heart disease.

The Karelians had tried, quite successfully, to change the agricultural production patterns. Dairy cattle did well, but one local delicacy was berry fruits, so they switched over a substantial acreage and now everyone helped out by eating berry dishes. Oh, they were wonderful; venison with cranberries, pale apricot cloudberries for dessert, redcurrants by the ton. The trouble was that the berries, mostly similar to blackcurrants, were fiercely tart and could not be eaten without cooking, and with a great deal of sugar. Most of the time they were incorporated into traditional Finnish pastries and custards with lashings of cream. That would do wonders for the cholesterol count, I thought, as I tucked into yet another yummy piece with my morning coffee. Clearly they still had a problem.

It was worse than that, they told me. The decline in the death rate had started to flatten out in the mid-1980s leaving Finland with figures still way above other countries. What now? Now we have hamburgers, they said, and certain well-known soft drinks; just like the rest of the civilized world. Our young people and working housewives are forgetting how to cook altogether, and we may have to start thinking it out all over again. A depressing prospect for them, but a helpful view for us. As I bought a very posh version of a Laplander's woolly hat, and some reindeer meat (low in cholesterol) at the airport, we agreed it had been a very worth while trip indeed.

*   *   *

Did the campaign work? It depends how you look at it. The first objective of the Look After Your Heart campaign had been to raise awareness of coronary heart disease and its risk factors – primarily diet. We certainly managed to do that. A 1986 survey showed that most people were aware of the illness and of the risks. That survey concluded: 'The English are aware of coronary heart disease as a serious illness, know of its major causes and ways of preventing them, have taken some steps towards changing their behaviour to protect their health, but are not sufficiently persuaded that changes should be made.' Hence the need for the LAYH campaign. It may be some time, however, before anyone can claim real success in changing habits.

In the late spring of 1989, the Health Education Authority were coming sadly to the view that the survey conclusion of three years earlier still held true. However, there is a 'softening up' process which is worthwhile. People change awareness first, then attitudes, long before they make the huge effort to change their whole life-style. So hopefully there is much more change to come.

'"Look After Your Heart" is not just a heart campaign – it is a strategy aimed at encouraging a healthier way of life. It will start by telling people what are the main health risks related to heart disease and how they can best be avoided. But it will develop from there and, as the campaign unfolds, we hope it will turn into a national crusade,' said Norman Fowler, in his April 1987 introduction to the Look After Your Heart campaign booklet. A few weeks later we fought a general election, and won, for an unprecedented third time in a row – this time facing stronger opposition – and romped home with a majority of 101. In South Derbyshire, George Brown's old stamping ground, my majority went up to 10,311. Oh yes, that campaign worked. The Department of Health made its contribution to that success, in my view. We had demonstrated that we cared about people, we had given leadership, we had shown courage. We had tried to look beyond the immediate demands of short-term electoral pressures to the health needs of people in every walk of life. On the political front the campaign worked, and I commend it to all future governments.

Some people thought the campaign worked even better than it did. The *Daily Express* of 15 May 1987 (three weeks after the LAYH launch) carried this story:

For the first time in many years, the death rate is plummeting. In England and Wales, more than a thousand fewer people than expected died each week, according to the Office of Population Censuses and Surveys. The first signs came last November when weekly deaths started to fall, and remained down for the rest of the year. Since then, there has been only one high death week during the record cold spell in January. The downturn could be the first sign that healthier life-styles are paying off.

One elderly gentleman rang my office in great excitement with his congratulations, which of course we graciously accepted.

There is always a price to be paid for success and it is campaigners who pay it, even if that's their job. Our efforts on health promotion began to attract international interest and I was profiled and interviewed by the foreign press. The 'No Smoking Day 1988' giant cigarette photo appeared all over the world, usually with headlines such as that in *Newsweek* of 5 December 1988 – 'Britain's National Scold'. Jean Rook, the First Lady of Fleet Street, called me a 'miserable-stomached daft little woman' and 'Britain's biggest gob'. Charming! You can make up your own mind. If the campaign saved any lives, reduced any pain, cheered up or encouraged those trying to improve their lives, then I can live with the carping and look back on those times with much pleasure and contentment.

By July 1988 some targets had been refined. By 1993, it is hoped, 90 per cent of the population will be aware of the campaign against heart disease – with 10 million employees enrolled in LAYH through their companies, and a 50 per cent increase in the number of GPs who routinely record risk factors such as blood pressure, smoking history and the like. I see no reason why these targets should not be achieved. They are, however, a means to an end. The aim, in line with promises long since made to the World Health Organization, is a 25 per cent reduction in mortality from coronary heart disease by the year 2000. It is possible – other countries have done it. Did the campaign work? Ask me then.

3

Government Health Warning

Tobacco . . . is commonly abused by most men, which take it as tinkers do ale, 'tis a plague, a mischief, a violent purger of goods, lands, health, hellish, devilish and damned tobacco, the ruin and overthrow of body and soul

Richard Burton, 1577–1640

I have never needed reminding of the ravages caused by tobacco. My family, like many in the land, has been affected by cigarette smoking: lives shortened, ending in pain, fear and misery. There were, however, many opportunities to be reminded in my time as a minister. Frequently, the gap between the victim's knowledge and my scraps of inside information yawned very wide. I began to understand why we have not been granted the gift of seeing into the future. It is too frightening, sometimes.

There was the occasion of the opening of a cardio-thoracic unit in Yorkshire. Most of the patients, coughing, breathless, grey-faced, were old men. In one side ward was a bright, cheerful young woman.

'What are you in for?' I had asked.

'Got a bit of a growth, like, on my lung,' she said, matter-of-factly. 'I'm here for radiotherapy. Treatment's rotten, makes me feel so sick.'

I froze. Most lung cancer patients are dead within two years of diagnosis. By the time it is detected, it's too late. Only seven in every hundred survive as long as five years.

'Any idea what caused it?' I asked, trying to talk casually. 'You're a bit young, really.'

'Oh yes,' she replied. 'They say it's cigarettes. I've been smoking since I was nine. I'm trying to give up now; you should be pleased

45

with me, shouldn't you?' and she gave me a cheeky, matey look.

We shook hands. 'Good luck,' I said, and meant it. I whispered a prayer for her as I walked away.

*   *   *

Lung cancer killed over 40,000 people in the United Kingdom last year. That is more than 100 people each day. Lung cancer is not as expensive to the NHS as heart disease because it kills people relatively quickly. It is caused nearly entirely (90 per cent) by smoking, and so are non-cancerous congestive lung diseases, such as emphysema, which add another 28,000 to the death toll every year. The costs to the NHS are in excess of £500 million per annum. Absences from work as a result of smoking-related illness are estimated at 50 million man-days per annum – twenty times the number lost to industrial disputes in 1987.

Britain is, sadly, the worst in the world for mortality from lung cancer. In Scotland seventy-one people in every 100,000 die of it each year, in England and Wales fifty-eight. Men are four times more likely to die of it than women. The average Scottish male is twice as likely to die from lung cancer as a Frenchman. Curiously, the death rates for it in Northern Ireland and Eire are much lower than on the mainland of Britain for both men and women: maybe they die of heart disease first?

Our death rates are a legacy of old habits long since abandoned by many. In the days of George VI most people smoked. Doctors offered a cigarette to a nervous patient; film stars puffed away; governments gave out free tobacco vouchers. Equally, it will be in the next century before the full benefits of today's non-smoking are felt.

It's not just lung cancer that smokers are playing with. The risk factors for CHD and strokes include cigarette smoking. Amongst the 400 components of tobacco smoke are many which damage the heart and arteries. Perinatal mortality is increased in women smokers, so is cervical cancer. The young woman who smokes and is on the Pill is many times more likely to have a heart attack than one who isn't. In fact, smoking is rapidly becoming more of a problem for women than men.

Of all the things we can do for our health, stopping smoking is the most important and the most effective. From day one the health risks start to diminish and within ten years, for most people, the ex-smoker is almost at the same point he would have been at if he had never had any. It really is worth trying to stop. And many people have. Smoking in this country is a minority activity and has been for some years in all the socio-economic categories. Broadly speaking, one third of people now smoke cigarettes, so every user is outnumbered two to one by a non-user. Many of the non-users are people who have given up over the years – probably about 14 million of them. ASH (Action on Smoking and Health), the pressure group which is funded by the Department of Health, claims there are more ex-smokers than current smokers.

We should not be too pessimistic about smoking in this country. The World Health Organization reported, in a survey of 122 countries in May 1988, that in Britain we had moved from being the highest cigarette-smoking nation in the world to one of the lowest. Cubans, Greeks, Cypriots, Poles and the Japanese are now amongst the heaviest smokers. Then come the Hungarians, Canadians, Yugoslavs, Swiss, Spanish, Australians and Koreans; the USA still has high levels of smoking, too. The Austrians, Czechs, New Zealanders, Italians, French (who also go in for heavy tar cigarettes), Germans, Israelis and Russians follow. All are heavier smokers now than us. The United Kingdom's cigarette consumption per head of population had dropped to half that in the heaviest smoking countries, and the average tar content of our cigarettes is now amongst the lowest in the world.

I was never the best person to advise people on how to stop. As an asthmatic I had never dared risk my wheezy chest with cigarettes, and as a teenager I reckoned there were more important things to learn about. I've told the story many times, to excuse my ignorance, about when my pals in 1963 (when we were sixteen or so) were busy behind the bike sheds at school learning how to smoke. I had somehow acquired a copy of *Lady Chatterley's Lover*, which was then on trial for obscenity, and was busy instead learning D. H. Lawrence's view of what to do with gamekeepers. I could never quite see why people needed extra stimuli like smoking, or wanted to vanish into the oblivion of alcohol. Life is what you make it, I thought, and using whatever talents and skills you may have to the full, not blunting them with drugs or self-neglect, might just help make it even better. Anyway, I enjoyed life without them. Simplistic perhaps, but defensible, and not a bad philosophy for life.

*   *   *

If we were to help those who were smoking to stop successfully, and to help people avoid starting in the first place, we needed to know more about motivation. I commissioned some work on teenage smoking, asking in particular why girls now smoke more than boys. We found that, for boys, there is no significant difference in attitude between smokers and non-smokers – the vast majority being non-smokers (they drink, though, some of them like fish). Girls, however, who in England are twice as likely to smoke as their brothers, see smoking in a positive light. It will keep them slim, it will help them with exams, it looks sophisticated. The psychology of teenage boys and girls is different. There is also plenty of evidence to show that if young people do not start smoking before they are twenty, then they probably will never start. That research forms the background to a long-term campaign aimed at schoolchildren, initially funded to the tune of £2 million a year, which was announced in the first days of 1989 by the Prime Minister. This is our major contribution to Europe Against Cancer Year in 1989, a campaign which is aiming for a 15 per cent reduction of cancer in Europe by the end of the century, and it should have long-term effects.

There are those who say fear of health risks does not make people change their behaviour. I think that is nonsense. Look all around, there are plenty who do change, every day. The Health Education Authority told me that in earlier days the most successful anti-smoking advertisement they ran showed an ordinary man, smoking in his armchair, reading in his newspaper about lung cancer. His little girl comes and puts her arms around him. It persuaded even heavy and committed smokers to stop; they wanted to see their children grow up. But there are plenty who, aware of the health risks, still are not motivated to change, so we explored their motives, and wherever possible substituted some other urge they might more readily accept.

For example, I think we have been successful in getting across the notion that masculine men don't smoke, only weak wimps do. I was aware of the finding in 1986 that smokers aged from twenty-five to forty-four are least happy with their habit, while on the whole the older people are less worried (perhaps because those who worried stopped – or died). I had a hilarious live phone-in, from London, with Piccadilly Radio in Manchester for No Smoking Day 1988. They had lined up a local strong man who claimed to smoke fifty a day. Live over the air, my conversation with the commentator (male, non-smoker) went something like this:

'Tell me, is he good looking?'

'Yes, not bad. Big and strong.'

'Can you get nice and close to him for me?' (Sounds of gales of laughter in the background. They were out in a busy city street somewhere in central Manchester. Heaven knows what they were doing.)

'Yes, I'm close. What do you want me to do now?'

'Smell his breath, I'll bet it's just like an ashtray.'

'Ugh!' (More laughter, and the sound of some equipment falling over.)

'And I'd guess his hair reeks of cigarettes, and his skin, and his clothes. Doesn't he know that real men, he-men, don't smoke? He'd be even more gorgeous if he stopped. I might even fancy him myself . . .'

And so on. Some of the nudges and winks must have verged on the obscene, but generally people know when there is a serious purpose afoot, even if dressed up with harmless humour.

In the West Midlands in 1982 there had been a campaign against smoking. The first item on the first agenda of the new Central Birmingham Health Authority in April 1982, which I was appointed by Norman Fowler to chair, was that all meetings should be smoke-free. As part of the campaign, smokers who had already successfully given up the habit were asked by local newspapers to write in and

explain how they did it. The results were collected in an excellent booklet (published by the Health Education Council and which I think is still available) illustrated with marvellous cartoons by Larry. I liked Mr J. T. of Shrewsbury who had smoked forty a day for two years: 'My wife and I banned smoking inside the house, the car, the pub, the shops, anywhere except in the fresh air. Oh boy, was it cold outside at midnight!' One lady went to bed when the urge came on – not a bad idea as cigarettes are a stimulant and many people find they feel tired while giving up, until the body adjusts. Mr T. of Dudley offered a different view: 'I thought one night of my old workmates. Twenty-six had died with chest complaints. I said, no more.' He had smoked fifteen cigarettes a day for forty-four years, and stopped for good successfully.

The staffer responsible for the booklet, Judy Berry, moved later to the North West Health Authority and did the same thing there. I left a copy of her second booklet on my husband's desk and, together with all the other pressures on him, mainly from our daughters, it helped him to stop in March 1987 after nearly thirty years and he hasn't smoked since. He succeeded with a London company called 'HabitBreaker'. His employers arranged for eight weekly one-to-one sessions with the company's trained counsellors for any members of staff who were interested. At the first session a target and a time limit were agreed. If the target was achieved, the employer paid. If not, the failed tryer coughed up – £175 back in 1987, quite a disincentive. My husband is now quoted in the HabitBreaker brochure, tongue in cheek, if not cigarette in mouth: 'If you want to stop smoking, HabitBreaker is the method. There is no easy solution but Habit-Breaker make it possible. It's also helpful if your wife doesn't smoke!'

The idea of No Smoking Day was originated by a Minnesota newspaper editor in 1974 and eventually developed across the USA into the Great American Smokeout, sponsored by the American Cancer Society. Our cancer charities still had some problems with smoking. Soon after I was appointed in 1986 the Imperial Cancer Research Fund showed me their facilities, paid for entirely by voluntary subscription, in Lincoln's Inn Fields. But, oh dear, there were ashtrays everywhere!

'Why don't you ban smoking in this building, here of all places?' I asked, sadly.

They looked a bit surprised at the question (it was still 1986). 'Well, you see, it's the maintenance men,' said one of the party. 'We wouldn't want to upset them.'

'Really?' I countered. 'It's OK for them to get cancer, is it? They don't matter?'

He lapsed into a safer silence.

Twenty minutes later I was introduced to the Head of Maintenance. 'Is it true that your chaps all smoke, and that this is the reason why smoking is still allowed in this building?' I asked, sweetly.

'No, it is not,' he replied indignantly. 'I'm a non-smoker myself, and the lads would be happy to keep a rule like that. It would help the ones trying to give up, wouldn't it? It's him,' pointing to the man at my side, 'he's the one as wants to keep it. Can you persuade him?'

Red faces all round.

Ashtrays have now gone from the public areas, I am told, but are still available in the staff offices.

The No Smoking Day idea was brought to Britain, therefore, not by the cancer charities but by the National Society of Non-Smokers, who suffered for a long time from a generally 'dotty' image. They attracted the main organizations involved with smoking prevention, especially ASH and the British Heart Foundation, and it has been an established event on the second Wednesday in March here since 1984.

Bill Caldwell

" National No Smoking Day is OVER now, Mrs Currie "

(All cancer charities do now support them.) I was involved in two of them, in 1987 and 1988.

The 1987 day was described (by supporters) as the most cost-effective health promotion campaign in the world. On a promotional budget of £150,000 – compared with an annual promotional spend by the tobacco industry of around £100 million – it achieved an awareness level among smokers of 88 per cent. I was told that, according to surveys, some 2.5 million smokers, about one in six, took part by cutting down or giving up for the day; about 800,000 of these succeeded in giving up all day; and some 50,000 were believed to have given up permanently. The organizers claimed that, as a consequence, up to 5,000 premature deaths from cancer, heart disease and lung conditions are likely to have been prevented in the long run.

My main contribution that first time, in March 1987, was to follow the example set by the Princess of Wales, who had been photographed a few days earlier at the Kentish Town Health Centre in North London blowing into a carbon monoxide monitor. The tell-tale machines measure the amount of carbon monoxide in the blood and will give the lie to secret smokers, even occasional ones. The Princess apparently recorded a normal non-smoker's reading. Mine, beeping away at around 11, indicated someone who had been stuck in London traffic for the best part of an hour, and took some time to get back to normal, at 5 or less. There was a huge crowd of reporters and photographers. One scrawny chap, notebook stuffed in mackintosh pocket in the time-honoured fashion, I knew to be a heavy smoker. Getting hold of him was like trying to catch a gerbil in a cage, but eventually he was latched on to the blower on the machine and encouraged by our cheers to give a big puff into it. It rapidly registered 58, squeaked and conked out. For months afterwards those present would swear to me that they had all given up that instant, but it was certainly an impressive demonstration of the damage smoking can do.

By the following year, Wednesday 9 March 1988, we were more sophisticated. The target groups by then were young women, children and middle-aged men. *Chat* magazine, widely read by young women, had a knitting pattern for an attractive white 'No Smoking' sweater which I duly modelled for them, wore all day and still have. We started off with the TV cameras at a school in the Dartford constituency of Bob Dunn MP, the big, solid Lancastrian who was then Junior Minister at the Department of Education. All very correct, as many ex-grammar schools are, school orchestra playing, headmaster concealing nerves beneath a formal exterior, young pupils sitting in immaculate uniforms in neat rows, very impressive. That sorted out the children.

From there to the last target group, the men. This was a lot more fun, for we had been contacted by Ron Pollard, the ebullient director of Ladbroke's who is often on television calling the odds. Prodded by Ron, who had recovered not long before from a heart attack and had become a determined non-smoker, the company had done its market research, and had found an unmet demand from customers for some no-smoking betting shops. So a dozen were selected and designated as smoke-free zones, and my job was to open one of them. That day there were soft drinks and buns available alongside the betting slips, and I allowed myself to put money on a horse called 'Warning' for the Two Thousand Guineas, and 'Attitude Adjuster' for the Grand National. Ron also offered me odds on George Bush winning the American Presidential race, but as the best he could do was evens, I politely refused. Mr Bush duly won; the others, as you will know if you are a punter, have had varying careers since and I lost my money.

That was a memorable day. In the end there was so much interest that I found myself working for twenty-two straight hours, way past midnight, despite having put a lot of pre-recorded material in the can. I hoped it would all do some good and, secretly, I half hoped, since we were running out of bright ideas, that someone else would be doing it in 1989. The latter wish at least was granted.

*   *   *

The UK Government's policy on smoking is influenced by a committee set up in 1973 by the Heath Government which struggles under the clumsy title The Independent Scientific Committee on Smoking and Health (ISCSH). Its chairman is Sir Peter Froggatt, professor at Queen's University Belfast, and its job is to undertake rigorous scrutiny of all the research on tobacco world-wide and then to tell the Government what to do.

Following previous ISCSH reports, Government action in Britain has taken various paths. The committee has recommended campaigning to warn the public against smoking. As a result, the number of adult men smoking in Britain has dropped from 52 per cent in 1972 to 35 per cent in 1986, and women from 41 per cent to 31 per cent in the same period. Who says campaigns don't work? The latest survey of smoking behaviour, for 1988, will be published in March 1990.

Another target of effort has been to get the average tar content down. The carcinogens are in the tar, and although doctors at first protested that this approach was giving in to the tobacco lobbies, it does seem to have worked, with a resulting fall from over 20mg of tar to around 13mg in the average cigarette smoked in this country. That's why Gauloises and other more powerful cigarettes now seem revolting to us; we aren't used to that reek any longer.

Tackling tar content is, however, nowhere near enough. Nicotine is an addictive stimulant affecting the heart directly, while carbon monoxide also forces the heart to work harder. Worried about additives? The ISCSH Fourth Report also has a seventeen page list of all the *permitted* additives which may find their way into cigarettes. They include aluminium, caustic soda, cocoa, coffee, cellulose, molasses, chalk, glycerol, tartrazine, iron oxide, liquid paraffin, shellac, titanium dioxide, triethylene glycol, hydrochloric acid . . .

There are also some controls on advertising – cigarette advertisements were taken off television in 1962 – mostly achieved by voluntary agreement between the Government and the industry. The effect of the agreement extant when I was a minister was to prevent the showing of cigarettes *in use*, so the advertisements became increasingly complicated and cryptic, but the producers were in practice also paying for large-scale government health warnings on 40-foot posters all over the country. The ban also applies to other advertisers, so if you see pictures of attractive people smoking cigarettes in adverts prompted by the pop music industry or by clothing manufacturers, please complain to the Advertising Standards Authority, who will start shooting from the hip.

The latest agreement ran out towards the end of Europe Against Cancer Year, in October 1989. Should we ban all cigarette advertising? I must say that I was fairly relaxed about it. The product is legal, its possession not a crime. We had done far better in reducing smoking and changing its culture than many other countries, such as Norway, which had banned advertising outright by law. Also, I'm not sure just how much support there would be in this country for a complete ban on advertising. Surveys in 1987, just as the debate on passive smoking was starting, showed only a slight majority (51 per cent) in favour of a ban on all forms of cigarette advertising, with the highest score, 61 per cent, in favour of a ban on outdoor hoardings and posters. The public would need a lot of softening up by political and local leaders to win support for a ban, but it is not impossible. In the North West, where smoking is heavy and the health authority determined, 67 per cent thought banning advertising and promotion of tobacco was a good idea.

The ISCSH Fourth Report, and the interim report which preceded it in 1987, produced one major change in approach. The term 'passive smoking' entered the nation's vocabulary.

For a very long time, it was non-smokers who were on the defensive. They might not like smoking, but that was no reason to demand that other people shouldn't do it. You don't like it? Go somewhere else, what I'm doing is legal and none of your business. Very gradually, however, it became apparent that breathing in someone else's smoke was not just unpleasant but could cause ill-health in the unwitting recipient. The ISCSH started to point the finger in 1983, when they showed that general respiratory problems in *non*-smokers could be traced to smoking spouses or to the smoky atmosphere at work. The children of smokers were more likely to have coughs and colds and chest problems, more days off school and, as a result, a poorer work record. The link between smoking in pregnancy and low birth weight, or a poorer prognosis for the baby was well understood and resulted in a series of hard-hitting advertisements in the early 1980s by the (then) Health Education Council. But the ISCSH now took the whole question further.

'Sidestream' smoke, from a cigarette in an ashtray, is more powerful, they said, than smoke exhaled by the smoker, since his body has absorbed much of the content. Also, the damage is the same to the passive smoker whether the smoke comes from cigarettes or cigars, whereas the smoker is less damaged by cigars or pipes since the smoke is less likely to be inhaled. The ISCSH looked at studies of non-smoking spouses of smokers from all over the world. It is tricky work as many were ex-smokers (or were fibbing about having given up), but quoting eighty-six international references in this part of their report and some 600 studies altogether, they said: 'The majority of reports conclude that passive smoking is associated with an increased risk of lung cancer in non-smokers . . . the findings overall are consistent with there being a small increase in the risk of lung cancer from exposure to environmental tobacco smoke, in the range 10–30 per cent . . .'

Let me put that in context. The chances of getting lung cancer are up to eleven times greater for a habitual heavy smoker compared to a non-smoker; say, 1,000 per cent. The risk to a non-smoker of regularly breathing in someone else's smoke, at 10–30 per cent, is therefore relatively tiny. Out of all the 40,000 deaths from lung cancer last year, passive smoking probably accounted for around 200 to 300. I felt so sorry for that small group of people who got cancer but didn't smoke, perhaps never had, or who may have given up so long ago that their personal risk should have been negligible. At this point, quite suddenly, almost overnight, the civil liberties were on the other foot. You can do what you like to your own lungs, chum, but you can't demand the freedom to do it to mine.

Early in 1988 the ISCSH report came to government and ministers looked at it carefully over the winter and discussed what to do. The Minister of State, Tony Newton, was a chain-smoker but is anti-smoking. His press release of 23 March 1988 accepted the thrust of the report. No doubt we will hear more in future. But my impression was that the ISCSH report in 1988 by itself changed the culture in this country. It needed no help from me – this was a change whose time had come.

Why do governments in this country hesitate when it comes to firm action and using the law on smoking? Here we are, with some of the world's toughest laws on drink-driving (and more to come); banning by law shopping on a Sunday, harmless enough; contemplating at one stage a ban on the sale of raw milk; forcing strict rules on pub opening hours; legislating the wearing of seat-belts; insisting on licences for both public entertainment and the ownership of private television sets and prosecuting non-compliants. Yet when it comes to smoking we hesitate, and witter on about the importance of voluntary agreements. They suit the manufacturers, of course. Perhaps they will suit the rest of us less in future.

Most people in government don't smoke. Most people in Whitehall don't. Most people in London don't, if it comes to that, and have coped perfectly well with enforced bans on smoking on the London Underground. Why are some unconvinced? I don't know. I suspect they will stay unconvinced of the appalling health hazards posed by tobacco until the day they have a stroke or a shadow on the lung, or drop dead in front of the rest of us.

I'm personally pleased now to see that 'smoke-free' areas are becoming much more common on buses, trains and planes, entirely for commercial reasons, because that is what the customers (often including the smokers) prefer. An opinion poll in November 1987 showed an amazing 85 per cent of the public in favour of restrictions on smoking in public places. Commercial hard-headedness is the best guarantor of clean air. The day will come when good restaurants, having toiled all day to give us the most delicate of tastes, object to the philistines who destroy their palates (and the enjoyment of the rest of us, still eating) with fags and request those few customers to go puff elsewhere.

*   *   *

A word of warning. European attitudes are changing and becoming more aggressively anti-smoking, which has become more apparent during Europe Against Cancer Year. I'm not sure that is a good thing and it sits uneasily with our gentler, more persuasive approach. The Eurocrats are trying to use the advent of the single European market in 1992 to change many of the rules, ostensibly because of the necessity to harmonize trade. If successful, they intend to harmonize to the highest health standard then extant in any country in the Community. That means, probably, a country which has legislated, which on the whole we don't do. Personally, I am quite relaxed about putting the Irish slogan 'Smoking Kills' on cigarette packets, but I can well understand that there are others who are incensed at the notion, especially as it will have to be done by law, not by agreement with the industry. The views of the latter are pretty obvious! There are battles yet to come.

*   *   *

And then there is alcohol. Whenever the public becomes aware of a health issue, there is often a backlash, as health professionals rush to tell us that we have got it wrong and something else is more important. This was the case with alcohol, about which concern rose steadily after 1986 – not as a result of LAYH at all, but because of fears about rising crime and violence, and because of the successful work on hard drugs described in Chapter Four.

'Alcohol is the major public health issue of our time, overshadowing even that of tobacco . . .' proclaimed the Royal College of Psychiatrists in 1986 in their excellent report *Alcohol – our Favourite Drug.* They went on:

There is at present a very high level of public concern about illicit drug abuse. During 1983, 77 deaths in Britain were attributed to the inhalation of glue and solvents, and 82 were attributed to opiates

57

and other illicit drugs. These figures are, of course, disturbing . . . Alcohol misuse is, however, annually associated with 4,000 deaths, 50,000 convictions for drunk driving and 5,000 first admissions to psychiatric hospital for alcohol dependence and alcoholic psychosis. It is our favourite socially acceptable drug . . .

Their comparison with tobacco is, of course, wrong – ten times as many people every year die from lung cancer alone as from alcohol directly. The psychiatrists were right to be worried, however. Mental illness may not be a big killer in this country but it is a big spender. It is estimated that the psychiatric services, along with their treatment, account for more money spent in the NHS than anything else. Here again, however, the causality – the link between cause and effect – is complex. Sometimes heavy drinking is a cause of mental collapse, sometimes a result, sometimes a symptom. What was being recognized slowly during the two years I served in the department was that excessive or persistent over-use of alcohol cannot any longer be ignored.

We aren't really heavy drinkers in Britain, when compared with the wine-drinking nations of the world. The French worry endlessly about their livers and they need to, drinking undiluted wine – often of dubious quality – with every meal except breakfast. What is noticeable in this country, however, is that drinking patterns vary in different regions, and amongst different groups, so generalization is fraught with danger.

The average Scots middle-aged housewife is abstemious. Her twenty-year-old son is not, but may well be sober all week and then go on a staggering binge on Saturday nights. As she cleans him up, puts him to bed and mutters over him indulgently, neither of them knows that his blood pressure is possibly now soaring off the graph and he runs a real risk of a stroke, not uncommon in young men after heavy-drinking bouts. Many of the inhabitants of our industrial cities regard ten pints a night as normal sociable behaviour, with a beer belly the sign of a man that can hold his liquor. A builder friend tells me that, working on a building-site when he was younger, he would regularly put away 100 pints a week. The prison officers' union in 1989 worries about the regular fourteen-pints-a-night man among its members. Medical students play brilliant rugby and go celebrating, roaring drunk in the college bar. Then they wonder why, in later life, doctors show statistics for mortality from cirrhosis above the national average. Another bad group – at three times the national average – are air traffic controllers. Now there's a thought.

The relationship between alcohol and illness is complex. Occasional drinking almost certainly is not harmful. Alcohol probably doesn't by itself cause cancer, for example; but drinkers who smoke too run a sharply increased risk of the disfiguring cancers of the mouth, throat, stomach and the rest of the intestinal tract, even those who are modest in their intake. Alcohol by itself probably doesn't have a strong influence on heart disease, though heavy drinking can bring on the flutters. There's even a recognized condition, noted in the medical literature, called 'Holiday Heart', in which palpitations and heart pain are brought on by excess holiday drinking. Possibly one link to heart disease for the heavy drinker is the encouragement to obesity. All alcohol contains lots of calories. You can bump them up nicely with soft drinks or sweetened fruit juice. Drink a lot, eat normally, and you could get fat without knowing why. Slurp the equivalent of your own blood volume night after night, and an increased work-load for your heart (let alone your bladder) is the inevitable result.

What alcohol does seem to cause is raised blood pressure, and that can mean strokes. Fluctuation in blood pressure and occasional 'highs' are probably part of a normal life. The dangers come if blood pressure is persistently high. Forcing the blood around strains the heart and prematurely ages it, while the fine tubes of the kidneys get damaged. A blood clot or haemorrhage in the brain produces a stroke, with its attendant wheelchairs and incontinence pads. Who would risk that? Diabetics seem to be particularly prone to high blood pressure. In Asians in this country diabetes is common, and the lethal combination may well be the explanation of their very high levels of heart disease, kidney failure and strokes.

The Royal College of Psychiatrists were not the only ones concerned. The other medical Royal Colleges pitched in too. According to a 1987 report of the Royal College of Physicians, three or four pints a day are enough to send the body's hormones haywire. I'm not kidding – in fact, the link between chronic alcohol abuse and disorders of sexual function in men has been known for centuries. The College claimed men who maintain a very high level of alcohol consumption may even become feminized. Many lose body hair, their sexual organs shrivel and up to 60 per cent develop an increase in breast tissue. You thought it was just obesity, didn't you?! 'Brewer's droop' is a real occurrence, and not in the least funny to those poor unfortunates who suffer from it. 'Keep sober – and sexy' read the headline in the *Evening Standard* that day in April 1987 when the Royal College's warning came out. I preferred the *Sun*'s somewhat livelier headline: 'Drink'll wrinkle your winkle'.

*   *   *

Excessive drinking was not just a problem for the drinker. During the spring of 1987 interest in drinking as the source of social problems was increasing, led mainly by the Home Office, responsible for doing something about the soaring crime and violence figures, and by the Department of Transport, whose Secretary of State was John Moore, with Peter Bottomley as junior minister. For years there had been a winter drinking and driving campaign which had proved to be so successful that there were, by then, more alcohol-related traffic accidents in the summer months, and in daylight, than in the dark hours of winter. People seemed convinced that they couldn't get drunk while the sun was shining. So I was invited with other junior ministers to help launch a summer drinking campaign, and duly did so with Peter in July 1987. The slogans were a little arch but the television ads pulled no punches. Within eighteen months we were getting fewer fatalities on the road than at any time since the 1950s, despite a huge increase in traffic since then, and our roads are now the safest in Europe.

This campaign worked to such an extent that people took the law firmly into their own hands. The young golf professional at one of the courses in Derbyshire had a bit of a drink problem. He was so paralytic one day that his mates took his car keys off him and phoned the police: shopped him, in fact. He was convicted of being five times over the limit and banned, and no one felt sorry for him.

After the reshuffle in June 1987, which followed the General Election, John Moore was moved to the Department of Health and a potent axis was created between his personal feelings about alcohol abuse and Home Secretary Douglas Hurd's deep concern that it lay at the root of much mindless violence. John quietly knew what he was talking about. An only child, he had grown up, he told me, in the back rooms of pubs in London, where his parents worked as bar staff. From this perspective he saw at first hand the effects of drunkenness. Eventually he gained a charity scholarship to the Licensed Victualler's School in Slough, where he shone; his subsequent career showed triumph over real adversity, though he was genuinely embarrassed if anyone said so.

Could we, therefore, do more to persuade the public that moderate use of 'our favourite drug' was best? Douglas Hogg (the junior minister at the Home Office), Peter Bottomley and I talked behind the Speaker's Chair late one evening about how to do it. Should we have an occasional meeting, or should we get together another ministerial group, under the aegis of the Home Office, which Douglas (Hogg) would chair? We rapidly came to the conclusion that alcohol was bigger than us. We spoke to our respective bosses, saying that this required a Cabinet decision, and that in our view it should be chaired by a member of the Cabinet, possibly someone akin to Lord Whitelaw (already busy with AIDS) who had no departmental axe to grind.

We could not have asked for a better outcome of these discussions. The press announcement by Douglas Hurd on 18 September 1987 admitted that up till then there had been no single mechanism for looking at the alcohol picture as a whole. A new ministerial group would be set up, with ministers attending (of junior rank, mostly) from the Home Office, MAFF, which was the sponsoring ministry for the drinks industry, the Departments of Health, Transport, Trade and Industry, Education and Employment, the Treasury and the Scottish and Welsh Offices. Representatives of the Northern Ireland office usually came too, and so did officials from Customs and Excise, the Health and Safety Executive, Her Majesty's Inspectorate of Schools and one of the Prime Minister's key advisers. The chairman was to be John Wakeham, Leader of the House of Commons. Soon John was so identified with the work of the Group that it became known as the Wakeham Committee. John had been Chief Whip in the previous Parliament and had been badly injured, his wife dead at his side, in the Brighton bombing. His shambling gait and stooped posture are the remnants of that terrible night – at one stage it was thought he would lose his legs. An accountant by profession, he is one of the nicest people in Parliament and his tactful manner and generally cheerful approach guaranteed a good presentation of the often quite radical proposals agreed by the Committee.

The first meeting of what was officially entitled the Ministerial Group on Alcohol Misuse (MGAM) took place in the Cabinet Office on Tuesday 3 November 1987 at 10.30 a.m. In all, there were seven meetings over the next year. They followed a familiar pattern, and they still continue successfully.

The Cabinet Office where we met is a rather drab stone building in Whitehall, with a small plaque saying 'Privy Council Office' on the door, opposite the Cenotaph and forming part of a block with

Downing Street. It is a maze of old corridors and odd unnumbered doors and it is possible to enter the front door and emerge a few minutes later, some distance away, from the front door of Number 10 or the Chancellor's house (Number 11) or the Chief Whip's (Number 12).

Come with me to the Cabinet Office. Cross over Whitehall from the Department of Health, carrying a red ministerial folder; up the stone steps, always exactly on time. There is such pressure on rooms that it is bad manners to be too early, you'll have to hang about in the corridor along with the wet coats and umbrellas. Through security; along a corridor, one side of which is a wall of the old Tudor Palace cockpit which used to stand on the site, complete with an ancient carved stone fireplace. We make bricks up in Butterley in Derbyshire and I loved the beautiful bright red of this old brickwork, the best, no doubt, that King Henry's money could buy. Past the suit of armour and through double glass doors, moving forward a couple of centuries, and so into Committee Room A. Its official title is the Treasury Board Room. It's not very large, but oh! it is handsome, with heavy green hangings, great portraits in heavy gilded frames, a magnificent carved marble fireplace flanked by columns and topped by a bust of William Pitt gazing out of the window. The huge square table, made in 1739, has majestic carved lions' heads, the cabriole legs shaped as lions' paws. It creaks under the weight of its age and the decisions made around it.

Places are already set. We don't have names on Cabinet Committees, but posts. Cards with our official titles mark our seats, and we address each other in the third person and through the chair, short crisp sentences, each word carefully weighed, discussed and cleared with officials, other ministers, for hours, days in advance. 'The Department of Health would agree with the Parliamentary Under-Secretary at the Home Office.' 'The Scottish Office is moderately content with the proposals as they stand.' 'Perhaps the Lord Privy Seal could be invited to resolve this small difficulty.' This is real politics, in a free democracy. Most of the people around the table are elected MPs. At the weekend, after the meeting is concluded and the minutes written, when the press releases have gone out and the media interviews are over, the ministers go back to their constituencies, hold their advice bureaux in local church halls and then, repairing to the Conservative Club for a little much-needed refreshment, will be greeted with 'Saw you on the telly last week. What was you goin' on about?'

And that's how it should be.

Broadly speaking the problems of alcohol misuse fall into three categories: (i) the anti-social; (ii) the heavy drinking which is dangerous to health; and (iii) the long-term dangers of *moderate* drinking. The first category now includes most of the behaviour British society has come to condemn, such as drinking and driving, football hooliganism, battered wives and children, carousing and violence in the streets on Saturday nights. In all these cases alcohol's main effect is to release inhibitions. We British must at heart be a collection of noisy and aggressive slobs if this is the result. In primitive tribes the effect of alcohol (which is not a stimulant) is to make people more relaxed, sleepy even, *less* troublesome not more. This was the main category of work which MGAM set out to tackle in 1987 as a matter of urgency, opinion polls showing that we had the full backing of the nation.

There were, however, other problems besides violence and anti-social behaviour. What, for instance, were the health effects of alcohol? Everyone had heard of liver cirrhosis and DT's. It was the view of some around the table at the early meetings of MGAM that there were relatively few people in the second category suffering such serious long-term ill-effects from inebriation. We could condemn them, or feel sorry for them, but their numbers were not significant. Confirmed alcoholics, we all recognized, had problems. The answer is better treatment facilities in the NHS – which are slowly improving – though no one likes working with drunks, understandably. Stricter legislation, stricter enforcement will also help. On the whole, such people surfaced in the first category as social problems – they wound up under the arches or in hospital casualty departments, one way or another, too drunk to give a sample, holding a bloody head and being sick over the nurses, victims of their own or their pals' stupidity and addiction.

In the Department of Health we felt that it was the third category which we would have to face sooner or later. Long-term steady drinking, well *within* legal limits for driving, perhaps; the daily or frequent drinking habits of law-abiding citizens who never kick the dog, never thump the wife or knock bits off the car (well, not often), was a contributing factor to our very high levels of preventable disease. These were the people who found it difficult to believe that anyone else could get through seventy pints of beer a week, yet they themselves would have a couple of pints at lunch-time, one or two on the way out of the office, most of a bottle of wine at that business dinner, three or four pints on a Saturday at the pub, and the same again, please, Sunday lunch-time. Anybody you know? As the Wakeham Committee got into its stride, the Royal Medical Colleges published new levels of alcohol intake which were judged to be 'safe' in terms of longer-term health. The guy I've just described would have been regularly polishing off rather more than twice that limit, week in week out, doing himself no good at all.

This is how it works, according to the latest medical advice. A 'unit' of alcohol, containing roughly the same amount of alcohol whatever its source, is half a pint of beer or lager, or a glass of wine, or a single measure of spirits or sherry or the like. Thus a pint is the same as a double gin and tonic, half a bottle of wine the equivalent of three glasses of port and lemon. There's no difference in alcohol content, though other ingredients mean a worse hangover from a glass of red wine than a vodka. A normal woman shouldn't regularly exceed fourteen units a week, so they tell us, a man twenty-one units a week. The only unfair thing about being female is that we can't eat or drink as much as a man even roughly the same size as ourselves; the different distribution of body fat, apparently, makes women likely to get drunker quicker. I can vouchsafe for that. So our chap described above – a model father, valued employee and abstemious citizen – is getting through twenty units (2x2x5) just at lunch-time in the pub during the week. His single quickie in the evening – let's say he misses the one when he goes to an evening class – adds another four units per week. His bottle of wine, not finished, gives him five units and the eight pints at the weekend, which leave him only slightly flushed, another sixteen. That's forty-five units and he hasn't been tiddly at all. Of course not. The liver sorts it all out at the rate of one unit per hour and he won't feel funny till he's pushing five or six units around his bloodstream at the same time. But he may be doing his health long-term damage at levels like that.

I read all this stuff and calculated my own consumption in the Palace of Westminster which, as Crown property, needs no licence, and is therefore well stocked with its twenty-three bars and restaurants open all hours. Quietly I decided I was doing myself no good either. Those extra calories were firmly unwanted and a clear head for a vote, a speech or an intervention at midnight would be useful. These days I don't drink when I'm working, so I have the added pleasure of associating a glass of something good with finishing the day's work. It also has the psychological effect that I feel I'm controlling my environment, not the other way round. Low-alcohol lager in these circumstances (brewed by constituents) is sheer joy, but so is finding that no one any longer thinks it's nutty to ask for orange or tomato juice, or to say, 'No, thank you, I'm driving'.

There is an easy way to find out whether you may have an alcohol problem. The following has been tested on a large group, and is well written up in the medical and learned press. We all love questionnaires, so try this one. It is known as the CAGE questionnaire, and has only four questions.

1 Are you ever *Concerned* about your drinking? (C)
2 Do you ever get *Annoyed* if someone comments on your drinking? (A)
3 Do you ever feel *Guilty* about your drinking? (G)
4 Do you ever start the day with an '*Eye-opener*'? (E)

If the answer to at least two of these four questions is yes, you may well have trouble and need some help. How did you get on? Still, there are plenty of other experiments that show even heavy and habitual drinkers can cut down successfully, particularly with the help of a sympathetic family doctor.

There was a great deal of beavering away behind the scenes during that Christmas recess, 1987–88. A host of good ideas were suggested and by January 1988 the Wakeham Committee had agreed a package of measures designed to, as the press release said, 'improve understanding of how alcohol works, encourage sensible drinking, and better co-operation between local services'.

The Licensing Bill, intended to liberalize the drinking-hours laws and which had come in for much criticism, was amended to strengthen the offence of selling alcohol to under-age drinkers. It meant that publicans have to be far more vigilant about under-age drinking. In future 'I didn't know he was only sixteen' would no longer be an admissible defence.

The portrayal of drinking on the TV screen was influential, too. John Wakeham met both the BBC and IBA and it was pointed out to them that it was not helpful to have endless soap operas based in pubs, or in which the first reaction of any character under stress, shoulder-pads and diamanté heaving, was to reach for the booze.

It was also decided to request the IBA and the ASA to take a fresh look at advertising codes of practice, in co-operation with the drinks industry. A new code was issued in September 1988. As a result the number of cryptic advertisements, where it is difficult to work out what the product is – the advertisers' revenge, perhaps? – has increased, just as for cigarettes. Humour has been toned down, sex reduced. Actors now have to bring their birth certificates with them to the set where ads are being shot, to prove they are over twenty-five and they must look it. No drinks advertisements should be shown in a cinema where the film has less than an '18' designation, so if there's an ad for alcohol on at your local cinema with *Beetlejuice*, complain. According to a report in *The Sunday Times* of 26 March 1989: 'Bass has been asked to withdraw a poster campaign showing fishermen with cans of lager because it fell foul of the ASA's new code. It was irresponsible to portray an activity such as fishing in connection with the consumption of alcohol, said the ASA.' In fact the ASA will not allow drinking to be associated with any work activities. The article continued, 'The Authority has also banned a poster campaign for Marston's Pedigree Bitter which asked, "Can you handle it?" because this kind of challenge is contrary to the Authority's code.' So the campaign against the campaigns is making progress.

The Chancellor, urged on by the MGAM (one of its members being Financial Secretary to the Treasury), announced in the spring budget of 1988 a small tax advantage for mixed drinks known as coolers and abolished the minimum duty charge on beer to encourage the promotion of lower strength beers. Six months later, according to the *Today* newspaper of 29 September 1988:

The nation's favourite tipples are being diluted as health-conscious drinkers demand less alcohol in their booze. The move may also mean savings in excise duty which are boosting distilleries' profits by millions of pounds a year. Yesterday the trendy coconut-flavoured rum Malibu became the latest spirit to have its alcohol content reduced. It follows a long line of leading brand names which have been diluted. They include Martini, Cinzano, Bacardi, Southern Comfort, Jack Daniels and Pimms. The result could mean safer, more sociable drinking, with a reduction in drunkenness – and cheaper prices. From next month Malibu's alcohol content will drop by 4 per cent to 24 per cent, bringing the owners, International Distillers and Vintners, a duty saving of more than 45p per bottle. Sales of more than 3.5 million bottles a year will earn more than £1 million extra revenue, while the cost of a bottle falls from £7.39 to £6.99. A spokesman for IDV said: 'Our research shows the public wants lower strength drinks. It's part of the general trend towards healthier living.' A spokesman for the makers of Pimms, Arthur Bell Distillers, said: 'For the first time in years Pimms is being produced at a profit. We're paying less duty to the government and we feel we are meeting public demand for lower strength drinks.'

That Committee did an enormous amount of work; Douglas Hurd and John Moore should be proud of their baby.

By the summer of 1988 the Committee was well into its stride and was pushing for the improved use of existing laws against alcohol abuse. Magistrates and police were reminded by John Wakeham and the Home Office that the law allows magistrates to ban people with criminal records of violence from named pubs. They can order the closure of all licensed premises in an area where trouble is expected. The police and courts can refuse licences, revoke them, insist on better behaviour. An experiment started in Coventry, with government approval, to ban the drinking of alcohol in public. There the kids had been congregating, aggressively drunk in the city centre and making the lives of passers-by and shopkeepers a misery. The experiment seemed to work and other cities started to copy it. In another move local licensees were encouraged to run their own identity-card schemes for young people and they became common in some parts of the country. Bad behaviour was clearly not just a problem amongst inner-city louts, though. Gangs appeared out of nowhere in sleepy well-off towns like Chard in Somerset and, drunk to the eyeballs, laid about others likewise, with a few plate-glass windows and policemen's helmets thrown in for good measure. Once the problems hit the Government's best voting areas, voters insisted that action must be swift and effective; it wasn't 'their' problem any more, it was 'ours'.

*   *   *

In February 1989, as I started the research for this book, I gave myself an hour off one night to watch a television documentary made by the Welsh journalist John Morgan about his own treatment for throat cancer. His face and accent were familiar from his years of reporting current affairs. He had always, he said, as he accepted another whisky and lit up yet another cigarette, had a party piece – that all this business about health risks and being careful was so much utter rubbish. The programme was originally intended to show that cancer wasn't so awful, that it did not automatically bring death, and that if people came forward soon enough, treatment was successful. Cancer could be openly talked about and should be faced without fear – a point I had often made. But Morgan, whose throat cancer had been detected at the age of fifty-three in 1983 and now, as the programme progressed, was accompanied by lung cancer, turned before our eyes from a vigorous, confident, handsome figure in the prime of life to a tragic, shuffling old man. He, to his intense surprise, did not make it. He died, five years after the cancer first showed itself, in December 1988.

He recorded the last scene in front of his old home in Swansea. The old house, though still serviceable, was shuttered as the dirt tip behind had started to move and it threatened to engulf the whole street. So life had been removed, the cherished garden was full of weeds, the gate hung off its hinges.

Morgan had been told there was no more to be done. This man, who had once taken refuge from the bombing in Viet Nam by hiding, laughing, in an ammunition dump, faced the end with awful courage – and anger. 'Rage is what I feel,' he said slowly to camera, 'rage – and after that, I am struck dumb.'

Rage, rage against the dying of the light. And then silence. There is no more, then, to be said.

4

The Innocents and the Cesspit

And I looked, and behold a pale horse: and his name that sat on him was Death, and Hell followed with him

Revelation, 6:8

Saturday morning at the advice bureau in Swadlincote in the autumn of 1986 was routine. The names on my list did not stand out, and the middle-aged couple now sitting in front of me were not particularly unusual either, though they were clearly more prosperous than the local coal miners, and from the look of his hands he earned his living by some other means. The man did not look very well, and I wondered what the problem was and whether I, with my limited powers as a local MP, would be able to help them.

'We have come to talk to you about AIDS,' the woman said. She had a pleasant face but looked worried. Under the table she reached for her husband's hand, which was trembling slightly. 'We have come to complain about the way it's all presented in the media,' she said. 'They talk about it as if it's all homosexuals and drug takers. It isn't. We've got it, and we're your constituents.'

I looked at her, wondering how in heaven's name we three had got caught up in the AIDS epidemic.

'He's a haemophiliac,' she said. A look of sheer misery crossed his face. 'He's been going down to Birmingham for his blood whenever he needed it, but he was feeling a bit off and they tested him. They said one of his treatments must have been infected. It only has to happen once, they said, and that's it. It's nobody's fault, I suppose; they have only been able to test the blood recently, and he's been going there for years.'

I knew the figures. As far as we could tell at that time about 1,000 haemophiliacs were infected in this country (in fact the number is greater, about 1,300). That works out at one or two per MP, and with the regional transfusion centre only forty-five minutes away I should not have been surprised to find one in my patch. I rehearsed in my mind what I knew about the disease and how it is transmitted. Normal social contact was all right, so shaking hands with him was not a problem. The only way I could catch AIDS from him was to sleep with him.

The full horror of the situation suddenly struck me and I turned to her. 'Have you been tested?' I asked.

'No,' she said. 'There's no need. We've been married twenty-five years and we have always had a good marriage. If he's infected, then so am I. I knew he was a haemophiliac when we married and we have learnt to live with it; the children are OK, thank God. I suppose we will just learn to cope with this, too, though it seems so hard. We live from day to day now. We'll manage.'

Lily, my helper, was tapping on the door to remind me that other people were waiting to see me, concerned about the dripping tap, or the neighbour's barking dog, or the pot-holes in the road. I asked the woman as gently as I could whether there was anything I could do for them.

'No,' she said, 'you have done enough by just listening. It's important that people like you should understand.'

With that, they rose to go. The man had not said a word. They were close together as they shut the door.

* * *

They were not in fact my first brush with AIDS and I should not have been so shaken. After I won my parliamentary seat in 1983 I kept up my contacts in Birmingham where I had been chairman of the Central Birmingham Health Authority. Friends there had been expressing their concern about the reports coming from America. I had started to put down parliamentary questions almost immediately. One question I asked in November 1983 was: 'What advice has been given to hospitals concerning the use of imported Factor VIII in the light of recent concern about its possible contamination with the causative agent of Acquired Immune Deficiency Syndrome (AIDS)?'

And the answer, from the then Minister of State Kenneth Clarke, was: 'There is no conclusive evidence that Acquired Immune Deficiency Syndrome is transmitted by blood products.'

Afterwards, whenever it was my turn to answer parliamentary questions as a minister I was extremely wary of suggested answers starting with 'There is no conclusive evidence that . . .'

I had had further contacts with AIDS during 1985. Several sympathetic back-benchers were approached by scientists from the pharmaceutical company, Wellcome plc, who were very excited and wanted to show us something; would we have dinner with them? The ensuing event, in Dining Room C, the smallest of the private suites in the Palace of Westminster, was not like many other company promotions. It was clear the company representatives could hardly wait to finish the meal and the general chat, and as soon as the plates were cleared we drew closer. Wellcome's board had decided with extraordinary perspicacity, some ten years earlier, that research into viruses was the thing of the future. With a flourish from under the table there was produced a small cardboard box, which was opened to reveal a collection of phials. 'This,' they said, 'is the AIDS test. There hasn't been one before, but this one will detect antibodies to the virus. We will be able to test every blood transfusion, and we can test people directly. Now we will know who has AIDS and who hasn't; this is the breakthrough.'

They were of course right, or almost right. (The antibodies develop some time after infection so the test isn't perfect.) The dinner took place in the summer of 1985; within weeks the kit was on the market, and in October 1985 we began testing all blood donations in this country. The tracking of the AIDS invasion had begun.

*   *   *

Let's get it right: it's AIDS, in capitals. It means Acquired Immune Deficiency Syndrome. It was recognized in 1981, but cases had been reported in the 1970s. It is not in itself a disease, and it is not itself a virus, though since 1983 it has been generally accepted that it is caused by a virus – or a group of viruses – which go under the name Human Immunodeficiency Virus, or HIV. The person with the HIV virus in his blood is HIV+. As far as we know, he will go on to develop the syndrome itself, though when precisely is in the lap of the crueller gods, probably within fifteen years from infection at most, usually more quickly.

This is not the place to set out in detail the full medical or scientific background to AIDS. Suffice it to say that the virus is acquired through contact with the blood or body fluids of an infected person, for example through sex, or through the transfer of blood – including blood transfusions – or by sharing hypodermic needles. Once acquired it seems to lie dormant for some time, for years in many people. During that time they are fit and well and, unless they are tested, they will not know they have become infected; there are no signs at all. But they are infectious.

At some point their immune system becomes compromised and they find themselves suffering from a range of opportunistic infections, often those whose bugs are with us all the time such as candida (thrush), and frequently several at once. They die eventually of general weakness and debility brought on by repeated bouts of pneumonia and other conditions, or through cancers such as Kaposi's sarcoma. This form of skin cancer was once known only rarely in elderly Jewish men before AIDS, but it, and another once rare form of pneumonia (*Pneumocystis carinii*), have become indicative of AIDS in Western sufferers.

I set this information out now, in the firm hope that in years to come we will have found a vaccine, and that AIDS will have disappeared and have been forgotten, as have cholera and smallpox. That, we understand, is unlikely for a long time yet. So I must state here that, as I write, there is no cure for AIDS, that as far as we know all those who become infected by the virus, by whatever means, will eventually come down with the syndrome, and after much suffering they will die.

They include children – haemophiliac little boys, or the babies of mothers who have been infected, some through prostitution, or by drug taking with infected needles. They include women married for years and faithful to their husbands – who perhaps weren't so faithful to them. They include the young doctor who died in Exeter, whose likely source of infection was the blood of his former patients in Africa. They include priests and harlots, homosexuals and heterosexuals, young and old; several patients being cared for by one of London's teaching hospitals are in their seventies. They include the frequenters of bath houses in San Francisco and New York, places with names such as 'Animals', 'Cornholes', and 'The Hothouse', where men would take several partners a night, usually complete strangers, in a welter of sweat and vaseline and stimulants. Many of their customers are now dead.

The people who die of AIDS include the innocents and the inhabitors of the cesspit; those who chose, even when they knew about the disease, and those who had no choice. The problem for government was a practical matter: how to stop it spreading, as it already had in other countries. This was the public health issue above all others in the period 1986–88, and if it has faded from the public consciousness somewhat now, that may just be because the steps taken then, particularly in public education, have been effective. Up to a point.

*   *   *

Following the Government reshuffle of September 1986, the new team at the Department of Health and Social Security consisted of Norman Fowler as Secretary of State; Tony Newton as Minister of State, who went thereafter to the Cabinet; myself, newly appointed, as Junior Minister; Baroness (Jean) Trumpington in the Lords covering both health and social security, a massive job; and the two Ministers for Social Security, John Major as Minister of State, also now with his own high post in the Cabinet, and Nick Lyell, the Junior Minister, soon to be promoted to the important post of Solicitor-General, with a knighthood. It was generally reckoned to be a good team, a judgement supported by the subsequent careers of all but the author!

Very soon after I arrived, Norman asked the health ministers quietly what our attitudes were to AIDS, and whether we would support a major campaign against it. We were all deeply worried and did not need to consult anyone. Without hesitation, we gave him our full backing. I felt the Government had no choice and that there was no time to lose.

Norman's method of keeping the mammoth DHSS under control and running smoothly was masterly. Every Monday morning at 11 a.m. there would be 'Prayers'. That is not in fact a session for communing with God, but a nice old-fashioned Civil Service name for a ministers' meeting with top advisers present. Other Secretaries of State take different views on the presence of civil servants at their ministerial team meetings, but for dealing with an issue as fast moving as AIDS, and where it was essential that official and political thinking should be at one, it was a first-class system. After the main meeting the civil servants would withdraw and ministers would go on to a buffet lunch, usually in John Major's room to which the parliamentary private secretaries and one or two other useful people, such as researchers from party headquarters, would occasionally be invited. We all had to pay for this lunch. Quite right, in a government committed to reducing wasteful spending.

At 'Prayers' and lunch, week by week, we discussed AIDS as the first item on the agenda. It became apparent very quickly that we could not cope with AIDS in the DHSS alone. For a start, there were the other health departments. Health in this country is not the sole prerogative of the Department of Health; despite its name it is responsible only for England. The Welsh, Northern Ireland and Scottish Offices are in charge of health care in their respective parts of the country, and life is complicated by the fact that they often have different legislation and ways of organizing their health services. (For example, the age of consent, sixteen for the rest of us, is seventeen in Northern Ireland.) And their residents sometimes had different attitudes to many of the problems we were to face. Bilateral discussions between us would take ages. Good links would also be needed with the Foreign Office in the international fight against AIDS, and with the Department of Education and Science. And if we were to spend any money, the Treasury would have to be closely involved too.

Clearly, however, the English Department of Health would have to play a major role in some parts of the work. In our department there was some discussion as to which minister should handle the issues. Jean Trumpington, perhaps, as her list of responsibilities included the Blood Transfusion Service? Me, as mine included prevention? I was adamant; this was deadly and serious, it needed someone with top-notch experience of government and should be dealt with at the highest level. This was no place for a brand new junior minister, not if we meant business.

After some discussion in Cabinet it was announced, to our relief and delight, that a major new Cabinet committee should be set up, the AIDS sub-committee of the Home and Social Affairs Committee, and it would be known as H(A). By tradition published references to Cabinet committees have been very limited since, owing to the doctrine of Cabinet collective responsibility, they weren't supposed to exist, though I could not see why the public or students of politics would expect the whole Cabinet to get through all the detailed discussions of issues necessary in a couple of hours on a Thursday morning. With AIDS, the convention vanished. The best news of all, however, was that Lord Whitelaw was to chair it.

Willie Whitelaw is one of the most civilized, intelligent and competent of men. The Prime Minister rightly relied on him as the Leader of the House of Lords, and as chairman of several major committees including H(A). I watched him at work several times. A large, seemingly ponderous Tory of the old school, he was amazing; under that lugubrious exterior was a razor-sharp mind and a kindliness of spirit which were to serve us very well indeed. I rapidly became an admirer, resolving not to talk so much and listen more when I chaired meetings myself – a resolve of short duration. The staggering amount of work that Willie put in for his many jobs, and the difficult hours at the House of Lords, damaged even his robust health, and after a slight stroke at the age of sixty-nine in December 1987 he retired from the front line of active politics. He was immediately very much missed.

The AIDS sub-committee, apart from Lord Whitelaw, consisted of twelve Cabinet Ministers. The attenders were Secretaries of State, men at the highest level of government, the most high-powered committee possible. I thought of them as the thirteen wise men. Their job, as announced when H(A) was set up on 4 November 1986, was to consider and co-ordinate proposals for measures to limit the spread of the AIDS virus in the UK and to deal with its effects. The terseness of the terms captured the mood – urgent, no nonsense, no fudging.

The H(A) committee was as close to a decision-making body as it is possible to get in Cabinet government. Our Department was a member of it, but only one. It reached conclusions which were then passed to the Department to carry out, but it did not replace nor supersede the work each Minister had to do.

*   *   *

By early November 1986 the UK's Chief Medical Officer, Professor Sir Donald Acheson, was saying that there were now over 500 cases of AIDS and an estimated 25,000 people in the United Kingdom infected with the HIV virus. The latter group was increasing by some twenty to fifty people per day and it was estimated that only one in ten knew they were infected. Some twenty-six children in the UK had already been born infected by the mother before birth, and it was believed that there were about 400 infected women in the UK. The number of AIDS cases was doubling every ten months. Acheson warned that if there were no change in habits and practices, especially of those most at risk, then at the end of five years there could be half a million carriers – at a sober estimate.

Right from the beginning the overwhelming majority of AIDS cases and carriers of the virus were homosexuals, around 90 per cent of UK AIDS patients. The bulk of the remainder, to start with, were haemophiliacs who had received tainted blood transfusions or injections of the clotting agent Factor VIII, which is manufactured by concentration from large volumes of blood. Some time before AIDS the homosexual communities of some cities in the USA, determined to show they were also worthy citizens, had encouraged the enrolment of their number as blood donors. By this route the virus went to many countries which were as yet unable to make their own Factor VIII and so were obliged to import it from the USA, the UK included. Subsequently, heat treatment of blood donations has made Factor VIII as safe as we can get it. Too late for many haemophiliacs.

Those involved had to combat at all times the nasty feeling of many of the public that as the disease was largely confined to homosexuals, it didn't matter. The Terrence Higgins Trust, named after a young British homosexual who had died in 1982 of AIDS, was set up by his friends to campaign for greater public awareness of the problem, and for recognition that it was not exclusively a 'gay plague', as it had been dubbed in the USA. In Britain the Government took the worthy view right from the start that it did not matter whether AIDS was solely a matter for homosexuals or not. First, they were citizens with full rights, paying taxes and entitled in every way to be treated as equals. Second, it can be quite dangerous, when dealing with public health matters, to assume that a condition or infection is confined to one group. The odds are that the boundaries with other groups are blurred and overlap, which was certainly true with AIDS. Bisexuals and drug users proved that. If it's a big enough problem, better to warn everyone. Third, once people are sick, they are all patients and need care. By then the route by which they contracted the illness is irrelevant.

By November 1986, however, it was beginning to be possible to put the disease into context. For a year all blood donations had been tested (some 2.6 million donations in all); fewer than 100 positives had been found amongst the donors and only three of them had claimed they were neither homosexuals nor drug misusers. Blood donors are quite representative of the general population, and those figures showed only 2 in 10,000 people infected. By mid-1987 it appeared that about 3 in 100 men and 2 in 100 women coming to STD (sexually-transmitted diseases) clinics were HIV+; they could be regarded as high risk patients. The history so far thus suggested only a slow leakage was likely into the general population. But what a problem for any public education campaign. On the one hand, public alarm about a runaway epidemic throughout society had to be allayed; on the other hand, it had to be made clear that such an epidemic could only be prevented by changes in the most intimate of personal behaviour, and immediately.

The H(A) Committee decided that there had to be a three-pronged approach: (i) to find a cure through research; (ii) until that were done, to halt and, if possible, reverse the spread – though talk of 'reversal' was clearly based on a misunderstanding, since, as far as we knew then, the only way the pool of HIV+ people diminishes is through death; and (iii) to care for those afflicted.

These honourable and decent men, who thought they had come into politics to fight socialism and to reform the trade unions, found themselves wrestling instead with some of the nastiest social problems of our time. As in much of the other public health activity of the eighties described in this book, a sensitive combination of vigorous government action, and encouragement of changes in private behaviour was required. Politicians don't normally get involved in issues of this sort and their background and early experience leaves them feeling ill-suited to the role. It was clear that a sustained public education campaign lasting many years was going to be needed, but the pressure on the Cabinet Ministers concerned – who did have other work to do in their departments – would be immense. It was decided, therefore, that the Health Education Council, which had been an independent body funded by government, should be reconstituted as part of the NHS, renamed the 'Health Education Authority' (HEA), and should eventually take over the job of public education on AIDS. The HEA did so in March 1988, but their campaigning was never, in my view, as effective as in the earliest days, when ministers themselves took a deep breath and told the nation to be careful whom they slept with.

*　　*　　*

At the end of December 1986 there were 610 cases of AIDS in the UK, of whom 293 had died. Two of the dead were children of infected mothers. Six hundred and ten and counting.

*　　*　　*

Norman Fowler worked very closely with the World Health Organization (WHO) in Geneva on AIDS right from the start. During the winter of 1986–7 the WHO made it clear that the then figure of 36,000 reported cases of AIDS throughout the world was totally unreliable. (The number estimated at the end of 1989 is more than 130,000 known cases.) Even then WHO advisers believed there were 100,000 cases, and that 5 to 10 million people were infected with the virus. They said this would lead to something between half a million and 3 million deaths by 1991. The bulk of these deaths would occur in Africa where, the WHO estimated, there were 2 to 5 million people infected with the virus. The other area seriously affected was, of course, the USA, where it was estimated nearly 180,000 deaths would occur by that date.

The pattern of transmission varies from country to country. In England and Wales, West Germany and the Netherlands, homosexuals and bisexuals are the predominant routes. In Spain, Italy and Scotland, drug misusers are the main group. In Spanish and Italian prisons, where testing is compulsory, fifteen in every 100 prisoners is HIV+. Three-quarters of them are drug users. In France and Belgium HIV is mainly passed on through heterosexual intercourse, as it is in Africa. I always felt deeply sorry for the Third World countries caught up in the AIDS epidemic. In parts of Central and East Africa 10 to 20 per cent of men and women in sexually-active age groups are infected with the AIDS virus. It shows up there as a wasting disease dubbed 'Slim'. For a while many of their governments denied they had a problem, except perhaps amongst foreign visitors and students. The Chinese spokesman at the WHO AIDS conference in London in January 1988 took precisely this line, too, and nobody believed him, either.

At last, when President Kaunda of Zambia's son died of the disease and, in his grief, he announced it to the world, Third World leaders felt able to admit that they had a problem running beyond their control. The lack of an administrative infrastructure in many states, particularly up-country away from the capital, meant that govern-ments had no idea how many people lived in an area, and the chances of finding out just how many were HIV+, or even the number of those who had died of AIDS, were remote. Trying to treat patients, except for a privileged few, would be impossible. Some of their spokesmen have expressed deep resentment at the notion that the disease may have originated from Africa, pointing out that the mode of transmission there is different. A plausible explanation may well be that in many parts of the world anal intercourse is the common form of contraception, and this is the usual method of sex for homo-sexuals, too. The walls of the anal passage are only one cell thick and it does not have the protection mechanisms against foreign material which would help avoid infection.

The real tragedy for Africa, which will emerge in the 1990s, is that social patterns mean the virus is widespread amongst their more educated groups. The apocalypse for some of these countries, struggling as they are, is that famine will get their poor and AIDS will get their well-off, so that their hopes of leaving destitution behind become more distant with every death.

However, some of the developing countries' governments did understand the problem, and had their own unusual ways of dealing with it. Nearly 150 nations attended the first WHO summit conference on AIDS in London in January 1988, 118 of them represented by their governments' ministers. There were also nearly 600 press representatives from all over the world, a breath-taking display of global concern. At one function I got chatting to a Minister of Health from a country which was governed by a military dictatorship. He was friendly and talkative over the canapés, and very excited. He felt he had discovered the answer, in conversation with others and by listening to the speeches, to a problem which had been puzzling him. Why were there pockets of 'Slim' all over his country, in remote parts which seemed to have no connection with the main sea ports and the cities, where the virus was endemic amongst the prostitutes, male and female?

'It's the roadside barbers!' he exclaimed. 'The lorry drivers take goods to the ports, and they spend the night with one of our adventurous girls; then they come home to their families next day, but before they enter the village they stop and have a shave and a haircut. The AIDS is in the specks of blood on the razor! The barber uses the same razor on the next man! There are barbers sitting at the roadside under sunshades all over my country. That is what is happening!'

I asked what he felt he could do to stop the barbers spreading infection.

'Oh, that's the easy part,' he said. 'In my country we can round them up and shoot them.'

And no doubt they did.

*   *   *

My personal involvement in the AIDS campaign was very limited as policy and decisions were being discussed way above my level, but I saw all the reports and Cabinet minutes and was encouraged to say my bit at 'Prayers'. (My main effort lay with the drugs campaign, in 1986 still seen as quite separate from AIDS.) The seriousness of the matter, and the way in which it was treated as such in this country, is shown by the effort put in by ministers. Between the setting up of H(A) on 4 November 1986 and the end of that year, it met seven times, with many other departmental meetings and 'bilaterals' (i.e., meetings between two departments) thrown in. It would be true to say that AIDS dominated our thinking for all those weeks, and indeed well on into 1987. Only the imminent general election at last wrenched our thoughts in other directions. There was this sense, therefore, which meant I had not needed to make any attempt to 'move the goalposts', to direct more attention to prevention and life-style changes. The move was made for us, by a scrap of protein probably derived from the green monkey virus, and which, as this book goes to press, has killed over a thousand of our fellow citizens.

The public education campaign of the winter of 1986–7 has passed into legend. It was the biggest government health campaign ever. Between March 1986, when the first tentative advertisements were put out, and November, 140 million copies of government advertisements had already appeared in newspapers and magazines – and that was before the campaign really got going. The summer's campaign had been evaluated, and had produced complaints that it was too low key, should be made more explicit and aggressive, and should be extended to television and radio. In mid-November 1986, that was what the Government decided to do.

One of the heroes of the whole business was Sammy Harari, managing director of, and brains behind, our advertising agency, Tragos Bonnage Wiesendanger Ajroldi (TBWA). A small, neat, soft-voiced man of Lebanese-French extraction, Sammy had been involved with Yellowhammer, the agency for the Government's anti-drugs campaign since 1984, and was strongly recommended by the minister responsible, David Mellor at the Home Office, as intelligent, honourable and sensitive. His material had a track record of originality and effectiveness, and he was used to working with the Government as client.

The AIDS campaign efforts of other countries were closely scrutinized. Leaflet drops had been organized in Austria, Switzerland, Greece and West Germany before ours. Advertisements abroad took many forms – we swallowed hard at the Scandinavian approach, using a character reminiscent of Wicked Willie, and decided solemnly not to use cartoons. The thirteen wise men felt that 'anything smacking of levity would be quite inappropriate'. I recall, however, sitting with the Chief Medical Officer and other ministers as the 'iceberg' ad was played to us for approval. It appeared on TV for the first time on Tuesday 3 February 1987. Whatever the later hoots of derision from the ultra-sophisticated, it had a chilling effect on me and I appreciated its sombre understatement, with its voice-over by John Hurt, bald, dry and painful.

The AIDS campaign in Norway asked: 'Are you dressed for all occasions?'

For a fleeting moment I understood how a nation felt in the few moments after war had been declared. One worried civil servant told me that the situation had no ready parallel in peace-time. Kenneth Baker at the Department of Education called it a 'national emergency'. In this war there was no jingoism, no jackbooted foe, only a sombre mood and a great unknown.

The wartime mood was also apparent in the general bipartisan approach and in the ready co-operation of the media, particularly television. Both the BBC and ITV agreed to have a whole week of programmes about AIDS including their own editorial material, which everyone hoped would bring home the information to the nation. There were endless articles and programmes, including a TV interview with Norman Fowler in a sweater. (Why a sweater? We never did find out, but I suppose it was a bit like a General taking off his peaked cap to talk to the troops.) The best programme by a streak, however, and one which caused an outcry at the time, was the excellent LWT *First Aids* transmitted in February 1987 in front of a live young audience. With the help of pop stars, *Spitting Image* puppets and some of our best young comic talent it explored many of the issues, with Rick Mayall demonstrating hilariously where not to put a condom and an earnest doctor showing how, using his finger, they should be used. We were to get accustomed to giant anuses and phalluses on television in the weeks to come. Goodness knows what today's teenagers, with their tight leather skirts and freaked-out hair-dos, made of the information that Casanova used animal membranes, with pink ribbons, as condoms or that the Japanese sell condoms door-to-door in smart packs complete with pictures of winking women, like seaside postcards. We found out pretty quickly what their elders thought of lines such as 'If you want humpy-pumpy it's pop-it-in-a-bag time'.

One scene, played by Hugh Laurie and Stephen Fry, in which a cocky young patient (Laurie) returns to the surgery to discuss his AIDS test with his doctor (Fry), showed that the producers understood the nature and the scale of the problem. The sketch opened and closed with virtually the same words: 'Good morning, Doctor. Are the results of my test back yet?'

'Yes, they are,' answered Fry. 'I'm afraid you've got AIDS and you're going to die.'

Embarrassed laughter from the audience.

The two actors then explored what medical science can do – hadn't it basically cracked the problem of disease? Well, no, actually, no more with AIDS than with a host of other killers for which there is no real cure, including cancer and heart disease. The camera played on the disbelief, complacency, then gradual, horrified, understanding of the young patient. At the end, the opening lines came again. 'I'm afraid you've got AIDS and you're going to die.' This time there was no laughter.

In the discussion at the end it was also interesting to see that the young people there were adopting very responsible attitudes, even while blushing furiously as they talked, in hypothetical terms of course, about their newly-restricted sex lives. I was delighted, how-ever, to see that a young Jack-the-lad who derided the whole business of personal responsibility, reducing the number of partners, saying

'Sod cutting down – *what* responsibility?' was almost set upon by some irate girls, who made it clear that he was no longer their idea of God's gift to women, even if he thought so! The advertising breaks offered coffee, lager, beds and multivitamins. Mike Smith, the presenter, summed it up: 'We never thought, it can happen to us.'

Not every member of the Government felt able to accept with equanimity these incursions into what had once been the nation's most intimate moments. I was asked on to a new breakfast-time television programme called *Watchdog*, to discuss the problems of condoms being sold without a 'Kite' mark (which shows that a product has reached the recommended British standard). It was news to me that there *was* a relevant British standard, but nevertheless I sat through reels of film showing how the things are tested – usually by filling them to vast size with quantities of water or blowing them up till they give way. The programme was live and I was acutely aware of cameras watching my face to detect the slightest twitch, as the monstrous things burst at the appropriate pressure. Manfully I did my bit, 'The Government was concerned', 'Of course we would take all steps necessary' etc. In fact the offenders, which apparently were full of holes, were taken off the market by the manufacturers very quickly and we all breathed a sigh of relief.

When I got back to the office, there was a very irate government minister on the phone to me, calling from Brussels, where he was at a meeting. A thoroughly nice and competent man, he was nevertheless known for being somewhat innocent. 'What in heaven's name are you doing, Edwina?' he yelled down the line. 'There I was in my hotel bedroom eating my breakfast, and suddenly you are on TV waving those damn things and dripping water all over my toast. I couldn't touch my sausages. How *could* you!'

In fact, ministers talked rather a lot about condoms both in public and private, trying to encourage their use. Even their proper name, abandoning euphemism, was unfamiliar. Their sleazy old image was challenged by bright new entrepreneurs such as Richard Branson. The latest fashion in jeans had a 'condom pocket' over the right hip.

Should we make them available free to everyone or not? No, said Norman Fowler. 'There's no evidence that those who understood the value of condoms are deterred by cost.' Free condoms were ruled out for prisons, too, as prisoners do not get privileges denied to the rest of the population. Nor was there much evidence that making them free would help much. The armed services overseas have long received a supply of free condoms. It is not quite clear what some members of the Queen's Own Highlanders, on duty in Kenya, did with theirs; but they ignored instructions that Mombasa was out of bounds and were returned to the UK in disgrace, more than one with VD, to be tested and retested for AIDS, a tour of duty some of them will never forget.

*   *   *

The first ever House of Commons AIDS debate was on 21 November 1986. It set out for the general public what ministers knew, what had been decided so far, what our approach would be. The debate was an essential link between the Government and the public, cementing a bond of agreement and common purpose which stood for some time, despite the words of James Anderton three weeks later (see page 95). It particularly helped to start turning the tide of opinion in Scotland. Six Scottish MPs had raised their concern about the threat posed there, not so much through sexual transmission but increasingly through drug misuse. Infected addicts up there were the largest single group of those infected, and in some areas more than half the addicts were HIV+, a proportion amongst the highest in the world – on a par with New York.

In Scotland, particularly in Edinburgh, the police had decided to tackle the drug problem with a fierce, but misplaced, efficiency. Possession of syringes and needles was evidence of possession of drugs (drug taking in itself in this country is not an offence, but possession and trading are). So they removed any equipment they found, forcing the addicts to share needles. That was safe as long as scrupulous cleanliness was observed – an impossibility for illicit drug users. AIDS meant that drug abuse slid from being anti-social and destructive of the personality and health of the user to being even more of a killer; and since one way in which the users would raise money for their drug was through prostitution, male and female, the opportunity for infection to pass to the general public was alarmingly apparent. Later, as the Scottish police also notched up some notable successes in seizures of heroin and cocaine, the drugs became more scarce in their major cities. Instead, the addicts came south for their supplies and by mid-1988 Scottish accents were heard in Liverpool and elsewhere, exchanging cash for a fix and leaving the virus behind.

Progress in Scotland was persistently hampered by the attitudes and prejudices, indeed bigotry, of some leading figures there. They condemned drug takers and fornicators: well, we all did, but we do not earn our place in heaven by shouting the loudest about these matters. Pragmatism and practical medicine, however, required that every effort should be made to attract the users into sympathetic centres for care and treatment, including weaning them off drugs, or at least off injecting, if at all possible. For those for whom it was impossible – or who were simply not ready yet to abandon their habit or way of life – support and effective help was needed to protect the rest of us, and for the users that meant clean needles and syringes in plentiful supply, and preferably free. For prostitutes (who of course did not have to be addicts to get and pass on AIDS) the same applied; their protection was condoms and the role of the public health authorities should have been to educate them to insist to their clients that they should use them.

Yet I was told, on a visit in 1987 to the Pollockpark Clinic in Glasgow, which specialized in the care of drug-using mothers and their babies, that the centre had been picketed by members of the church opposite on the day it had opened. The women there faced real fear and prejudice, and showed enormous bravery by agreeing to meet me, some with their babies, others pregnant, to tell me of their experiences. I felt a little out of place in my city suit – it was the kind of place where the staff make an effort to look just like the clients – but sometimes when the men are absent women can weep together and I believe we all learned something that day. The gaunt face of one girl, in her early twenties but in the classic local way already minus her teeth, will stay with me. Part of her rehabilitation, I was told, was to get her some decent looking dentures!

The wisdom of getting that centre going was demonstrated by the fact that the women did not lose their babies, a worthy end in itself in an area with very high levels of perinatal mortality. Later, however, it was discovered that the AIDS antibodies which the babies acquired from their mothers before birth in many cases disappeared from their blood sometime later, with the children subsequently testing as negative for AIDS. That in itself was marvellous news – that an HIV+ mother could have a healthy normal baby – but it is also of enormous significance in finding a future protective mechanism for the general public. It is a pleasure to pay tribute to the staff and those who backed them on the local health board; they needed vision, courage and compassion and did not find them among many who should have been backing them to the hilt.

*   *   *

The British Government's leaflet drop of January 1987 is now famous, but distributing 23 million leaflets, one through every front door in Britain, was a breath-taking idea, which also had its hilarious moments. The problem was the text.

If AIDS was as serious and nasty as we said it was, then the leaflet would have to be explicit. The more explicit, the more it would offend people, cause a real row, possibly have us all scuttling for cover in the backlash of enraged public opinion only months before that ever-present general election. If, however, we baulked at the task, people would laugh at it and us and, worse, would not take the messages seriously. Subsequent campaigns, particularly the work we did on AIDS and drugs with the help of Sammy Harari, were carefully, indeed exhaustively, researched and I learned *not* to trust my own instincts when we were trying to get through to people whose values might be different from my own. When we first started, however, we had very little time (though research was done). It was important to explore what words meant to us, at the Department of Health.

So, there we were, the Department of Health ministers, sitting round Norman Fowler's table in the appalling Alexander Fleming House at the Elephant and Castle one Monday morning in the autumn of 1986, complaining yet again about the ministers' lift not working and the impossibility of getting any of our offices to a reasonable working temperature somewhere between freezing and roasting. 'We have to agree a text for the leaflet,' said Norman, a former journalist, who perhaps more than the rest of us knew the dangers of the wrong word.

The Department of Health press officer, a redoubtable lady of considerable experience and worldly wisdom, had dutifully collected some leaflets from other organizations, including the Terrence Higgins Trust, and proceeded to pass them around during the conversation. You could tell how far the leaflets had got as the eyes popped. I will admit I learned things that day as I read the material; I cannot for the life of me imagine how people could get pleasure from some of the practices described, but that was none of my business. Our job that day very firmly was not to comment or pass judgement, but to work out whether we wanted to adapt any of this wording to our own purposes, or use instead a civil service draft which had also been circulated, and which was very close to the one eventually used.

Someone, John Major I think, pointed out that it would be helpful if we all at least attributed the same meaning to some of the more significant words. What, for example, did 'promiscuous' mean to different people? Solemnly we went round the table. One said that promiscuity meant sleeping with more than one person, another said that was not enough to qualify. As a student in the sixties I recalled hearing that it meant more than five a year, and that was my offering. Others reckoned it was far more than that! As each person chipped in it was clear that we had no idea what view the general public would have and we were going to have to take a real leap in the dark.

We also parted company somewhat on the question of 'safe sex'. My understanding of the AIDS virus was that it was found, as would be any other virus, in all the body fluids; that it was a weak virus and did not appear to survive long outside the body; that the most effective way to acquire it was by injection straight into the blood, with anal intercourse being almost as dangerous because of the thin wall of the anal passage. Ordinary kissing was OK – at least there were no known cases of infection by that route. But any rough play which might draw blood could be dangerous.

So it seemed to me that urging 'safe sex' – or even 'safer sex' – was problematic. Since we couldn't even agree what we all understood by 'promiscuous' we were going to have a real headache with 'safe'! In my view, the only safe sex – to avoid catching AIDS – is no sex, and I was far happier *on health grounds* alone advocating celibacy for those who had not settled with a regular partner. There were enough dead lovers in the world already. If it elevated affection and friendship to a higher position than sex as the foundation of human relationships, so much the better, but that was not our purpose.

We all crossed our fingers when a piece from the respected *New Society* writer, Jeremy Laurance, appeared at the end of December (before the drop). It said:

> The leaflet's realism about people's sexual (and drug-taking) behaviour is commendable. It pulls no punches, sticks strictly to the medical facts and eschews moralizing . . . Critics will complain that it is too wordy (more than 1,000 words) and does not use the street language necessary to give it maximum impact (there are no four-letter words). On the other hand the government is likely to get plenty of flack from the moralists among its own supporters and from those offended by details like the risks of semen in the mouth. Politically speaking, then, at least, it has probably got the balance right.

It transpired that the decision as to whether to do this drop or not had, in a way, already been taken out of our hands. The 23 million envelopes, complete with their warning on the cover about their explicit content, had already been printed on the orders of some minion who had sought to be helpful. So if we didn't use them, we had some explaining to do. Obviously we also wanted to do the drop as soon as possible, but the only organization capable of the delivery was the Post Office, which at that time was up to its eyes in Christmas cards and turned us down flat. We were offered February, presumably because the postmen all needed a rest after Christmas, but after a little arm twisting they agreed to go ahead in the week beginning Monday 12 January 1987, and all the leaflets went out in the two weeks after that. The leaflets for parts of Wales were to be in Welsh, but somebody demonstrated their ignorance of that fair country by arranging delivery of some of the Welsh leaflets in the areas where no one spoke Welsh, and of the English version in the Welsh-speaking areas.

We did seriously discuss whether they should go to every household, for fear of offending people of a sensitive disposition or those to whom the leaflet would not apply. Should we remove all the names of elderly people – or perhaps those who might be, with names such as Daisy, Gladys and Albert? It sounds daft, but in fact political canvassers do it all the time when trying to spot houses where people are likely to be in during the day and less likely to answer the door at night. We sought the views of some elderly people, who promptly registered their indignation at being written off in this way. A more sensible objection was put to me by a grey-haired constituent, who said simply that she hoped to discuss these questions with her grandchildren, who might be more willing to talk to her than to their parents, so please, could she have her leaflet?

Their indignation was quite real and revealed a side to our retired population that many of us younger people, I confess, thought they had long ago given up. At a meeting held in the House of Lords, Lady Jean Trumpington, once Mayor of Cambridge, now a Junior Health Minister, finished her earnest description of AIDS and the campaign with a heartfelt sigh, 'I must say I am glad that I have reached the age when these things don't matter any more.' Also present was the bright, snappy little Welsh MP, Lewis Carter-Jones, who retired at the election. He piped up: 'You speak for yourself, Baroness! I'm sixty-six, and I'm still going strong.' Jean drew herself up to her full height – even her friends would call her formidable at times like these – gave him a look, and said, 'Well then, you're a dirty old man.'

The Innocents and the Cesspit

Royston men in the far south
Are black and fierce and strange of mouth;
At Over they fling oaths at one
And worse than oaths at Trumpington.

At the end of December 1987 there were 1,227 cases of AIDS in the UK, of whom 697 had died. Twelve hundred and twenty-seven and counting.

*   *   *

Did the campaign work? In February 1986, before we started, the proportion of the general public claiming to know something about AIDS, or to have seen, heard or read anything about it, stood at less than 44 per cent. A year later that figure stood at 94 per cent. As the campaign progressed 98 per cent of the adult population claimed to be aware that the disease could be transmitted by sexual intercourse and drug injection. We had thus created one of the most successful campaigns in the field of public health that this nation had ever seen.

What was also remarkable about the whole campaign was the way everyone rallied round. No advertisers withdrew their commercials from a TV slot also running the AIDS advertisements. The media took the advertisements and offered extra space, often free; they ensured that for months on end we had a clear run and our choice of sites and prime-time spots. The *Financial Times*'s media correspondent commented on 29 October 1987:

> The UK's speedy and whole-hearted approach to fighting AIDS has led the rest of the world and its experience is being copied in countries like Belgium and Italy . . . the campaign has also changed attitudes in the media. For once the advertising world has managed to act for the public good with a unity that has won it approval and respect.

Television advertising was easily the most potent source of awareness, with over 80 per cent of the British public claiming immediately that they had seen it. So for all the complaints about the triviality of icebergs, chisels and gravestones, the images must have struck right home. It helped that the ads were shown on both BBC and ITV in prime time. Proven recall of the advertising reached the highest levels of any social persuasion advertising so far undertaken in Britain – far higher than most advertisements for cornflakes or cars. Those darned leaflets, which had given us so much trouble, were, however, the jewel in the crown, seen by 81 per cent of households. A whole nation had picked up its envelope, opened it and sat down to read. Overwhelmingly, the public supported what we had tried to do and how we had done it. Only one person in twenty said they found the things we said offensive, whereas 90 per cent felt that it was right that the Government should pay for advertising of that kind. Would that we always got an approval rating like that!

But we had really set out to change not just attitudes and knowledge but behaviour. There is much evidence that the majority of the British public is faithful to one partner for long periods of time. One of the surveys done in the early stages, as part of the evaluation of the advertising, involved detailed face-to-face questionnaires and inter-views with carefully selected samples, done under strict market-research rules by reputable companies. They told us that around 20 per cent of adults aged 18 to 64 in this country claimed they had had no partner at all in the last year; almost 70 per cent had had just one; and of the rest, the roughly 10 per cent who had had two or more, some six-tenths had reduced their risk by cutting down the number of partners, for example, or by using a condom, or both. Thus, although the numbers who had claimed to change behaviour were small, they were a relatively large proportion of those who admitted to being at risk. I commented at the time that I found it hard to believe that the British really were so well behaved, but the lack of progress made by the virus in this country since suggests that many of them must have been telling the truth.

It was one thing to raise public awareness, another to get across the essential information to different groups, particularly those at risk. The campaign inevitably had to move into longer-term strategies to change behaviour, with a divergence of approach. Drug misusers were seen as a priority for future stages of the campaign, and so were homosexuals, but, to avoid driving the problem underground, it was decided very promptly and properly not to make AIDS compulsorily notifiable by doctors. It was, however, a pity that as we moved away from raising the awareness of the general public to tackling the particular groups, we faced the criticism that we had lost interest in the campaign. This was not true.

Advertisements and information were made available to these at-risk groups; for example, material on drug abuse and injecting was put into the 'youth press' and I allowed my own children to go on buying some of the appalling, mindless rubbish which passes for publishing for the teenage market, so that I could check that our advertisements were appearing and whether they had the desired effect on the teenage market. Material was also produced for schools. There was more than one heated argument, particularly later in 1988, between HEA staff and ministers. We were not prepared to allow explicit information to fall into the hands of young children; even for us there was a limit to the AIDS risk.

It was particularly important to target homosexuals, who really needed our advice, particularly as it became apparent that some had been indulging in wildly promiscuous and dangerous behaviour, which put them at risk of catching and passing on hepatitis and parasitical infections, let alone AIDS. Anyone who didn't know what homosexuals did to make love certainly knew by the summer of 1987. With the welter of publicity it was also hard to remember that many homosexuals have monogamous and loving relationships, and were as appalled as everyone else at the revelations about the bath houses and wild life in such places as San Francisco and New York.

Amongst gays interviewed in the gay bars for the tracking research by the British Market Research Bureau changes in behaviour were widely claimed. Before we started in February 1986, three-quarters had claimed to have slept with three or more partners in the previous twelve months, and only 3 per cent had been celibate. A year later, the picture had dramatically changed; now one in eight were celibate and a quarter had been faithful to one partner for a year at least. In total the proportion who were still being stupid and sleeping around – by which I mean, in this context at least, three or more partners – had dropped to barely half. We must have saved some lives, but it also goes to show that some people are beyond saving, though most of the target group approved of the campaign.

The work needed to collect such data involved experienced interviewers going to find the subjects, in gay bars and other meeting places. Apparently there was no problem, for the men were only too happy to give their views and, in many cases, a substantial discussion ensued. It was hard to picture the middle-aged housewives with their neat hair-dos who do this kind of market research seeking out their nearest gay disco and, amid the noise and after-shave, holding detailed conversations about sexual practices, often for hours on end. Still, we had no complaints from either side. The men were watching their friends die; they knew how important it all was.

*   *   *

Screening for HIV antibodies was also an issue which was tackled right from the very first meeting of H(A). Testing was always offered to any patient who requested it. All blood samples were screened. Should we test other people routinely? That could tell us about the progress of the disease, but it could also give ammunition to the forces of discrimination. Voluntary testing would have a built-in bias, but compulsory testing raised awful questions of civil liberties, and there was also the problem of what to do with refusers. Compel them? Or deem them to be positive? On the other hand, the thought of the cost of testing millions of people, when the odds were that only a few would be found positive, would put off anyone who gave it a moment's thought. That money could be better used in pursuit of the same objectives via different means, for example, by paying for more research. One suggestion made in the press was to take all positives and refusers and dump them in the Isle of Wight. A constituent of mine suggested to me that we solve two problems at once, as it were, by taking them all to Hong Kong and allowing all the inhabitants of the colony to come here. He did not feel we should check with the people concerned first.

But what about international travellers? In a table of AIDS cases per million of the population in European countries in 1986, the UK was in tenth place. Other countries had more AIDS than us. Should we screen visitors from Africa? Or from particular countries there? The idea of screening inward travellers was kiboshed when it was realized that, in terms of sheer numbers, it was visitors from the USA who posed the greatest threat. And once it was decided to screen all the arrivals from a particular country, including, of course, British citizens returning from business or holidays abroad, no exception could be made in all fairness. The thought of having to insist that President Reagan or other distinguished visitors from America should undergo an AIDS screening test before being allowed out of Heathrow was too ludicrous to contemplate: no more was heard of it.

That we abandoned very quickly ideas of compulsory screening for visitors was, to my mind, very much to this country's credit, and our decision gave a lead to the rest of the world. AIDS was not some miasma being brought in from outside; it was here already, and we could not keep it out by sending people home on the planes which brought them. If its spread was to be halted, or at least slowed, it would be the behaviour of people already in this country, indeed the everyday behaviour of millions of ordinary people, that would achieve it. Since behaviour was to be tackled through the public education campaign, further messing about at airports, with all the queues and frustration – and cost – could not possibly have added anything much to the programme to protect the British public.

In November 1988, however, H(A) agreed to the anonymous screening of routine ante-natal blood samples given by pregnant women. That put paid to scientific arguments for the moment, and would certainly help track the progress of AIDS in the general population of the UK.

*   *   *

For an illness without a cure, research was clearly going to be important. Very early on, Sir James Gowans, then Secretary of the Medical Research Council (MRC), was invited to a meeting of H(A); he was asked to bring with him a couple of doctors engaged in research, but it was made quite clear that they were invited to speak on research work generally, and not to lobby for their pet projects!

The MRC is the Government's main channel of funds for medical research. It had already set up a working party on AIDS in 1983, but the usual approach to government-funded research, in which the MRC carefully considered requests made to them and allocated whatever money they had, was clearly going to be too slow, too hit-and-miss. After much discussion in H(A), a radical new approach was devised. Instead of sitting back and waiting for bright sparks to come forward, the Government decided to commission, through the MRC, a substantial programme of work, linking public and private laboratories along lines which scientists agreed looked the most hopeful. This was to be the first occasion in peacetime that this 'pro-active' approach was taken. By the autumn of 1987 research was under way in twenty-two laboratories. Some ideas came from unexpected quarters, for example centres which specialized in animal work, for the HIV was similar to the bug which causes fatal leptospirosis disease in cats.

Britain could take the lead in this research work, partly because we were strong in immunology and molecular biology, but partly because of our generally helpful legal scene. The USA, where huge sums would normally be expended on research, both from the public purse and from the pharmaceutical companies, was stymied by the fierce threat of litigation. The far-distant creation of a safe vaccine, with all the years of testing required and the huge risks involved, was not a realistic commercial goal for many of their businesses. I don't criticize their boards of Vice Presidents for being cautious – though the Federal budget for AIDS is huge – but this work needs a steady hand and real courage, and a virtually bottomless purse. H(A) decided over £14 million was to be allocated to the MRC over a three-year period. In fact, by March 1989 £27 million had been committed in AIDS research by the British Government, with a further £14.5 million for AIDS research in 1989–90 alone, far more than anyone expected.

Government money for research for a vaccine and a cure was, however, a good investment. The costs to the NHS of treating AIDS patients were already horrendous as more HIV+ people started to develop the disease. In the USA, even in the last days of 1986, it was estimated that the cost of treating one AIDS patient, from the date he was first tested as positive, to his death, was around $140,000. The arrival of drugs such as azidothymidine (AZT – also called zidovudine), which was licensed in the UK in March 1987 and which helped prolong the life of sufferers, and better management of patients, added to this bill. By 1988 sums of the order of £400 million *per year* to treat and care for AIDS patients in the NHS were being discussed for future public spending rounds. Even if the public education campaign were successful the money would be needed for many years to come because of the long gestation period of the virus.

*   *   *.

Two speeches at the time sent a shiver down my back. Both were well-meaning, both by distinguished and decent people, one of whom, at least, I admire very much.

The Princess Royal, Her Royal Highness Princess Anne, accepted our invitation to open the joint UK Government-World Health Organization conference on 26 January 1988 at the Queen Elizabeth II Conference Centre in Westminster. It was a remarkable event, the first of its kind, where governments from all over the world finally realized the global tragedy facing us. British government ministers waited nervously in the foyer of the brand-new show-piece Centre. Her Royal Highness, hatless, cool, elegant in a long yellow and navy check jacket and high-necked navy blouse, carried a bouquet presented to her by the little daughter of another minister. She went down the line as we bowed and curtsied. Being presented to Royalty is always a thrill and I am always nervous, though curtseying elegantly is impossible.

The usual practice with Royal speech-writing involves government ministers and officials offering material thought appropriate, but the Princess Royal writes her own speeches. President of the Save the Children Fund, she is worth listening to – erudite, thoughtful, sharp and compassionate, sometimes off the cuff, and frequently right. This time the audience was riveted. 'The real tragedy is the innocent victims, people who have been infected unknowingly, perhaps as a result of blood transfusion and a few who may have been infected knowingly by sufferers seeking revenge.'

She spoke of the impact of the epidemic on children: 'This has affected me deeply. In the course of my work with the Save the Children Fund I have seen evidence of this in many parts of the world, including the United Kingdom . . . It could be said that the AIDS pandemic is a classic own-goal scored by the human race against itself. There is a saying that prevention is better than cure. When there is no cure prevention is the only answer.'

The Princess's remarks were the first public statement of the view that some of the victims were 'innocent'. So who was guilty? The finger was pointed by James Anderton, Chief Constable of Greater Manchester, in Manchester on Thursday 11 December 1986. In an impassioned speech at a seminar on AIDS and hepatitis, Anderton 'bared his soul', as he put it, and accused homosexuals of 'degenerate conduct'. He went on, looking and sounding like an Old Testament prophet, 'As the years go by I see ever-increasing numbers of them [homosexuals] swirling around in a human cesspit of their own making . . . I am speaking as a man, a Christian, a husband, a police officer, a father, a lover of the human race and a believer in God's creation . . . why do these people freely engage in sodomy and other obnoxious practices, knowing the dangers involved? These are the questions we should ask instead of publicizing the wearing of condoms.'

Oh, heavens. He hit the headlines in no uncertain terms with that. His police authority in Manchester, part of a left-wing Council, were beside themselves with rage and ordered him to silence. But he had, nevertheless, touched a nerve. In a telephone poll for the London LBC radio station, 74 per cent of callers agreed with him. The *Sun* said: 'Three cheers for James Anderton. For the first time, a major public figure says what the ordinary person is thinking about AIDS.'

Personally, I preferred the intelligence of Tony Newton. Challenged to respond, he said gently: 'People who sleep around in a promiscuous way are running great risks. In the end it is for people to make their own moral judgements. I feel considerable compassion for those dying of AIDS.'

Later Anderton claimed, or allowed himself to be quoted as claiming, that he had been told by God to utter these words. Quite why he should have been chosen in this way defeated his listeners, but there is no doubt that he articulated a feeling of revulsion and anger against promiscuity and homosexuality (which he did not distinguish from each other) which was widely held amongst some sectors of the public, particularly among those who were looking for someone to blame.

We were, and are, under constant pressure to make the campaign more 'moral'. But counselling sexual fidelity in itself, or advising celibacy for homosexuals, or anyone else, is not a complete programme for the public health by any stretch of the imagination. It was awareness of that fact that led to my somewhat sarcastic remark in February 1987 – 'Good Christians don't get AIDS'. I was both amused and amazed at the diverse reactions, which again showed how strong many people's feelings were, just below the disciplined surface.

I had in my mind the strong words of the US Surgeon General, Dr C. Everett Koop, a born-again Christian, who, despite his own highly moral views, felt that the public health demanded a realistic approach to those not amenable to the Christian ethical code. The 'Surgeon General's Report on AIDS' in October 1986, written at the request of President Reagan, was a call to arms against the epidemic, complete with marching orders. He told the members of the Moral Majority, a pressure group trying to improve moral standards, that they were not his first concern. If they lived according to the religious tenets which they so powerfully advocated for other people, then, barring accidents (such as tainted blood transfusion), they would not be at risk. His public duty, analogous to that of British ministers of health, was to reach out to those who did *not* live according to Christian religious faith, nor indeed to any other code which advocated chastity and fidelity to one partner for life. That meant saying 'Use a Condom', and it meant saying it to people who were not married to each other or who slept around. If he and we were to protect the health of the rest of the population, we had no choice but to say things that were unpalatable to us personally and to people whose personal behaviour we deplored.

The Innocents and the Cesspit

What I actually said, in response to a question from a reporter, was: 'Good Christian people who wouldn't dream of misbehaving will not catch AIDS.' I see no reason to resile from it. Of course, good Christians *do* get AIDS, and of course other religious groups, such as Moslems and Jews, are equally protected if they observe their own moral codes. I did not need the huge post-bag which followed to tell me that! Nor did I mean, or intend, to set myself up as the voice of the moral majority in this country, despite the many letters which I received thanking me for my willingness to stand up and be counted; rather the reverse in fact. In the end I got fed up trying to explain, and let the remark lie on the table. I could live with it in all its forms and interpretations, and was content that it should provoke discussion from time to time on what was safe behaviour and what wasn't.

My other personal 'contribution' to the AIDS debate also took off in an unexpected way, and even appeared in the WHO world-wide newsletter on AIDS some time later. I had been at a lunch in the Midlands in the autumn of 1986, the sort of event I attended frequently and still do; a good lunch for 100 or more local business people, mostly men, at which a Conservative speaker would talk and answer questions. These events raise a lot of money for the party and are good fun. (Even though Julian Critchley, the journalist MP, once said the meals consisted of endless rubbery chicken. It's not true.)

As at virtually every other engagement at the time, all the questions were about AIDS; the guests were earnest and concerned, and I reflected not for the first time how basically decent the British people are. All except one man at the back, somewhat florid of face, who had perhaps enjoyed the luncheon wine a little too freely. He stood up, took a deep breath, and let loose a torrent of unpleasant invective. What did we think we were doing, spending all this money on an AIDS campaign to warn the general law-abiding family-loving public about a horrible disease they were not going to catch? There was a murmur in the room, which seemed suddenly a bit too warm. Some felt his intervention was bad manners, others felt relieved that he was saying what many were thinking.

I started to explain the intricacies of AIDS, how it appeared to be almost accidental that it was passed on through gay sex and drugs in this country, mentioned haemophiliacs and babies. 'We don't distinguish between patients in this country,' I said, beginning to feel a bit desperate. 'If we did, we'd have to stop treating all sorts of people whose illnesses could be proved to be linked to something they had done, such as smoking, wouldn't we?'

He took a belligerent puff at his cigar and said, 'That's not the same thing and you know it. Nobody here is going to catch AIDS. Why are you spending our money – wasting our money – telling everybody about it?'

I looked at him. I hate people like you, I thought. Cutting you down to size will be a pleasure. 'Tell me,' I said, 'are you in business?'

Affirmative grunt.

'And do you travel abroad at all on business?'

'Yes, a lot,' he said rather proudly.

'Do you travel to places like New York, or Paris, or Milan, or Naples?'

'Yes.'

'Lagos, perhaps?'

'Yes, once or twice.'

'And would you like to know our advice, on what you should take with you when you go to these places, where there is more AIDS than here, so you can avoid catching it?'

Nods all round, they were all eager to know.

'You take the wife,' I said.

For a moment they all fell about laughing, the gentleman in question good-humouredly, too. They were honourable people as I had thought at first. Then his mates at the table were looking at him and there was alarm in their eyes; one guest visibly shifted his chair, put

'Tell Fifi it was not my idea to bring the wife – it was Madame Edwina Currie.'

distance between them. I thought with a *frisson* of horror that maybe he really had been stupid in some far-off city, tired after a long day doing business with strangers. He would not be the first, or the last. Maybe he had already read our warnings in the leaflet for travellers, and had taken as much notice as of the health warnings about smoking.

When the comment 'Take the wife' became well known I received a shoal of mail and was, as ever, both amused and bemused at the reactions of my correspondents. Many wives seemed to think it was a grand idea and insisted on going on the next trip! Lots of husbands agreed but grumbled about the cost, and wanted to know if the Chancellor would reinstate tax allowances for foreign travel, preferably including the spouse. I reflected idly on just how many 'Mr and Mrs Smiths' that would cover. A few wives and feminists were most indignant that I should suggest that a wife's job was to service her husband in this way. Married myself, I wondered why not, if it made him happy and kept him out of trouble. But the letters I had not expected came from numerous well-known companies and business associations, and usually started: 'My chairman has instructed me to write to you about the insult you have just paid to British business, in suggesting that our businessmen do nothing all day on overseas trips but pick up foreign women. In this company they work very hard selling British goods . . . etc., etc.' One company secretary had the grace and wit, after signing one of these pompous monstrosities, to scribble 'Good on yer!' in his own hand at the bottom.

The issue, however, is serious. The simplest way of contracting AIDS in many countries is to go into the bar of a smart hotel and pick up a girl, or a man, who gives the visitor a friendly smile. In many of the great trading cities of the world a large proportion of the prostitutes have the virus and no one, but *no one*, can tell that they are infected without a test. The individual need not be a prostitute or even a drug addict, though these are the common routes by which infection occurs. They may simply be good-time girls or boys, who regularly sleep around. It's as easy as that.

The whole tragic business is vividly described in Randy Shilts's chilling book *And The Band Played On*, published in the UK by Viking, which should be required reading for anyone interested in AIDS. Shilts was a reporter on a California newspaper and became aware, in the early 1980s, of the extraordinary sicknesses and the increase in deaths amongst otherwise young healthy men in this part of the USA. In the age group most affected, the thirties, the death rates should have been amongst the lowest in the whole American community. And these were not drug addicts, but ordinary citizens. The only distinguishing feature in almost every case was that they were gay, and had often come to the West Coast for the more liberal attitudes and freedom that it offered.

The control of the transmission of the disease was hampered by the gay community's fear of discrimination. Shilts describes how some thirty-five gay elected councillors and other leaders in San Francisco came together to sign a letter demanding the resignation of Paul Lorch, editor of the *Bay Area Reporter*, a gay newspaper, who had pilloried them for their reckless approach to the disease. Lorch obtained a copy of the letter and pinned it up on the wall of his office. As the men who had signed died of AIDS over the next couple of years, he crossed their names off, one by one, till nearly all had gone.

I asked for the book at the House of Commons Library as soon as I heard about it; they had to send to the States for a copy, so that, apart from reviewers, I must have been one of the first people in this country to read it, occasionally surreptitiously under the table at more long-winded meetings! It reminded me, over again, that governments have roles in public health which they cannot shrug off. Even if the illness affects only a tiny proportion of our people, a minority despised or not, we have a responsibility to take whatever steps may be necessary to help them, even if there is an outcry. It is not enough to leave it to the minority to deal with themselves, for they may not have the vision or the power, and they may be under too much pressure from partial interests within the group. The skill, the really clever business, is for government to take those steps and gain public approval at the same time. We certainly did that with AIDS, at least in the years I am describing.

*   *   *

The relationship between drug taking and AIDS was understood as soon as the causative agent was identified as a virus. From 1984 onwards tremendous efforts were being made to get to grips with the heroin addiction problem in this country, and the Ministerial Group on the Misuse of Drugs (MGMD) was formed, consisting of ministers from the same Departments as those on H(A), but all at more junior rank. I joined it on my appointment in 1986 and was genuinely impressed with the commitment and effort of the civil servants, including police and customs officers, who came regularly to report on progress or otherwise. Often they would bring the latest methods of concealment to show us, including on one occasion a collection of impeller motors from Nigeria which had had heroin ingeniously packed inside; the bits of greasy equipment lay littered among the biscuits and remains of the ghastly Home Office tea, as we talked. I learned just how much cannabis is used in this country (a lot), I learned about 'ecstasy' and 'crack' and 'chasing the dragon'. I learned that many addicts hold down jobs and are very different to the usual image. And I became increasingly pessimistic, though without our efforts the problem would be vastly worse.

My first meeting was on 18 November 1986, with David Mellor as Minister of State, Home Office, in the chair. It was, as ever, well attended, with twenty-one officials, six ministers and two special advisers. The topics covered were typical of the fare of the group – customs, assistance to South America, drug liaison with India, the size of the Pakistan poppy harvest (up four times over the previous year), a forthcoming UN conference on drugs, liaison with the USA, the latest meeting of European ministers (David had addressed the European Parliament on drugs in October 1986), GPs and drug addicts, Scottish health education, police attitudes, a schools video on drugs, teacher training, inadequate Department of Health statistics and a host of other topics. No one could ever accuse us of not being thorough.

The committee worked hard. It was also systematic and well informed. Six-monthly assessments of the drugs problem in the United Kingdom were started in the spring of 1986. It is sad to read now that by November of that year a feeling of cautious optimism was apparent. Heroin abuse seemed at last to be at a standstill, with a fall in seizures, and cocaine supply was being kept low through enforcement successes. Many treatment agencies were then far more worried about the incidence of amphetamines. 'Crack' was unknown.

Police attitudes were crucial. There was a clear conflict of culture between regarding the addict as a criminal and getting him to come for treatment. The most careful recruitment and training of police was needed – for men and women, who put their lives at risk, particularly for underground work. It is amazing now to think that at that time there was no separate drugs wing anywhere on the Scottish crime squad. Other people were doing better, in my view. I attended a meeting of the South Derbyshire Police Liaison Group, in the little local police station. These groups were set up on the recommendation of Lord Scarman following the 1981 riots and were intended to promote good relationships between the public and the boys in blue. I've no idea how successful these were elsewhere, but the best one in my constituency, a generally law-abiding area, met in Swadlincote, in the patch where a single pub brawl was front-page headlines for weeks. There were always a few strangers at these meetings, which were attended by representatives from all the political parties. We were studiously polite to each other; political knockabout is not really approved of in Derbyshire, and quite right too. There was an empty seat in the front row, which I headed for. Next to it was a very scruffy man in jeans and a dark sweater, in his late thirties at a guess, hair lank, lying greasy on his shoulders, his body thin, twitching slightly, rather pale. Drugs were on the agenda. I wondered, with slight misgivings, who this guy was, and what he might have in his pockets as I sat next to him. Perhaps he was just the latest representative from the Labour Party (they seemed to change frequently), but there was definitely something not right about him.

The agenda wound its way through the other items, then came to the report of the regional crime squad. The inspector, resplendent in his uniform, spoke with some pride; the force was cock-a-hoop at catching several drugs-laden vehicles belting up the M1, acting, as they say, on information received. The Asian communities in Derby were also helpful. Generally law-abiding like everyone else, they were incensed at the pollution of their young people by the dealers on the make from Leicester and elsewhere, and shopped them regularly.

The man next to me shifted, coughed. Heavens, I thought, I hope he's not going to start taking something in here. He was standing up. 'And this is Detective Sergeant X,' said the inspector. 'He works with the youngsters in Derby.' My man shambled over to the desk and started talking, and I realized that I had been sitting next to the bravest man in the county, who lived with the chance of a knife in the guts every day of the week. Now I understood what had not been right about him; his hands were a bit too clean and he had not reeked of cigarettes. Apart from that his disguise was perfect, for he had served in that self-same police station as a uniformed officer for several years, and not one of the locals had recognized him. We were all fooled. Later I took him off for a drink in the Conservative Club, and he introduced me to low-alcohol lager. 'Good stuff, this,' he said perspicaciously. 'It'll take off, you mark my words.' He was right about that, too.

By June 1987, after the election, when Douglas Hogg replaced David Mellor as its chairman, the MGMD had shown itself an excellent vehicle for decision making in a complex area cutting across several departments. Douglas was the President of the Oxford Union back in the days when I was a starry-eyed 'fresher'. He hasn't changed a lot since. Pugnacious and kindly, a fine debater in an older tradition, you'll spot him bending over the Despatch Box, chin thrust forward, spectacles on the end of his nose, tearing the Opposition to shreds. Now, as chairman, he was seen as taking a key role both in presenting the work of the Group to the rest of the Government and to the outside world, and in resolving any problems between departments. For example, when there appeared to be a demarcation dispute blowing up between Customs (run by the Treasury) and the Police (run by the Home Office), Douglas thumped the table in a splendid imitation of his father, Quintin, and told them to sort it out, to ringing cheers from the rest of us. The tactic worked, too.

Somewhat nervously, at my first meeting I had presented a paper on the next round of the public education campaign which we undertook each year. By this time the Government had already done two annual drug campaigns. AIDS was looming over us and I explained that we had started looking at possible anti-injecting messages. At this stage AIDS and drugs campaigns were still seen as separate. How optimistic we were! We were thinking, too, of extending the campaign to cover stimulants such as amphetamines, although in fact this was not done till 1988. I was also able to report that 'cocaine, although a threat, had not so far produced widespread problems in this country' and I advised that there could be a real danger that advertising would draw attention to it and create a problem by so doing. The discussion on cocaine in the file is underlined in red ink by me; perhaps I had a premonition of the deaths and misery cocaine would cause in this country before much longer.

By January 1987 we were being warned by our researchers, Andrew Irving Associates in particular, about new trends appearing: the glittering image of cocaine, which was seen as less dangerous or addictive than heroin; the increasing use of drug 'cocktails'; the increase in under-age drinking, with fears that in some instances this was the precursor of unplanned, impromptu drug use. Cocaine in 1987, we were told, was too expensive for general use and was not seen by users as good value for money. Its image was glamorous, jet-set, in contrast to the everyday image of amphetamines; and 'speed' could be obtained for less than a bottle of whisky, and equally readily by the knowledgeable. How bizarre, how sad, I thought, that these kids should take the same 'value-for-money' approach to drugs as their mothers do to sausages in a supermarket. Amphetamines could be made anywhere relatively easily; when one factory in the East End of London was raided in late 1986, 17 kilos of the drug had been seized. I needed no more convincing of the danger of this aspect of the drugs problem, after a factory making 'speed' was discovered in a house in fashionable Spondon in Derby. If it's a problem in Derby, it's a problem everywhere.

By that spring we were thinking hard about our third annual drugs advertising campaign. We were beginning to feel experienced in this kind of work, using public money and advertising campaigns to get a health message across. The television campaigns of late 1986 against drugs certainly got noticed, with 80 to 90 per cent of young people claiming to have seen something on television. Posters came next, with recognition by 74 per cent. Nothing else came anywhere near. We thus had our techniques in a pretty refined state. It was no accident that the concurrent AIDS campaign used similar methods. Even if expensive, the ads had to be on television; the more money, the more prime time.

Sadly, the Health Education Authority (HEA), which took over AIDS work in 1988, seems to have forgotten these lessons – which are not based on prejudice or personal opinion but on reams of basic research and evaluation of public response. The HEA's AIDS campaign in the winter of 1988–9 has ignored television and concentrated on one of the least effective modes, newspaper advertisements. No wonder the Consumers' Association has criticized them for an overly intellectual approach; they deserve it. Their campaign, in my opinion, verges on a waste of public money. If you're going to do it, do it properly.

We had learned some unexpected lessons from the drugs campaigns of 1985 and 1986, too. Young people's values and driving forces are often different from those of their elders. What really upset girls about the anti-heroin advertisements was the lank hair and the lack-lustre appearance of the addicts. What upset the boys was spots! So we ran more advertisements like that in the youth press and they clearly had an impact. Later, however, we were warned that the horribly pimply youth who was the main focus of some of the 1986 advertisements was in danger of becoming a cult hero, with requests for his poster coming in, so we put a stop to that and his face disappeared from our campaigns.

* * *

The bringing together of the AIDS and drugs campaigns was inevitable, and happened in the spring of 1987 when Norman Fowler decided that both should be run by Sammy Harari's agency, TBWA. One advantage was that the total budget for the campaign had been increased and £5 million was spent in 1987 on the 'Don't Inject AIDS' campaign. A staggering amount of work went into it over the next few months. Getting the two campaigns against AIDS and drugs together was going to be very tricky indeed and demanded advertising skills of the highest order. Our confidence in TBWA turned out to be very well placed and the campaign won them over forty national and international awards. It was copied by other governments, almost word for word. And by the time the June 1987 election was over the material was almost ready. I recall now the meetings where we discussed the material being offered to us, and I marvel at the freedom we were allowed. The researchers and the advertising agency on 'Don't Inject AIDS', led by Sammy Harari, explained the background. There were, they said, three groups. The 'refusers' – most of the kids, regularly over 90 per cent of all teenagers, in Britain; they needed their resolve strengthened and reassured. The 'might-tries' – a small group, which had already shrunk during the course of the 1984–6 campaigns from 11 per cent of young people to 4 per cent. They had different motivations – I'm not a junkie, and I don't steal or anything like that. Asked whose opinion they feared most, they said 'Mum'. A separate campaign was devised for them showing how people *do* deteriorate. Then there was the third lot, the 'users' – tiny in number, using drugs already, knowledgeable, cynical, often anti-authoritarian. But research showed something interesting. Both the first and the third groups wanted a hard-hitting campaign. Influenced, perhaps, by the AIDS hype, where the endless criticism was that we were being too nice, young people said, tell it like it is; show the dirt and degradation, show the bloody needles. And use the street language for once, can't you? Then we'll believe you mean business.

So we did; and the 'bloody needles' campaign, with photographs by Don McCullin and Clive Arrowsmith, came into being. We (the Junior Ministers on the MGMD) held our breath at some of the suggestions for those 40-foot posters – the body in a morgue, label tied to toe, for example. But when Sammy suggested a picture of yet another bloody needle with the slogan 'It only takes one prick to give you AIDS' we goggled.

'You're kidding?' we said.

'No kidding,' he replied. 'The testing shows this is the one above all the others that they all remember.'

We gulped. 'Well, we're game if you say so, but we'll never get that past our Secretaries of State.'

Sammy, however, knew his stuff and the programme gradually gained approval higher up. I was in the courtyard of the House of Commons one afternoon when I spotted two dazed characters staggering slowly towards the public exit. I recognized them as two very senior officials from our Department.

'What's up?' I inquired, ever solicitous of their health.

'We've got it!' they said.

'Got what?' I pressed, thinking the worst.

'Approval for the bloody needles campaign,' they whispered. 'From the top.'

It transpired that they had been at a meeting of H(A).

'All of it?'

'Yes, the lot.'

'Including . . . ?'

'Oh, yes, they liked "Only one prick." We're going ahead with that. What is the world coming to?'

It worked, and that's what mattered. There were the television advertisements, too; directed by John Amiel, whose previous work included *The Singing Detective*. A boy comes down the stairs to collect his card, brought by the postman, for his hospital appointment, where he discovers that he is HIV+. The street-wise kids loved it, complaining only that the house was 'too clean'. There was one for girls, too, warning them of the dangers lurking in a syringe offered by a friend, with the powerful image of a wax doll, stabbed over and over again with pins, falling dying at the end. My twelve-year-old daughter Debbie saw it on television at her boarding school and wrote me a long letter – 'it was awful, Mum; we talked about it for ages, and we all said we'll never, never try drugs. Did you have anything to do with it?'

The whole campaign was launched by John Moore at a press conference in September 1987 – more than seven months after the original decision to combine drugs and AIDS – and created a huge impact. It was the best and most professional campaign on any topic I had ever been involved in. The evaluation research later showed we had achieved greater awareness, and more strengthening of the desired attitudes amongst the target audience of young people, than anything since the work against drugs, the first modern public education campaign, had got cracking three years before. In Scotland, however, where it was decided for the first time to run the same campaign as in England, the effect was very powerful indeed. They had seen nothing like this. All their material had been mild by any comparison and probably ignored by the growing number of addicts; so the drug users were largely unaware of the risk of AIDS that they were running not only by injecting, but by sharing equipment. Andrew Irving reported that the effect of the 'bloody needles', all too accurate a picture for Edinburgh and Dundee, was to create panic and near hysteria amongst the addicts. For many it was too late. Others, however, did change their habits, and gradually, as needle exchange schemes came in, alternatives began to emerge for at least some of these lost souls. And for their children. The agency reported various comments from drug users in Scotland about the 1987 campaign: 'It's painful just looking at the size of that needle. When you see things like that you can see what you could turn into . . . I wouldn't jab now since I've seen that.' One comment from Merseyside said it all: 'That advert even looks dirty. I look at that and I cringe.'

Irving summarized the evaluation of the campaign: 'It generally placed a frightening AIDS halo over the hard drugs scene. It clearly communicated the risk of contracting AIDs through injecting and sharing needles.' And he told us we didn't need to worry that the impression was gained that it was all right to take drugs by some other means – they were all put off by the sordid pictures. As the needle squirted blood, so the nation's young people hardened their hearts against drugs of any kind.

I played some part in the 1988 campaign, too, with its grainy black and white TV adverts, the pulsating red spot showing how AIDS could be transmitted from user to user. Those 1988 advertisements were the first to refer to drugs other than heroin. That change had become necessary as heroin was virtually unobtainable in many parts of the country. By mid-1988 injecting amphetamines had become the norm in parts of London and Wales, with benzodiazepines also being widely misused by addicts. Now it's cocaine and 'crack'. Perhaps next year, and the year after, it will be something else, as the user looks ever onward for his fix.

*   *   *

We agonized for months about those needle exchange schemes. The Dutch were very quick off the mark in giving out free needles, while the Swedish authorities gave out free condoms to young people. The problem about free needles was not the cash, which was only marginal. (Indeed, in Scotland, the only schemes which worked eventually involved the pharmacists *selling* the equipment to the users in large quantities.) The point was rather that the exchange should be made easy, private, confidential and non-judgemental so that it attracted the users. That would give us a better chance of reaching a higher proportion of them and gave the opportunity of advising them how to reduce their own risk, let alone ours. It would also mean the dirty equipment could be collected and safely destroyed. That opportunity for counselling by trained staff was regarded as crucial by Ministers in England; I believe my colleagues in Scotland did their best, but the public there just wouldn't have it.

I was always a firm supporter of carefully managed needle exchange schemes and I was glad that the national drugs and alcohol charity Turning Point, with which I had done some work as a back-bencher, went ahead, along with other bodies, and set them up all over England and Wales, including, quietly, in Derby. Many were funded by local health authorities with money provided by the Government, a brave and wise move. When we first tried to set up a drugs counselling service in Derby, using volunteers, we held the first meeting at my house. Despite its being fiendishly difficult to find – one reason why we had bought it! – scores of people turned up, and that service is now up and running. My experience was repeated in much of the rest of England, but constant control and supervision was needed. At least one drugs clinic had to be closed when the pushers got in, bringing violence and mayhem in their wake.

By mid-1987 things were changing. It looked as if the threat of AIDS was far bigger than the threat of drug taking, both to the individual addict and to the fabric of society. That point of view was put to us, as firmly as anything could be, by the Advisory Council on the Misuse of Drugs (ACMD), chaired by Mrs Runciman. Their report on AIDS and drug misusers was published on 29 March 1988. AIDS is more dangerous to individual and public health than drugs, they said, in a stark and unqualified statement. That means, you must help the addicts, not condemn them. That means, too, that funding for drugs campaigns should not be competing with bids for the programme against AIDS – they are a major part of it. And it means, maintaining the attitude that drug taking is very dangerous. That is indeed the approach which has been adopted since.

Are we likely to win the battle against drugs? Without world-wide co-operation, I doubt it. Tim Eggar, the Junior Minister at the Foreign Office, described to MGMD in September 1988 the visit he had just made to South America. He recalled his flight along the Huallaga Valley in Peru; a valley 100 miles long and 10 miles wide devoted to coca production, in which there were fires everywhere as yet more jungle was cleared. A vigorous man, he had tried to pull out a two-year-old coca bush and found it already firmly rooted. I fear for my own children; I fear for yours. I hope that complacency never sets in on this topic, perhaps more than any other topic in this book. The route from innocence to the cesspit down the shaft of a needle is both certain and deadly.

*   *   *

By May 1988, some thirty months after HIV testing became possible in this country, over 6 million samples of blood supplied by donors had been tested, with only a handful of positives being found. About a quarter of a million people had come forward for testing. I liked the approach of the clinic in Liverpool, which insisted that all clients have a counselling session first as to why they wanted the test. That provided an excellent opportunity for a discussion on the methods by which AIDS was transmitted, and the ways it wasn't. Often people were then able to go away reassured; they could use the same crockery as someone HIV+ in the canteen at work, they could sit next to them, and they wouldn't catch it. The clinic doctor would then ask two more questions. 'What will you do if you're HIV+?' and a discussion would ensue as to possible options for what might be a bleak and limited future. The key question came next. 'What will you do if you're not?' There must have been many, sitting uncomfortably in front of the kindly doctor, who would then be forced to think about their life-style, about the occasional use of drugs, or the sleeping around, or the pal who boasted bisexuality.

There was, of course, another argument: that the public were smart enough to decide without help whether or not to test themselves, but to me this was *laissez-faire* taken too far. I hope and, indeed, am sure, that our approach to counselling and testing was effective in producing a change of direction for many people at risk long before the infection could take hold in the general population. By 1989 the time for doubling of new cases had slowed from ten months to fifteen months. Maybe the campaign was working.

*   *   *

AIDS dominated our discussions on drugs. But a few items had their own significance. The last main topic that was dealt with by our worthy MGMD while I was a member also showed (in my humble but biased view!) the foresight of the team. Colin Moynihan, appointed in June 1987 as the new Minister for Sport, knew his business, as a former Olympic cox. Drugs in sport were on our agenda in September 1987, a full year before the scandal at Seoul. With some prodding from Colin, the Sports Council had endorsed a determined programme to eradicate drugs from British sport at their meeting earlier that month. They had some clout, for they could withhold grants from any sport which failed to comply. That still left the sports which did not receive grants, such as snooker or motor racing; Colin found himself on television explaining why a sportsman might take not a stimulant but a drug to slow down the heart beat, so that his hand might be the steadier as he took his shot. He is a doughty fighter on behalf of honesty in sport, was worried about the long-term health of athletes taking terrible risks with drugs, and his persistence has paid off.

*   *   *

At the end of December 1988 there were 1,982 cases of AIDS in the UK of whom 1,059 have died. Eighty-two per cent of all known cases are homosexuals, 6 per cent haemophiliacs, 3 per cent women. Nineteen cases were children infected by their mothers; of these sad babies, eight were already dead. One thousand nine hundred and eighty-two and counting.

How many people in the UK really have AIDS? No one knows. There's no way of finding out. Dr Anna McCormick, a medical statistician with the Public Health Laboratory Service, spoke at the London AIDS conference in March 1988. By analysis of the death certificates of young men she showed that perhaps the number who had died from AIDS was really twice as high as reported. 'I don't know any other reason why the mortality rate among single men is going up,' she said. Unmarried men account for 90 per cent of the extra deaths.

Sir David Cox's Committee on the forecasting of AIDS cases reported to the Department of Health at the end of 1988. You can expect at least *ten thousand cases* of AIDS by 1992, they said, mostly from people already infected. Don't be surprised if the rate of infection appears to be tailing off. It could mean simply that the most vulnerable have been removed from the group – in other words, they are dead and can infect no more. Ten thousand and counting.

We will fight the next election against that background. And what happens after that – into the next century – depends on what people do now.

*   *   *

There was no doubt that AIDS changed everything for a great many people. I have been struck in reading back through the files, how much we now take for granted was the subject of agonized and lengthy discussion only a short while ago. AIDS changed what we taught our children, what we advertised on television, what we spent on public health, how we dealt with drug addicts. It changed the conversation at every dinner-table in the land. Worried parents gave their children condoms to take back to college, consumer programmes discussed the merits of this bit of rubber versus another, while the sexual practices of what many would regard as deviants and perverts were widely and exhaustively discussed on prime time TV. Dentists took to wearing gloves and masks, surgeons switched to thermal lances from scalpels, companies sprang up to store a customer's own clean blood till such time as he might need it, princes took pints of their own blood on tours abroad where the local supply was suspect, princesses bravely shook the hands of dying men in hospital beds in London. Thousands, perhaps millions, of people looked at their way of life and changed it. The old-fashioned virtues of chastity and fidelity once more came into their own and the illiberal liberties of the permissive age were rightly put away.

The problem of AIDS will not go away and, indeed, will be worse for many years before it gets better. But as I have done my research for this book I have been struck over and over again by the honesty and earnest desire to do right on the part of almost everyone involved. The problems were not hushed up or ignored or denied. They were, and are, tackled with vigour and vision in this country. The leap in the dark was taken with a sure-footedness which augurs well for the future. If we could take a similar approach to some of the other subjects covered in this book, which were part of my effort to move the goalposts, then the ordinary people who play the game of life would enjoy the very best of health.

5

The Other Half

I suspect that Woman will be the last thing civilized by Man
George Meredith, 1859

The room was small, cramped; it was full of the smell of freesias, a deep, sickly perfume. Underneath was another smell. Death was sitting on the bed, almost visible.

The girl in the bed was in her late twenties. She was thin, pale, and must once have been very pretty; even now her big dark eyes and wide mouth suggested warmth and generosity of spirit. Another woman, the girl's mother, sat tight and miserable in a chair, face crumpled, fighting off tears.

We were in the Marie Curie home in Woolton, on the suburban edge of Liverpool. I had promised to visit ages before. Most of my visits to the city were private and I had begrudged the time taken from seeing my mother, who lived nearby, to do official functions. But this one was different.

Jeanette Smith was an ordinary Liverpool woman, with two children, a close family and, no doubt, everything to look forward to. In the normal way of events her life would have attracted no attention and I would never have met her. I did not like to ask, and never found out, exactly what her story was; it didn't matter. Her pretty, drawn face, the flowery dressing-gown, the agony in her mother's eyes, the smell of the flowers and the stark whiff of cancer were the reason for my visit; they were a potent confection.

The matron popped in to see if we were getting on well, concerned that the presence of a visitor should not tire her patient, and promptly pulled me out, commenting that even Health Ministers needed to know when they had had enough. A month later Jeanette was dead of cervical cancer.

In 1988, 2,000 other women in this country died of cervical cancer. Yet of all the cancers, it offers the most hope of recovery: provided it is detected early enough, it can be treated and probably 90 per cent of those deaths could be avoided. I do not know if Jeanette had had the smear test, or had had it early enough to detect the condition so it could be treated to save her life. But twenty-five years after the development of the Pap smear test, decades after the WHO called on governments to institute mass-screening programmes, and long after the establishment of well-organized pressure groups in this country – such as the Women's National Cancer Control Campaign, which spends a lot of its time persuading women to have a smear test, and persuading professionals to persuade them to – this cancer remains a significant killer of women before their time in Britain, and our figures are amongst the worst in the world.

* * *

When I was first appointed to the Department of Health in September 1986 there was no separate official approach to women's health in this country and it was not treated as a topic, or group of topics, in its own right. It seems hard to believe now. When I asked officials for a list of the subjects under the title 'Women's Health' which concerned the Department, they obligingly cobbled together a large collection of more than forty jumbled titles, ranging from 'Rape' to 'Perinatal mortality', in no particular order. There was no general section of the Department called 'Women's Health', and no officials designated to deal with it. The only exception to the rule was the medical speciality of obstetrics and gynaecology, which merited a section with officials of its own.

This approach was leaving gaping holes in any worthwhile discussion of the health of women. It would be misleading to suggest that all women's particular health problems could best be dealt with under the general heading 'Gynaecology'. It could be dangerous to assume that all the health problems experienced by a woman are due to her hormones, with the implication that she might just have to put up with it; a totally different cause of the problem might be missed because of this outdated prejudice. The whole business seemed to me most unsatisfactory. Long before I came on the scene, there had, of course, been plenty of work done by the Department of Health, and by male ministers, in some of the fields relevant to women, much of it very far-sighted. What was missing was a systematic approach to the health needs of the 'other half' of our population – while remaining very aware, as all good politicians should, that this 'other half' in fact comprises rather more than half the voters of this country.

I wanted to know whether there was a distinct female angle to health, whether the pattern of women's health was different from that of the men, and thus whether, for preventive purposes, we should expect to give different advice to women and girls than we do to men, or to the population as a whole. The answers to questions like these surprised me very much, and led to major rethinks in our Department and elsewhere.

'May I indulge a particular interest of mine?' I asked Norman Fowler. 'Can I do Women's Health?'

'Of course, if you want to,' he replied.

Thus, in late 1986, the new title in the Department was born. Although I did not know it till recently, Britain thereby became the first member country of the United Nations to appoint a minister with special responsibility for women's health. I gathered together a great bunch of civil servants from all over the Department, several at Deputy Secretary level, including doctors and a nurse, and we started to meet regularly. We rejoiced in the obvious name of 'Women's Health Group'. The civil servants were so proud of it that they briefed me – quite unusually, for they usually keep their heads down – to mention the Group in the debate on women's health which was called nearly two years later, in Government time in the Commons on 10 June 1988. There was, of course, a token man, one of the doctors, whom we tolerated with easy grace. He was invaluable, not because he was a man, but for his wise mixture of erudition and caution. He confessed that the friendly atmosphere, in which ministers and officials would toss ideas around, arguing with each other, challenging, probing, teasing, was quite unlike the usual briefing meetings for ministers. 'Ah,' we said. 'We're women; that is what makes the difference.' And it was different, and very special, and it is the main thing I miss. A bunch of women together is quite different from a bunch of men. We are more like sisters, less hierarchical, less authoritarian, perhaps – who knows? – more committed, more open-minded, less ambitious, more naive.

You will read in this book of numerous ways in which ministers discussed policies with civil servants and advisers. There was the Cabinet Committee (or, at least, sub-committee) for AIDs, chaired by a Cabinet Minister, attended by Secretaries of State. There is the Ministerial Group on Alcohol Misuse chaired by a non-departmental Cabinet Minister, John Wakeham, and attended by junior ministers; and there is the longer-established Ministerial Group on the Misuse of Drugs, with similar attendance but chaired by a junior minister from the Home Office. There was a Ministerial Group on Women's Issues (MGWI) which was set up in May 1986 in response to the United Nations Decade for Women. That event had ended in 1985 with a world conference in Nairobi with all sorts of ringing declarations and 372 recommendations, most of which (like having decent maternity services) we were already following. The MGWI had middle-ranking ministers in attendance, chaired by the Minister of State at the Home Office, since that Department is responsible for equal opportunities legislation. None of these bodies has decision-making power; decisions, and the implementation of them, belong to the Departments. They do not cut across the collective responsibility of ministers – they help make that collective responsibility effective. The groups are talking shops. They are, however, the quickest way of 'testing the water' across Departments, sniffing out the opposition, winning allies; they are thus not needed where the control of a policy, such as for women's health, lies entirely within a single Department. The Women's Health Group (WHG) paralleled one on preventive medicine, the Prevention Strategy Group, already in existence in the Department of Health, which I started to chair. The WHG was thus entirely my baby and I was well pleased with it and its efforts.

The first questions we asked were: 'What do women die of?'; and 'What do women die of prematurely?' – by which I meant, vaguely, dying in middle age or earlier, with the implication that such deaths were not simply caused by old age or heredity or general deterioration.

Every year there are around 600,000 deaths – of men and women – in this country. Seventy per cent of our people get to seventy years of age; more of them women than men. Of the 292,000 deaths of women of all ages in 1986, 142,000 (or nearly half) were due to diseases of the circulatory system and 67,000 (nearly a quarter) due to cancer. That's a lot of heart disease and a lot of cancer, but the bald figures didn't mean very much.

Go into it a bit deeper: look at the death *rates* per million population by age for women in 1985. These show how likely a particular cause of death is. In the 25 to 34 age group, the killer is *cancer* – 163 deaths per million, compared to 56 for heart disease, 118 for injury and

115

poisoning. Cancer persists as three times more common for women than heart disease up through the age groups until the late sixties. By then the cancers account for 4,411 deaths per million, heart disease for 3,300 deaths per million, and chest problems (other than cancer) for 665 deaths per million. We all have to die of something, and these illnesses become more common in older women, but these are substantial death rates for women still young enough to get indignant if anyone tried to write them off.

How do these figures compare with those for men? Ask the same questions and you'll come up with different answers. Amongst young men (25 to 34) the largest group (again in 1985), deaths from injury and poisoning, accounts for 438 deaths per million people – though these data predate AIDS, which may well overtake other causes of death amongst young men in Britain as it has already in some cities in the USA. Cancer for this group stands at 132 deaths per million, well below the female figure of 163. By the time men get to their late thirties, circulatory disease – mainly heart disease – has overtaken cancer and is racing ahead; as they get to retirement age (65) there are far more heart disease deaths than cancer deaths amongst men.

In this country, therefore, to generalize, middle-aged men die of heart disease and middle-aged (and young) women die of cancer. That alone justifies looking at women's health separately. We do not clearly know why there is such a difference. It is thought, for instance, that women may well be protected by their hormones from heart disease in their child-bearing years, when the heart has to be strong enough to cope with enormous and rapid changes in the strain put on it during pregnancy, including a substantial increase in the blood supply. Once that protection dies away after the menopause, heart disease for those who might be prone to it, or who encourage it with the typical British diet, may be as much a risk for women as for men.

Let's poke around in that cancer figure a little more. When the Women's Health Group started, back in 1986, any gathering of informed and concerned women, if asked which was the commonest cancer, would, without hesitation, have nominated cervical cancer. They would have been wrong, and very wrong indeed. In England and Wales, in 1986, around 67,000 women of all ages died of cancer. The largest single group turned out to be breast cancer, with 13,641 deaths – around 15,000 for the UK as a whole. There are some 24,000 cases of breast cancer reported every year, but the mortality is not as fearsome as it looks; we know that, if it is caught early, nearly two-thirds of the women treated will survive to that magical five-year mark when they are regarded as being free of the disease.

The number two cancer among women, to everyone's surprise, was now lung cancer; over 10,000 deaths in England and Wales, over 11,000 in the whole country. That is over 200 a week. I was amazed as I looked at these figures, sitting in my office in the Elephant and Castle back in 1986. 'Why don't we women know about lung cancer? What are we doing about it?' I demanded of officials.

'It's worse than that, Minister,' they said sadly. 'Those figures are going up, we have nearly 30 per cent more deaths from lung cancer amongst women now than in 1979, whereas the death rate for the men is dropping. They are doing better and women are dying in larger numbers, and younger. Oral cancer among women is rising sharply too. And it is going to get worse, because more young women are now smoking, and smoking more than they used to. That is the price of female equality.'

Going further down the list, bowel cancer accounted for nearly 9,000 – it is a major disease in men also and is alleged to have demonstrable links with a too-refined diet. Leukaemia still took over 4,000 women per year, stomach cancer almost the same number.

I realised with surprise that I had got this far down the list and, with the obvious exception of breast cancer, none of these diseases was particularly associated with female bits. Most of the deaths were from cancer in parts of the body common to both sexes. Leaving out breast cancer and lung cancer, the two top-notchers, women in fact suffered *less* from cancer than men of the same age. Now that really was a puzzle. Is it because of some other protective element in our make-up? Or is it really because traditionally we have always smoked much less than men, regarding it until very recently as a rather butch habit? Perhaps those cigarettes have a link of some kind with many cancers, not just the obvious ones, or have some overall effect on the immune system. The thought, as I watch colleagues take another puff, makes me shudder.

If you're an expert in this field you probably know the answers. I can only convey to you how puzzled I felt as I pored over the charts and tables. Perhaps you can get a whiff of my frustration when there were no simple sturdy replies to my questions, and of the feeling of dismay as I realized just how much we were taking on, if we were to persuade women to change their life-styles and those of their whole families, and to take up with enthusiasm new schemes for screening

– of which neither they, nor their friends, sisters or mothers (to whom many women still turn for advice) had ever heard.

Our efforts on cervical cancer certainly seemed a little out of proportion. It is down towards the bottom of the list, at around 2,000 deaths per year, one of the rarer cancers accounting for only one in thirty-five deaths from cancer among women every year, or substantially less than one in a hundred deaths of women from all causes. Looking for cervical cancer was in fact a classic needle-in-a-haystack quest. And yet there was Jeanette.

*   *   *

There was no doubt about breast cancer. This is the big one. The cancer women fear most of all; the one talked about between mother and daughter, sister and cousin; the one which insults, disfigures, destroys a woman's very femaleness, where the treatment for years was amputation and radical excision of lymph nodes, leaving disablement and scars, an inability to raise one's arm ever again, to brush one's hair without pain. It is a cruel and evil disease which returned again to kill. The incidence in Britain is amongst the highest in the world. There is no geographical pattern whatsoever, no apparent link with other risk factors such as smoking; only a vague idea, difficult to research, that there might be an inherited link, so that if one sister gets it, another is more likely to – and yet it appears out of the blue in other women. There appeared to be no means of preventing breast cancer, no advice we could give women to help them avoid it. All we could say was check yourself for the signs regularly. Sometimes it's a dimple, or a discharge, or an ache; but for most women it's the lump, found perhaps while in the bath, tiny, firm and persistent.

I was told that nine out of ten lumps are benign, and there are 25,000 cases of breast cancer every year. That must mean that a quarter of a million women every year get a lump. Some get them quite often – they are 'lumpy ladies' – but that's no comfort. As for those lumps which are benign – just milk cysts in a blocked duct – the average woman simply cannot tell by feel at all, and every single one ought to be checked. The doctor can often tell in ten minutes by fine-needle aspiration, i.e. putting in a hypodermic and drawing the fluid off.

The picture is not all gloomy by any means, and it is at last beginning to dawn on the professionals concerned (mostly male) that the psychological well-being of their patient may be promoted by judicious application of current knowledge. I was invited to dinner with the South Derbyshire General Practitioners; they shared their table in a local hotel regularly with the local surgeons. The chairman, male, bow-tied and cheerful, leaned across the table as the coffee came. 'You were right!' he said to the surgeon, also bow-tied, who reached for the sugar. 'It works!'

'What works?' I inquired.

'Breast lumps. Getting rid of them. It's easy, and the patients are tickled pink.'

What had transpired, it appeared, was that the surgeon had advised the GP to exercise some discretion in sending him young women with lumps; despite recent scares, they are unlikely to be cancer, or anything else very serious. Only send the ones over thirty-five. As for the rest, the young women, aspirate the lump; it will only be liquid, not solid, and as long as there's no blood in the liquid, it's OK.

'What do you do then?' I asked, breathless.

'Oh, chuck the liquid down the sink and send the patient back to her husband,' was the casual answer.

I wondered if they realized what a staggering relief that was – simply to go home, lump gone (probably never to recur), instead of the weeks of waiting to see the surgeon, the tests, biopsies, fear, terror, that had been their lot before. You lot are gods, I thought to myself, and you are acting like saints. Bless you. But I didn't say it.

*   *   *

If there is no primary prevention (avoiding a disease completely) then we have to try secondary prevention (detecting it early enough to stop it). During the 1970s researchers in Sweden, in New York and in the Netherlands were experimenting with different methods for the early detection of breast cancer. Breast self-examination (BSE) looked promising, and so did heat-spot detection; and there was a revival of interest in low-dosage X-rays, 'mammography', which in skilled hands can detect the tiny hard lumps and the minute deposits of calcium typical of early cancer.

We knew that it was no use if we merely found cancer in its later stages. Find it in a lady of eighty, and she may well die later of something else. The key was to find it early enough to save lives and to give real improvements in mortality and quality of life. On the other hand the condition, rare in younger women, is, in them, much harder to detect as the breast tissue is very much more active – the mammogram is foggy and harder to read. Our quest would have the most promising effects in the middle years. In the age group 50 to 64 the incidence of breast cancer was seven times as high, and the death rate twelve times as high, as in the women twenty years younger. No country therefore did regular screening of women under forty. Sweden's system did the age group 40 to 49 every eighteen months, and the fifty-plus ladies every two years. Some of the USA experiments started at forty-five. We felt that fifty was the appropriate age. As I was forty a few weeks after I became Minister, I can assure any critical readers that had there been, in the state of our knowledge and the available technology at the time, any evidence that regular screening could have helped our age group, we would have done it; it was not a question of money. We didn't rule out older women, either, but their response to call and recall systems was weaker, so we decided that those over sixty-five could carry on coming if they wanted to, knowing the keen ones would. If, later, it is decided to extend the age range in this country, then it would be my view (which I expressed as a minister) that we should go upwards to seventy, not downwards to forty or forty-five. It's easier to detect then, we'll find more of it in the older women, and the life expectancy of an otherwise healthy woman in her sixties these days is nearly two decades.

In 1978, following the publication of some of the New York results, it was decided to set up long-term trials in this country, to see whether screening did work. Eight centres were designated. Two did BSE, two (Edinburgh and Guildford) did mammography, and the other four were controls. The cautiously optimistic results were published in the *Lancet* in August 1988. Some time before that doctors were already getting excited about mammography, though BSE, on the other hand, was increasingly reckoned to be a waste of time, except insofar as it encouraged a woman to take a general interest in her health.

In July 1985, Kenneth Clarke, then Minister of Health, asked Professor Sir Patrick Forrest, the Head of the Edinburgh unit, to chair an expert working group to report on whether breast cancer screening really was a good practical idea for the UK. Their report was duly received in November 1986 and concluded, in that cool, laid-back language which often conceals a real breakthrough, that 'deaths from breast cancer in women aged 50 to 64 who are offered screening by mammography can be reduced by one third or more'. They recommended a nation-wide system of mammography screening for all women in this country, every three years, in that age group, with computerized call and recall systems so that no one was missed. They made careful recommendations about the extra surgical and radio-therapy facilities which would be needed and, to my delight, urged the inclusion of counselling and after-care for the women affected. If we were to introduce a complete system within three years it was reckoned we would be saving around 4,000 lives by the end of the century.

The day we met to discuss the report in January 1987 was a busy one in the House of Commons. We ministers were on a 'running whip'. That means, votes may be called at any time and it is not a good idea to be stuck in traffic ten miles away when they are. The voting record of even the most distinguished minister matters when promotion comes up. The meeting was therefore held in the Large Ministerial Conference Room, in the bowels of the House of Commons. Despite its name this is no grand salon but a bit of a dump. The Commons was bombed during the last war and the replacement was built during the age of austerity under Attlee; I doubt if it had been refurbished since. The walls are a grubby, lifeless, sour-cream colour, the pictures obscure prints, the thin green leather of the table top marked with ancient ink blots breathing disappointment. The ghosts of ministers long since passed into obscurity, trimming here, cutting budgets there, lurk in its dusty corners.

Norman Fowler, Secretary of State, was in the chair. I was very new, very junior, and very keen indeed that we should accept the Forrest report's proposals. In medical terms it was worth doing. In political terms, with the election no more than a few months away, it was also attractive. What would, however, mess it all up would be to make the same mistakes as with cervical cancer. But if we were to approve the system, we must not leave the health authorities to get on with it themselves, trying to find the money by postponing other activities. That simply would not do, and we all knew it. Yet digging money out for something new, for 'growth', in an economy which, in early 1987, was still struggling – and for what? for women? – should have proved very tricky. My private view was that if we weren't going to do it properly, I'd rather we didn't do it at all. The argument raged around the table. That was me they were talking about, in a few years' time; the girls I went to school with; the lady who did my housework; the cheerful women in the House of Commons tea-room; my mother; my daughters.

Despite their importance, these decisions are always taken against a time deadline. We kept half an eye on the television monitor in the corner of the room. It is a closed-circuit system which, unbelievably and gloriously antiquated, shows only the name of the MP speaking in the Chamber. When the minister responsible for the issue under discussion rose to his feet, a vote was not far off, and our discussion would be curtailed.

'Ping!' went the warning tone from the monitor. There was a stir and 'Ping!' again. The Minister's name came on the screen. 'Well, do we go ahead or not?' asked Norman. Yes, we agreed, provided the colleagues in the Treasury came up with new money. That was a tall order, for departmental budgets were long-since settled. 'Ping! Ping!' went the tone again, and 'DIVISION' flashed up. We broke up and headed for the stairs to the voting lobby. There was no division between us on this issue.

Only too aware, as Tony Newton put it in a note, that the programme would not carry credibility without any money, Norman and Tony managed to persuade the Treasury to fund the lot, starting with four regional centres which would be used to train staff for the whole country, and one centre in the first year for each of the fourteen English regions, with plans to cover the whole country by 1990. The money would come from central funding and would be new money. The cash would be 'ring-fenced', that is it couldn't be used for anything else – hurrah! – and the total investment was likely to be around £55 million. The announcement was made in February 1987 by Norman Fowler in the House of Commons, with me sitting grinning like a Cheshire cat at his side, so very happy. The good Professor Forrest, who sat up in the gallery with a more modest smile, commented with approval that we were clearly going for a high-quality service. There was no point in doing otherwise.

It also meant that, when combined with our nation-wide cervical cancer screening programme, we were now the leading nation in improving the health of women. Finland had only cervical screening, Sweden did not yet have nation-wide breast cancer screening, and apart from those countries no other government had taken these two steps. We are world leaders. It was a good feeling.

One of the training centres was King's College Hospital at Camberwell and I was delighted to be asked to open their little screening centre in the Butterfly Walk shopping mall. Screening using the mammography machines could be done virtually anywhere, so shops and mobile units parked in shopping-centre car parks should become a common and welcome sight. The main requirement was trained staff, virtually all female, who could handle the equipment and be nice to the customers. The films could be developed on site quickly, so the woman would know it had been done properly, and then she

122

could go home. Reading the X-rays was a very skilled job indeed and was done elsewhere, usually (then) by chaps who spent all day looking at thousands of bosoms of all shapes and sizes. I wondered if women's greatest asset lost its savour for these guys but I never liked to ask.

At Butterfly Walk there was enormous local interest, with chattering women queuing up clutching their computerized invitations on the first day.

'Do you have any problems?' I asked the staff.

'Well, no, they are all very keen,' I was told. 'The only difficulty is that they are big around here. We've had several ladies who didn't fit on the machines at all; they are designed in Sweden, you know, they must be minuscule. Anyway we have to take a picture of every bit of flesh and our record so far is five pictures each side for one lady.'

We giggled together about that. 'What did you say to her?' I asked. 'Oh, we just told her she was very lucky and so was her man, and she went away very pleased,' they replied.

In the West Country another problem developed. There was nowhere to store the X-rays, which are quite large and bulky. As an emergency measure it was decided to ask the women concerned if they would keep theirs at home, and have them ready for the next time they were called, in three years' time. That had an unexpected bonus. All over the area, matronly women in their fifties confessed their new experiences to their friends over the tea and scones. Passing the clotted cream and the home-made jam, they shyly brought out their X-rays and explained how they were produced. Envy stirred in the teacups. We couldn't have asked for a better advertising campaign; the response rate rose, the support was solid and we had to fight off demands from their pals to do them *right now*.

The first seventeen centres were up and running very quickly and another forty or so were developed in 1988–9. The full service is expected sometime in 1990. By that date, the first women in the first centres will be receiving their second round of letters, and it will be 1993 before every woman in the relevant age group in this country will have received an invitation. If the high response rates, typical of the early centres, persist, then breast cancer will cease to be the frightening killer in the hands of the Reaper it is now. And I am well pleased.

*   *   *

As a result of the breast cancer screening system, we found there was a lot of interest in the methods by which patients give consent for surgery and in what they were giving consent for.

It had turned out that it made precious little difference for many cases, in terms of survival, whether a surgeon did a full mastectomy, or just took part of a breast. If the lump was big enough, then the odds were that secondaries had already seeded elsewhere in the body, so full amputation would not improve the woman's chances. In a tiny lump cancer cells would be restricted to the immediate area, so careful moderate surgery would have the same life-giving effect as more drastic work, particularly if combined with chemotherapy and radiation treatment. That meant women really had a choice, on cosmetic or convenience grounds.

The media had a field day with surgeons who allegedly said, 'Trust me, dearie, I'll do what's best for you' and then whipped off both breasts just in case. It wasn't just hype. There was more than one well-publicized case where this happened and compensation in large amounts hit the headlines. The surgeons, however, were changing their practices – though I met at least one who was 'knife-happy' and made a mental note never to be referred to him! A study of eighty centres doing cancer surgery showed that the ratio of mastectomy to conservative surgery in 1980 had been about 50:50. By 1986 it was 20:80 in favour of conservation. But the results were interesting and varied around the country. One hospital, which biased its advice in favour of retention, still found that half its women patients opted for mastectomy. It was easier, they thought, and involved less 'messing about'. The US President's wife, Mrs Nancy Reagan, took that view as well, and I had some sympathy for her. Personally, I would not want to go through the months of plastic surgery offered to women in many centres and I could understand those who simply wanted to walk away from their cancer and get on with their lives, minus a bit.

Ministers are never too happy about campaigns which demanded one form of treatment as opposed to another. I had reacted with some antagonism to the Jeannie Campbell Appeal, which set itself against amputation. When they wrote to me as a back-bencher in 1986 asking for support I said no; Jeannie Campbell may well have 'kept her figure', as they rather tweely put it, but after refusing a mastectomy she eventually lost her life to her cancer. I did feel it was too simplistic a campaign and perhaps misleading.

By early 1988 they were on to a better topic. Peter Hawkins, their chairman, had written to both the Prime Minister and myself suggesting a special consent form to be signed by patients about to undergo biopsy for suspected breast cancer. This would prevent the surgeon proceeding straight to amputation without allowing an opportunity for discussion of the less drastic alternatives. He referred to 'wretchedly old-fashioned' consent forms. In the briefing they prepared for me, civil servants surprised me somewhat by saying we were ahead of him there, as they had been working on a new form for some time, in particular insisting that the doctors should discuss the options with their patient and should encourage (and respect) informed choice.

Consent forms had been introduced for all types of surgery at the behest of the British Medical Association in 1969 to protect doctors from being sued by their patients. In those days no one thought any patient would want to know they had cancer, let alone discuss the possible treatments. The whole style of medicine was different then. Doctors were gods and the guardians of the truth, which was best kept from patients who, like children, could not be expected to understand it nor to be rational about it. That was, of course, in the days when cancer was automatically a death sentence and pain control was in its infancy. We found we needed to revise the consent forms, partly because these attitudes were changing, partly because of the difficult ethics surrounding teaching and drug trials, and partly because the Campaign for Freedom of Information, which was demanding access to medical records by patients, presupposed a much more open relationship between patient and doctor.

The feeling of having control over their bodies seemed to be increasingly important to women, and my post-bag suggested it mattered to men, too. 'How would you like to wake up and find half your gut has been taken away, and you'll have to cope with a bag for the rest of your life?' asked one male correspondent. So when I talked more fully about the new consent forms to the wonderful members of the Breast Care and Mastectomy Association on 20 September 1988, they gave a rousing cheer and produced banner headlines the next day. I waved the new forms at them and they crowded round. We had asked the unit which specializes in the design of these things, and which has won several awards from the Plain English campaign, to help, and the result was a most elegant improvement over the previous tatty photo-copied bit of paper which had given patients virtually no rights at all. In fact the real benefit to patients would come, not with the form itself, but with the discussion between patient and doctor beforehand which we intended to make routine.

In the back of my mind I also had surveys that had shown a lot of unnecessary surgery going on, not just for breast cancer. Doctors were sometimes afraid to appear to be denying dying patients anything, however gruesome, which might be regarded as necessary treatment. There would in future, I knew, be some patients who, faced with a serious assessment of the odds of success of surgery, would say quietly, 'Thank you, doctor, but no thank you. I want to go home now.' And that would help the doctors, too, to come to terms with their entirely human powers and no longer force them to pretend they could cure everything.

There was almost inevitably a zanier side to all this worthy work. We made a real effort to include all the consents that would face most patients on one form, including, for the first time, consent to chemotherapy and radio-therapy, and for patients' records to be used for research. One day I sat discussing all this with officials in my new office in Richmond House, that splendid edifice in Whitehall which had once belonged to the explorer Henry Stanley, ever the master of understatement. I looked more closely at the bottom of the form.

'What's this?' I asked. 'It says here, "I understand that all implants are and remain the property of the NHS, and may be recovered at any time".'

The officials shifted uncomfortably and glanced at each other. 'Yes, Minister,' they said.

A bizarre picture flashed through my mind. 'You have got to be kidding. Do you mean that we are going to send women patients away worried that we might demand back their silicone gel anytime we're a bit short? What on earth are you up to?'

The officials, who are nice people, looked even more unhappy. One was nudged by his fellows with a '*you* bell the cat' look on their faces. He took a deep breath. 'It's heart pace-makers, Minister. We are having problems with the funeral directors,' he explained earnestly.

I must have looked puzzled. Warming to his theme, he ploughed on: 'You see, Minister, pace-makers have mercury in them and have to be removed before cremation or they blow up. That will damage the ovens. And then there are the hip and knee replacements, especially the latter; they are made of best chromium steel and cost £700 new, and are worth a lot as scrap. And we think we should make it clear that all implants are and remain NHS property, not theirs, so we don't have to pay the crematoria people for recovering them.'

Now it is rude and cruel to mock civil servants but I confess I nearly fell off my chair laughing. Go talk to the funeral directors, I told them, and work something out with them; but we are not putting out a consent form leaving the people of this nation scared stiff that I'm going to come and demand their bits back any time I feel like it. And that suggestion I vetoed.

There was also the case of the missing nipple. At that meeting in September 1988, I gaily told the women present that the NHS was becoming much more conscious of their needs.

One attractive lady came up to the top table and prodded me. 'Oh no, you're not,' she declared. 'Do you know you can't get nipples on the NHS?'

I goggled.

She went on, as everyone nodded, 'If you need a prosthesis [false breast] the NHS will give you a bland nipple-less one. If you want a nipple you have to go private. And you can only get white ones, too – what do black and brown women do?'

Good question! My officials were looking at the ceiling, at the floor, everywhere but in the eye of the indignant lady and her companions. So I set the wheels in motion back at the Department, but with no great success. The only UK manufacturer interested in non-white skin tones has ceased to make them and nipples are only available outside the NHS. So what? you may say: the patients don't expect to go round flashing their new spare parts. I just wonder how white women would all feel if told only black boobs were available! Bureaucracy can be very cruel sometimes.

*   *   *

Mass screening tests for cancer, or anything else, should meet the ten criteria laid down by the WHO in 1968. These are: (i) that the condition should be an important health problem, not something trivial; (ii) that the natural history of the disease should be well understood – and in every screening programme I have been involved in, we have learned significant and awkward facts about the illness *after* we started; (iii) that there should be a recognizable early stage, at which (iv) treatment is more beneficial than treatment started at a later stage – hence, we rule out screening for lung cancer, for by the time we can detect it death is usually not far away and treatment can only be palliative; (v) that there should be a suitable test which is (vi) acceptable to the population concerned – acceptability of testing is a major hurdle, in my view, but doctors do assume that all patients will automatically say yes; they won't; (vii) that there must be adequate facilities for diagnosis and treatment; (viii) that the cost of screening should be balanced against the benefit it provides; (ix) that for many diseases where the criteria are otherwise satisfied, repeated testing at intervals will be necessary; (x) and that the chance of physical or psychological harm to those screened should be less than the chance of benefit.

I think these criteria are quite brilliant; I quoted them often as a minister. Breast cancer, in the light of the knowledge we had in 1986–8, and with the Forrest report recommendations to hand, seemed an ideal candidate for a screening programme. Cervical cancer, with its intimate test and its comparative rarity, was more problematic. AIDS screening fell at the hurdle of physical or psychological benefit to the patient. Lung cancer screening falls down on all criteria (except the seriousness of the problem). Ovarian screening has problems over the acceptability of the test, too. Screening for osteoporosis by bone scanning might be horribly expensive; but then, so is the cost of orthopaedic surgery. Cholesterol testing for certain at–risk age groups looks promising and may well come. Many general practitioners have started screening their patients regularly for high blood pressure, as they have done for years in the USA. A successful screening programme, coupled with other efforts at prevention, and treatment, will eventually put the screeners out of business, of course. That happened to the programme of mass screening for tuberculosis, and hopefully it will happen for some of today's killer diseases, too.

There was no shortage of enthusiasts for schemes which wouldn't work. Take ovarian cancer, for example. It kills around 4,000 women in this country every year and is something of a mystery. It is commonest in developed countries, yet Japan is at the bottom of the list. The United Kingdom's figures are similar to those of the United States, neither the best nor the worst. A woman with a female relative who has contracted this cancer is twenty times more likely to get it than another, yet only 5 per cent of all cases seem to have a genetic input. It creates vague symptoms, perhaps similar to the menopause, and may well be missed or misdiagnosed. Benign ovarian cysts, which are quite common, may produce similar symptoms. By contrast with cervical cancer, where virgins don't get it, virgins and childless women do get ovarian cancer. Women also seem to be protected by having lots of pregnancies. All of which means we don't know much about it and haven't the foggiest idea how to prevent it.

The attenders at the meeting of the British Gynaecological Cancer Society, one autumn Saturday morning at a new, characterless hotel near my home, knew what to do. They invited me, I'm sure, to persuade the Department to cough up the money for a mass screening service for ovarian cancer. We drank our coffee and I listened politely. Then in we trooped to the airless meeting room, the coffee cups were stashed away under the chairs and the discussion began in earnest.

They were all such nice people, so keen. They have machines, now, I was told, which would show up the lesions and bumps which might be caused by ovarian cancer, using non-invasive ultrasound. The problem, they admitted, was that the ovaries are pretty bumpy anyway and there was no simple way of finding out whether that lump was benign or not. There was laparotomy, of course.

'What's that?' I inquired, innocently.

'Er, well, it means opening somebody up to see what's inside,' they said.

'That would mean an operation for every single bump which showed up on your screen then, even though most aren't cancer?'

'Precisely, yes,' was the answer.

Oh, great stuff; I could just see women queuing up for it. Wasn't there any other way?

'Yes, there is,' they said, looking sheepishly at each other. 'Bimanual pelvic examination.'

'Please explain that one, too,' I said, and 'You know, by hand,' came the answer.

I must have sounded like John McEnroe. 'You cannot be serious!' I said. 'If we go for the same target group as for breast cancer – that's just women between 50 and 64 – then we could be talking about screening 13 million women. With your hefty false positive detection rate using ultrasound, that is a lot of "pelvic examination" to do. And – bearing in mind that this condition is found in middle-aged spinsters and childless ladies – do you seriously think I'm going to encourage you to go poking up the vaginas of all those women? More to the point, do you seriously think *they* would let you? The whole idea is ludicrous. That won't do as a screening service. Forget it.'

They did look sad, these good people. Perhaps I was unduly harsh to them, but it would have been a diabolical waste of public money and demonstrated how some people really go too far. In years to come, I hear, a tumour-marker system may be developed in which radioactive antibodies may seek out the cancer cells which could then be detected by X-ray. I'll welcome it when it comes. Meanwhile, my apologies to the nice doctors with warm hands, and to the makers of rubber gloves.

*   *   *

We should go back to Jeanette. Cervical cancer is cancer of the neck (cervix) of the womb. It is found all over the world. The highest incidence rates are in South America, the lowest in Israel. Our mortality, though not the worst, is relatively high compared with the rest of Europe and the USA. There used to be over 3,000 deaths a year here in the 1960s. Now there are around 2,000. In those days treatment always took ten days in hospital – now it's a few minutes with a laser in out-patients. What was apparent from any international comparison, however, was the rapid downward trend in a number of other countries over two decades, compared with only a very slow decline – recently about 1 per cent per year – in this country.

When the WHO recommended in 1964 that governments should start mass screening using the simple 'Pap' test, named after its inventor, Dr George Papanicolau, in which a small sample of cells are taken from the cervix for microscopic examination, we thought we knew rather a lot about this disease. The exciting thing then was that, unlike most cancer, if found early enough and treated, 90 per cent of cases could be cured. The condition usually takes many years to develop and the mean time in the United Kingdom between the point at which it becomes life-threatening and the first date at which cell changes can be detected is about twelve years. Testing women every five years should therefore be highly satisfactory, and is the foundation of effective systems in the Scandinavian countries. What we didn't realize was that we knew precious little about the natural history of the disease, and that the condition was changing. Perhaps, in the 1980s, it is now more than one condition, for in younger women it can develop and kill within eighteen months. We also found that governments can propose, and even send out weighty circulars, but local health authorities frequently suffer from the Nelson syndrome. And we should have remembered that successfully screening the entire female population of, say, Iceland, all quarter of a million of them, is not quite the same thing as doing it in our hefty overcrowded island at all.

The idea was to call in all the women in the at-risk age groups regularly, take a smear and check it, and send them for treatment if necessary. Couldn't be simpler, right? But cervical cancer screening has caused more headaches and taken more government and managerial time than almost any other condition mentioned in this book, and for the relatively small number of cases, many of whom refused the test or ignored the offer, I honestly sometimes wondered if it was worth it. The whole saga demonstrates in my view how not to go about a health programme. In mitigation, no one knew that till some

130

twenty years after they had started. Fortunately, by 1985 other benefits had emerged, including getting the Family Practitioner service computerized. My apologies if I sound grumpy about this, but breast cancer kills seven times as many women as cervical cancer, lung cancer more than five times as many. You make up your own mind.

Cervical screening became available in this country in October 1966 when a health circular went out asking health authorities to introduce screening for women over thirty-five every five years. Hardly anything happened. It was then announced in 1971 that recall would be done by the NHS central register in Southport. That was also a disaster, with a response rate by the women of only 20 per cent. Local schemes, however, produced a response of 60 per cent and in areas where the doctors were keen, as for example in Aberdeen and Oxford, 80–90 per cent rates were achievable. So in 1981 another circular (the files are thick with them) announced a change from national to local recall, asking health authorities (which run the treatment services) to co-operate with their Family Practitioner Committees (which organize the general practitioners and keep the patient registers) to set up local schemes by 1 April 1983.

Oh yeah, thought some health authorities. I remember going, as a member of the Birmingham Health Authority, to visit Birmingham Family Practitioner Committee, which was housed in some sheds out in a suburb. At that time we didn't talk to them much; virtually their sole job was to pay doctors their expenses. The Chairman was the delightful Dr Llew Lloyd, a local GP. A small, neat, talkative, dapper man, who for years looked after patients with his doctor wife in one of the roughest parts of the city, he proudly showed me the Family Practitioner Committee's patient records, row upon row of dusty little cards in filing cabinets stretching for miles. Of course it would not be ethical, he said, to give the health authority the names and addresses of patients – even for their own good – as confidentiality was much more important. We're going to have trouble with this little lot, I thought, and so it proved, for Birmingham was one of the last parts of the country to get their system computerized and on-stream after a lot of 'encouragement' from my officials.

However, in April 1985 the Health Minister they had to contend with was Kenneth Clarke, who told the health authorities to get cracking on introducing computerized call and recall systems. In the following January new planning guidelines were issued which at last took into account that laboratories and treatment facilities are not cheap, and set a deadline no later than the end of March 1988. Then the fun began, for Ministers meant it. A target had been announced and it was clear that for political reasons, if nothing else, the shilly-shallying had got to stop, and an effective system be introduced. By 25 February 1987, when Norman Fowler made the announcement about the new breast cancer system, he also said that the age for screening for cervical cancer was to be dropped from thirty-five to twenty.

Sir Roy Griffiths, the Prime Minister's adviser on the NHS, was asked soon after to lead a team to ensure that the health authorities at last did as they were told (he was also in charge of a team with similar purposes for breast cancer, and deserves much of the credit for successes in both fields).

The essence of computerization is to put all the names and addresses of millions of patients, with their sex and birthdays, on to a computer, which can then produce lists of selected people as required. The real benefits lie far beyond cervical cancer screening. With such a register it is then possible, for example, to produce a list of all fifteen-month-old babies in an area for immunisation, or all fifty-year-old women for cancer screening, or all forty-year-old men for blood pressure testing. Doing the same thing by hand is slow, and makes it impossible to trace any gaps. Scandinavian countries have such patient registers as a matter of course, often maintained by their cancer societies. We had only those records of patients registered with a doctor, kept to calculate the per capita payments to which doctors are entitled. That was fine for stable areas but gave problems where people moved around a lot; in Salford, for example, the registers were 30 per cent out, with whole streets appearing which had been demolished in slum clearance years earlier (and for which the money was presumably still being paid to the GPs). Getting the patient lists computerized and brought into the latter half of the twentieth century would also speed up transfer of patient records between doctors – by hand it was taking months. For all these reasons I was keen to see the new system brought in. I knew it meant, in particular, that we would be able to start the breast cancer programme with no messing about at all.

The pace really began to hot up after April 1987, for we realized that if we were to achieve the deadline, in England at least, of having full computerized call and recall in every single one of 191 health authorities by the following March, we were going to have to get a move on. At that time only fifty-eight district health authorities had their system in and running and we would not get to 100 – just past half way – until the autumn. Another thirty-two said they would not be ready by March, and four said they hadn't the slightest notion when they would be ready, and implied that they didn't care much either. One health authority in the south of England resisted strongly the blandishments of the Department of Health and seemed to ignore the non-cervical-cancer benefits of the scheme. They protested that they had had only one death from the disease in the previous year and that they could think of other ways to spend the money, thank you.

We did get our way in the end, for there was no mileage in having a national scheme with holes in it for certain fortunate patches of the country, but in getting the cervical cancer screening system in on time it seemed to acquire a life of its own. During the winter we acquired £10 million-worth of computer equipment for Family Practitioner Committees and some 750 VDUs were eventually installed, while five different computer companies transferred 35 million records on to the computers. Ministers and officials lived, breathed and ate cervical cancer progress reports for the next few months and a staggering amount of work went into getting the thing done. I seemed to be answering parliamentary questions on it every two minutes, usually from the Labour spokesman Harriet Harman, an armchair socialist if ever there was one. Slim, fair and pretty, dressed in Battersea chic, she was woefully ill-informed and I tended to keep her that way. Knowing that we were going to be successful I let her rabbit on, despite getting very irritated by her, eventually telling her bluntly at the end of 1988 (in what John Patten called 'an exhibition of controlled venom') that the women of this country had been calling for a system for more than twenty years, that we had given them one, and that she ought to say well done. In the end we made it. Most of the systems were indeed complete by 31 March 1988 and the stragglers were all on stream a few weeks after that. I was able to announce completion of the programme in the debate on women's health on 10 June, with a sigh of something like relief. But it was not easy. Ministers are not supposed to single out individual civil servants for praise, and indeed it is not fair to the others whose work I did not see, but they know who they are, and they should be well pleased with themselves.

* * *

Meanwhile the image of Jeanette, not yet thirty, still haunts me. Although most of the women who contract the disease and die from it are over thirty-five, the numbers of younger women involved are rising slowly. But, between 1975 and 1985 there was a 42 per cent increase in the death rate from cervical cancer in women aged 15 to 44. Over a longer period, according to the *British Journal of Cancer* in 1984, the most striking change in mortality was in the age group 25 to 34 where the mortality rate more than doubled. What in heaven's name was going on? I badgered officials and medical advisers for more information. Was there some cause of this change, which might lead to advice we could give to younger women on how to reduce their risks of cervical cancer?

The answer was 'yes' and it led again to one of my so-called gaffes. The officials gave me the published articles containing the research of the Medical School at Oxford University. The classic work of the team, led by Martin Vessey, was published in 1980 and 1984. I met Professor Vessey later on several occasions; an erudite, patient, charming and sympathetic man. If his students don't love him they are crackers. He is also a fine scientist and the papers are a model of how to do this kind of research. They carefully isolated various possible antecedents of cervical cancer, comparing the condition in patients with other gynae-cological disorders, and came up with two outside links.

First, cervical cancer was clearly associated with sex. We knew that already, for nuns and virgins don't get it. That was virtually the first fact established about the disease long ago. But the more partners a girl has, the more the risk of catching cervical cancer, along with other sexually-transmitted diseases like herpes – and, of course, AIDS. The same, it transpired, applied to her male partner. Even if she were impeccably behaved, she stood a greater risk if her husband or boyfriend played around *or had played around in the past*. Both findings suggested a transmission agent – a virus perhaps – and more recent laboratory research has identified the papilloma virus, which causes genital warts, as at least one strong contender. There may be others. That's good news in the long run, for viral infections open the way to possible vaccines.

There was also a bit of work done elsewhere which indicated a link with men in certain industries – in heavy-duty workshops and in shipyards – and it was suggested that mineral oil might be a causative agent. There are carcinogens in certain kinds of oil, but shipyards, it occurred to me as a Liverpool girl, tend to be found in ports, and ports have always had more than their share of certain diseases. I was struck, as my 'gaffe' generated a lot of letters from perfectly respect-able ladies who had always been faithful to their husbands but had still contracted cervical cancer, how many of them mentioned that their partners were, or had been, in the armed forces and had served overseas. They might have been virgin soldiers, I reflected, feeling a terrible sadness about the whole business, or then again they might not. The Oxford team's work certainly suggested that male behaviour, now or in the past, had a lot to do with cervical cancer.

The second link which the research demonstrated beyond doubt was the link with smoking. The girls who smoked were several times more likely to get cervical cancer than the non-smokers, with the heavy smokers well up there in the figures. What is it about cigarettes, I wondered, that produced this weakness, this inability of the body to resist damage? We don't know, and I'm darned sure the tobacco industry will not fund the research to find out. But other workers, such as Albert Singer at the Whittington Hospital, have shown that cervical cells are damaged in a very fundamental way by smoking.

I sat next to Albert at a lunch at Christmas 1986, organized by the Women's National Cancer Control Campaign. Handsome and elegant, like most male gynaecologists, and a complete enthusiast for his subject, he never stopped talking and drew for me diagrams of the sexual organs on the table napkins right through the meal. We agreed that it was utterly disgraceful that smoking should be allowed at these fund-raising lunches. It took some while to persuade the committee (one famous lady told me we should not insult the guests) but we got what we wanted and at the same event, in 1988, to cheers and applause, I ceremonially threw away the ashtray on top table.

*   *   *

Perhaps ministers should not read original research; perhaps we should leave the messages which glare out of the pages to be delivered quietly by earnest people at learned symposia. Perhaps the public should not know. Some, no doubt, would rather not know. It would certainly make life easier for ministers, who have the ear of the public, not to have to say anything. But original research goes to the heart of the work we did, and it is of the essence of the Conservative philosophy that people in a free democracy should not be constrained by unnecessary barriers but, as far as possible, should be provided with sound information and left to make informed choices about their own lives. Even if some people get upset at what has to be said.

The interview was for the May 1988 edition of *Family Circle*, a magazine widely sold in supermarkets, which takes a lively interest in health matters. What advice would I give to young girls? Was there anything they should be saying to them, as a responsible magazine, about how they might improve their health and avoid nasty things like cervical cancer?

'Yes,' I said. 'Don't screw around, and don't smoke.'

It must have been a quiet week for news. The first moment I realized the fuss this would create came on 31 March 1988 as my ministerial car was stuck in the traffic at the lights in Parliament Square. On the corner of Whitehall is a newspaper seller. I glanced idly at the headline on the billboard. 'Don't screw around, warns Edwina' it read. Oh, Lord! Well, never mind, at least it will get the topic talked about, and it did. But I had not counted on the anger of the older women who had been treated for cervical cancer and who were not, as one put it, 'old lags'. It was not then, and indeed never has been, my intention to add to the pain and fear of sick people or those whose illness has been caught in time. Even women long widowed get (and die from) cervical cancer, the saddest legacy of their happier days. Perhaps I should have remembered the line from *Antony and Cleopatra*: 'Though it be honest, it is never good to bring bad news; give to a gracious message a host of tongues, but let ill tidings tell themselves when they may be felt.' On the other hand, the advice was particularly aimed at youngsters for whom the screening service, into which we were putting such effort, was less useful. I had a Liverpool girl working in my office, a lovely bright bouncy lass with an accent you could spread thick on bread. I asked her if she thought it was too strong, saying 'don't screw around'?

'Naah,' she said. 'We all torhhh like da where I coom from', and coming from the same place, I knew she was right.

*   *   *

We worked hard in the Women's Health Group and were able to share our increasing knowledge with women nationally, by linking up with the voluntary organizations, by holding a debate on Women's Health in the House of Commons and by a major day conference on Women's Health in Westminster in June 1988. Many articles which are still appearing in the national and women's press stem from those events.

Our concern was not just cancer. There were other topics, not perhaps major killers, but problems which caused a lot of misery. One was the menopause – osteoporosis and hormone replacement therapy (HRT); another was mental illness.

If men had to suffer a proper menopause, instead of the excuse for a climacteric which they claim to go through, there would be laws

against it. Once many women died before they reached the age of menopause. Now, every year 300,000 women start their journey through it. Many are lucky and sail through with no trouble. Three-quarters suffer some kind of symptoms, with hot flushes and night sweats being the commonest. Around a quarter of all women have real problems, including pain and discomfort, moodiness, depression and a loss of libido. Sometimes the physical problems, which are quite genuine, are mixed up with psychological troubles, as children grow

137

up and leave home, as husbands enter the peak time for illness such as heart disease, as women face the fact that they are now too old to have children and the next stage is to go grey and become a grandmother. For others the menopause is the lifting of a great burden just as the menarche was a curse. No one finds it easy, however, particularly if they suffer some of the worst symptoms and get neither sympathy nor practical help.

As the 1987 election loomed, the Conservatives in Billericay had to find a new candidate fast and their choice fell on Teresa Gorman, a successful forty-seven-year-old business woman who was, it was said, so right wing she made the Prime Minister sound like Chairman Mao. I had known Teresa and had shared platforms with her, but I did not recognize the bright and bouncy lady who soon took her seat with such glee; she had been rather forgettable before. Others commented and soon she gave an interview in which she confessed to being rather a lot older than forty-seven, and said it was all due to HRT, or hormone replacement therapy.

Strictly speaking it isn't hormone *replacement*; the dosages of the female hormones needed to suppress the menopausal symptoms are a lot higher than normal doses. But HRT does work in circumstances where sedatives and tranquillizers don't. It also carries its own risks and costs. There is a great deal of controversy about both.

Teresa put her point of view far better than I could in the debate on women's health on Friday 10 June 1988 in the House of Commons. Fridays are often dead days when colleagues clear off to their constituencies. The Whips' Office is sometimes hard put to find a nice safe topic which can be handled with the minimum effort, preferably by one minister. They had already offered me one such date, in October 1987, when I had opted for a general (and very successful) discussion on prevention. This time the conference I had organized on women's health (for 22 June) was looming, so here was a grand opportunity. 'It won't run the whole five hours from 9.30 a.m. to 2.30 p.m., of course,' the Whips said, helpfully, 'so we'll organize someone with another health topic you can take to fill up the rest of the time.' They needn't have worried, for many of the forty-one women MPs cancelled other engagements to come and speak, and we were delighted to get strong support from the chaps, too. Maybe it is time for the Conservative Whips' Office to appoint its first woman, so they might learn about a whole world out there which clearly doesn't penetrate at present!

The gallery was full when Teresa rose to speak, as it often is on

Fridays, when spectators frequently outnumber MPs. This time they got a treat. Small, short-sighted, blond, barbed, she reminds me of a bright little hedgehog; always smartly dressed, though this time in a yellow and black outfit that I wouldn't dare wear for fear of the alternative adjective 'waspish'. As a Conservative she sat behind and to the right of me and I had to crane my neck as, arms waving and ear-rings a-jangle, she got cracking.

'When we are cute little babies,' she said, 'everybody loves us. When we become older and become pregnant Mums, everyone cares for us. Who cares for women when they become menopausal?'

. . . Women in this age group are often embarrassed and feel guilty . . . Women tend to put up with a great deal that a man would normally go to his doctor to complain about . . . There are the awful hot flushes, which are embarrassing when one is in a room full of people. The woman might say, 'Oh my God, it is hot in here'. Everyone looks round and says, 'It is not really. It is you.' It is rather like saying to a crowd of strangers, 'I am getting old'.

She described her own experiences:

. . . My wrists and ankles began to hurt. My ankles became so painful that I could hardly get to the top of my house. My wrists became so painful that I could not cut a slice of bread . . . I was running a business and when I returned home at about 7 o'clock I was knocked out, as it were. I was tired, listless, dreary and irritable. Worst of all, I started forgetting things. This meant I missed appointments. I began to think that if these were the symptoms of becoming old at the age of about forty, I would rather be dead. I felt that I could not face another thirty years of them.

And so she had done something about it, and was brave enough to say so out loud. Back-bench members of Parliament have no power, only influence. They have access only to the 'megaphone effect': whatever worthy point they make, it can be magnified just by virtue of their being MPs. Teresa has taken to telling everyone when she has had a new 'patch' and she does deserve some credit for getting people talking. After that original interview she had received 10,000 letters from women and has become an ardent campaigner for HRT. Why, then, don't I share her enthusiasm? Possibly, no doubt, because I have not yet had the experience and I might feel differently in ten

139

years' time. I do not decry the misery of the menopause or the relief given to many by HRT, but do we really want to take artificial hormones for the rest of our lives? Many of us who have no choice about long-term drug therapy, such as asthmatics and diabetics, would say how hard it can be. And should it be available to *all* women – which I have heard advocated by some doctors – or just some, and, if so, which? Perhaps there are alternative treatments. Some of that improved appearance might well have come from realizing a dream, or from having more money to spend on clothes and hair, or from eating better, or stopping smoking, or taking more exercise. Some improvements might have come anyway as the menopause passed on, to what many women regard as the prime of life. The cautious view I expressed in the debate reflected my feeling that for many women there may be other ways to feel good. (For the sake of completeness, I should add that HRT is available on the NHS and no woman has to go to a private clinic for it; finding a knowledgeable and sympathetic doctor to recommend it may take a wee while longer.)

Probably the most serious condition which comes with the menopause is frail bones, the condition known as osteoporosis. It affects one woman in four and is ten times more common in women than in men. In 1986 a National Osteoporosis Society was set up and from 1988 I was delighted to ensure it a regular grant from the Department of Health. They made me the honorary 5,000th member in return. I met several sufferers at their meetings, including one lady who had shrunk six inches in a year. She told me how she had been gardening and had bent down to pull out the root of an old rose bush. Giving it a sharp tug, she felt her back give way and there was a sound like two pistol shots; two of the vertebrae had collapsed, and more were to do so shortly. She had turned virtually overnight into a little bowed old lady. The condition used to be known as 'Dowager's Hump'. After hearing her story, as we drove back to the office I looked at people at bus stops, carrying their shopping home, standing in the street chatting, and I realized just how wide spread the condition is, seeing so many bowed women, often quite disabled, seriously at risk of further damage. It is very common indeed.

Living bones are stronger than stainless steel, partly because they can repair themselves. As natural hormones decline with age something goes wrong with the repair mechanism and the bones lose their mass and mineral (especially calcium) content. This condition is called osteoporosis. Both men and women lose bone as they get older but women far faster than men, and the process occurs steadily, often rapidly, after the menopause. The result is bone fractures, particularly of load-bearing joints such as the hip, the wrist and the shoulder, and the neck and spine. A Danish survey found that by the age of seventy more than 25 per cent of women have suffered an osteoporotic fracture. In England and Wales it is estimated that around 150,000 such fractures occur every year, nearly all of which involve hospital treatment, often for months, and frequently result in permanent disability, sometimes (for example, when an elderly person has fallen and not been discovered until too late) in death. More women, most of whom are old, die from the results of these fractures each year than from breast and cervical cancer combined.

It's probably a disease of civilization – commonest in Sweden (for both men and women) and virtually unknown amongst the blacks of South Africa. The explanation must be partly longevity (we used to die before it manifested itself), but also partly exercise – or the lack of it. For much of our lives that living bone responds to stress by becoming stronger. Heavy manual work, energetic exercise and good diet, especially in youth, will build up a good bone mass which can be maintained by continued activity – walking the dog will do, anything that makes the bones bear weight. On the other hand, the thin, cigarette-smoking, car-driving modern woman who never carries any weight, not even her own, is likely to have delicate bones as a teenager and as a grown woman, and broken bones after the menopause. The cigarettes damage her hormone levels, too, so she enters the menopause on average five years earlier than her sisters, and that means five years more bone loss at the same age. Astronauts get a version of osteoporosis after prolonged weightlessness, but bone strength does seem to return to these fit young men after a while under normal gravity. Teenage girls with their penchant for cigarettes and soft drinks (instead of milk – rich in calcium) are probably asking for trouble, though the evidence that calcium later in life helps is highly contentious. For all these reasons, my response to Teresa and the other advocates of HRT was, 'I'm afraid it's on with the track suit, girls, and leave those fags at home.' And that – more than any other of the endless bits of advice with which I bombarded the nation – is advice I try to take myself.

*   *   *

Lots of my friends have happy and uneventful lives. On the whole, we love our husbands, dote on our children, worry about our mortgages, wonder whether we can cope with a full-time job, and do our best to look after ourselves. When illness strikes we feel bewildered, unready. When it happened to – let's call her Annette – she was, instead, mortally terrified.

As a trained nurse she had been a great pal to me during my pregnancies. When, like many another new mother, I got panicky, Annette was there with good advice, gentle, calm-voiced, sensible, managing. She was a coper: I could not imagine her in any trouble, but soon after the birth of her own second baby she came down with a savage attack of puerperal psychosis, that mental illness which hits a tiny proportion of recently-delivered women. She described it to me:

> Edwina, it was horrible, terrifying; I was convinced that I was going quite mad and would lose everything, the babies, my home, the lot. I had felt a bit depressed after the first baby, but I put it down to anti-climax, or feeling tired, you know. Then this one came along and it hit me with a great whoosh. I felt completely out of control. I started hallucinating, the craziest things. One time I was in church and suddenly the candles all seemed to be growing, the flames were getting higher and higher, the church was going to catch fire; I looked around and everyone else was just carrying on as if everything was normal and I started to scream at them, 'Look! Look!' Then I looked down the aisle and it was – oh! I can't describe it, I was out of my mind with fear. There were some creatures coming towards me, like something out of a horror movie, headless, horrible, voodoo creatures, but this wasn't a movie, this was real, and they were coming for me. I felt that I had to jump out of the window to get away from them. It was almost a relief when people took me away.

She was admitted to a local psychiatric hospital with her younger baby and I went to visit her there. She had a side ward off one of the ordinary female wards. The smell of disinfectant was overpowering. There were no pictures, no flowers, no visitors. The lino floors were shiny except where someone had dribbled; inmates stood along the walls, hooting and gibbering as I tried to find her. By contrast her little room, with its cot, baby bottles, and brightly-coloured toys was a haven of normality, but my visit was a waste of time for Annette was doped to the eyeballs and hardly recognized me. I came out white and shaking and sat quietly in my car for a long time.

And yet, a year later, she was back at work part-time and now, some years on, it is as if it had never happened. What is this strange condition? We don't know. It isn't the same as 'baby blues', which affect more than half all recently-delivered women, nor quite the same as the 10 to 15 per cent of those women who suffer serious depression, enough to require treatment, perhaps as many as 75,000 people every year. For at least half the 750 or so women who end up in hospital every year like Annette, this will be their first mental illness. Some will never have the problem again, while for others it may mark the start of a lifetime of mental illness, with all the attendant misery for their families, and most of all, for their children.

In the past century the physical health of mothers may have improved but their mental health has not. The rate of admission to hospital for puerperal psychosis is virtually the same now as it was in Queen Victoria's day. If ever something merited more research this does, and I would not be surprised to find it linked, like osteoporosis, to (perhaps abnormal) fluctuations in hormone levels. So despite my dislike of those who blame women's hormones for all our ills, there is no doubt that some conditions are linked to them. I'd like to know which and how many, and whether hormone treatment – and possible early detection of deficiencies – might be helpful. Meanwhile, I am well aware that Annette was lucky. Apart from anything else, in most areas she would not have been able to take her baby into hospital and would have been separated from him for months, with all the future damage that might cause.

We discussed mental illness amongst women in the Women's Health Group, and as we got the cancer screening topics sorted out I took far more interest in it. Once I had been in charge of Birmingham's housing and had been distressed so often, as yet another young mother clutching her baby jumped off one of the city's 429 tower blocks. As Minister, in autumn 1988, I went to the Bethlem Royal Hospital, where Dr Kumar is a consultant (more disinfectant and shiny floors, but a warm and kindly atmosphere) and I asked him to advise on a simple check-list which might be used at the baby's 6-week clinic check, to see whether there were any signs in the mother, such as sleeplessness, lack of appetite, irritability and so on, which might just point to a clinical depression or anxiety state which could be gently treated. I commend this work to my successors.

My friend Annette was probably treated with the major tranquillizers. Many other women, who came to their doctor with worries, problems, anxieties, some of which were mental illnesses and some of which weren't, were given prescriptions for the minor tranquilli-zers, the benzodiazepines. Lots of women, in fact. In 1979, the peak year of their popularity as a treatment for almost all the ills of a sophisticated society, GPs in this country wrote out *31 million* scrips for tranquillizers. It should be more widely known that in the UK, some 70 per cent of the hypnotic benzodiazepine drugs are prescribed for women, and around 40 per cent, again representing millions of pills, for women over sixty-five. That is not just a British phenom-enon, either. World-wide, prescribing of tranquillizers is twice as high for women as for men. If a man turns up at the surgery with the same complaints and symptoms, he is more likely to be referred to a consultant in an out-patient clinic. Honestly.

The development of many excellent psychiatric drugs has helped since the war to empty the dreadful old institutions, and has made a normal life possible for many people, such as epileptics; don't decry all the drugs. Tranquillizers, however, were the wonder drugs, or so they were hailed when they were introduced in the 1970s to replace barbiturates, which had been lethal in even small overdoses, especially if combined with alcohol. But the 'tranx' turned out to have a different danger, almost as sinister. They are addictive. Instead of removing a problem they can create it. Getting off them can be horrendous, often worse than the original misery which gave rise to the request for help. One organization, the Women's National Commission, talked about 'lace curtain junkies', and I received some heart-rending letters, includ-ing some from men, describing the awfulness of withdrawal–especially 'cold turkey', and expressing their outrage at the damage done to them and fellow sufferers by these seemingly harmless little helpers.

Add to that the fact that while tranquillizers are useful for *anxiety*, they have for years been wrongly prescribed for *depression* – which is the commonest form of mental illness. There is even research (such as the Nottingham study reported in the *Lancet*, 30 July 1988) which suggests that one of the most popular tranquillizers, diazepam, is less effective than self-help. People would in many cases get well just as fast, or even more quickly, after a quiet chat with a trained nurse so that they understood their own feelings with more insight and could control them better. Even a placebo was more effective. Perhaps, therefore, we were lucky that many patients were a bit suspicious from the start, for research also showed that around one fifth of all tranquillizer prescriptions written were never dispensed and that of those pills dispensed more than a quarter were never consumed.

Fears about too-ready prescribing of tranquillizers, amongst other things, led Kenneth Clarke, the Minister of State in 1985, to remove the branded varieties from the permitted list which the NHS would pay for. It was reckoned that doctors who had to look up the proper generic name for the drugs might just think twice about prescribing them inappropriately. There was a huge, flaming row, with GPs signing standard letters put up to them by the drugs firms, doing the image of the pharmaceutical industry in this country a great deal of harm. It left many of us, I suspect, with a degree of cynicism about the professional ethics of some doctors. A lot of money was saved, and the number of scrips dropped – a bit; by 1987 some 25.5 million a year were being written, and it was estimated that half a million people, at least, were dependent on benzodiazepines. We knew that nearly one prescription in five was for at least 100 pills, a lot more than the dosage recommended. By that time the doctors themselves were getting very worried, too, and our efforts at improving services for hard drug users had thrown up addiction to tranquillizers, and a lot of unhappy people, all over the country.

Advice on how to help withdrawal symptoms had been issued to doctors as long ago as 1984, but in January 1988 the Committee on the Safety of Medicines, an official and powerful group of senior doctors and pharmacology experts, issued an official 'Bulletin'. Prescribe these things for new patients for anxiety or insomnia only, and then not for more than four weeks, they said. There are, they added firmly, better drugs or other forms of treatment for depression and other mild mental illnesses. One woman MP, Dawn Primarolo, called for a complete ban. During 1988 the pressure mounted, with me pushing in the background, and we discussed the matter several times in the Women's Health Group. I asked the Chief Medical Officer formally for his advice. These drugs clearly helped some people. Was the risk of damage small enough, or controllable enough, to carry on using them? In November 1988 he called together a meeting on tranquillizers and invited the Royal Colleges of Physicians, Psychiatrists, Surgeons and General Practitioners, the British Medical Association and the General Medical Services Council. They pointed out, rightly, that only recently had the problem of habituation been understood. It was relatively easy to advise new patients: for them the drugs should be prescribed, as the Committee for the Safety of Medicines advised, for a short time only and then only for insomnia and anxiety. (That recommendation does presuppose that GPs can differentiate between various mild mental illnesses correctly, of course, and I'm not too sure about that, either.) It was also the considered view that there was little evidence that the long-term use of a single sleeping tablet at night was harmful. But, they said, we are less certain about the best approach to the existing long-term users, since withdrawal itself is a problem, and helping withdrawal is a complex and skilled task. (In fact about one third of patients can wean themselves off, perhaps with a bit of help, with no ill effects. In many other cases the underlying illness, which may have been masked for years, reasserts itself and needs treating.) There are probably no simple solutions for all the patients currently on tranquillizers.

I was warned against a general campaign to encourage withdrawal, as it might have the effect of pulling patients off useful drugs – including some quite unconnected with tranquillizers – thus leaving conditions untreated. A campaign might also be counter-productive: if patients think it will be difficult to stop they might not even try.

Still, one of the few powers available to junior ministers is the power to make grants, so on 9 November 1988 I made £70,000 available for a telephone helpline for tranquillizer victims as part of the series on BBC TV's *Daytime Live* programme, to run throughout the winter and spring of 1989. The whole business attracted a lot of interest and, although I was convinced by the sensible advice not to try for a ban on these drugs, it focused the dissatisfaction felt by many people over doctors who gave repeat prescriptions, often for years and without seeing the patient, instead of a decent service.

This is one area where I am pretty sure that matters will improve. Trained counsellors, a useful alternative to drug treatment, will become more commonplace in general practice soon, now that the rules are changing so that they can be employed in the local GP's surgery. And computer checks of prescribing patterns will highlight any doctor who reaches too easily for the scrip pad – for tranquillizers as for anything else. So that is where I left it, still feeling sad that so many people had been hurt, so much money wasted, so many women fobbed off with a little bit of paper instead of proper consideration and care.

*　　*　　*

We have a lot of work to do yet in this country, in my judgement, on mental illness. Bear in mind, then, that most people admitted to mental hospital are women; that most are in fact old women; and that the commonest mental illness diagnosed is not Alzheimer's disease or something more florid, but depression. We have an image of a typical mental patient as someone young, male and schizophrenic. In fact the crazy old crones in Annette's ward are closer to being typical, for the largest single group of mental patients in Britain today are depressed old ladies. Heaven only knows how much, if any, of their depression is preventable, but there must be risk factors that encourage it. There must be a stage where early detection and intervention would be helpful. It must be possible to promote better mental health alongside better physical health.

*   *   *

Right! What next? Trying to develop and encourage breast-feeding straddled the line between the welfare of women and that of their children. It was also an example of an area of work which previous governments had signed up for but where progress had been slow, and where the dictates of fashion were beginning to go in the wrong direction.

There's no doubt that breast-feeding is best for the baby. However good the manufactured milks – and they are excellent in this country – they are not made of human milk, so problems with allergies and other reactions can arise even in otherwise healthy babies. The artificial milks also lack one crucial ingredient, human antibodies, which are normally transmitted to the baby in the first few days of breast-feeding. There are obvious hazards to making up bottles, too, and I really was puzzled by the argument that bottles were more convenient than sitting quietly in a corner. Of course, it *is* perfectly possible to bring up a healthy infant on artificial feeding, as millions of children in this country and others can testify. But breast-feeding is better.

It's also much better for the mother, too. The usual result of natural feeding is to cause the uterus to shrink faster after childbirth, and to use up the fat reserves which are laid down during pregnancy. In other words, the mother returns to normal more quickly and in a more natural way. Having fed one of mine for several months, while the other would simply not have it, I did understand mothers who were unable to carry on after trying, but I also understood the rather vague and emotional point made in some of the literature, that natural feeding created a very strong bond between mother and baby: it does, and it is glorious, and very special, lasting and private.

The Department was galvanized into action eventually by the arrival of the five-yearly survey on breast-feeding from the Office of Population Censuses and Surveys. The report covering 1985 was published in July 1988. We had a problem, it said, for although breast-feeding was still the choice of the majority of mothers, it was getting less popular. Amongst first-time mothers, for example, the numbers who wanted to feed their babies had dropped since 1980 from 74 per cent to 69 per cent, and amongst women from working-class backgrounds, barely half now expressed that preference, even though the better-educated women showed scores way up around the 85 per cent mark. It made no difference whether the women had jobs or not. The study showed, broadly, that whereas two-thirds of mothers said at the beginning that they intended to breast-feed their babies, within six weeks of birth two-thirds of babies were being bottle-fed. Most mothers had given up within two weeks of birth, and many had stopped even before leaving hospital, despite there being plenty of help, presumably trained and wise about the value of breast-feeding, on the spot. Or was there?

The change-over to bottle-feeding was a fashion, no doubt about it, encouraged by some less-well-informed professional staff. I recalled a visit to the Scotswood clinic in a poor part of Newcastle upon Tyne in the autumn of 1986, which to me summed it all up.

The clinic was very busy. The smell of cigarette smoke was in the air.

'So do you run an anti-smoking clinic?' I asked and the health visitors laughed.

'We'd have to start with the doctor,' they said.

I sat in with him as he did the six-weekly examination for one baby, checking its hips and so on. The mother, I was told, was typical of the area, very young and a single parent. The doctor was not required to check on her health. He started to fill in the baby's forms. 'Will you be having the child vaccinated?' he said, not looking at the mother.

'No,' she replied. 'I don't believe in them things. I don't like needles.' And that was the end of that.

The rest of the main clinic was equally depressing. At about four o'clock, however, there was some action. Virtually every mother dug into a shopping bag for a bottle and without more ado thrust it into her baby's mouth. Most of the many toddlers were also clutching dirty bottles, having discarded the dummies which were tied or pinned to their jackets. There was the sound of happy gurgling.

The mother I had been chatting to, an articulate and thoughtful local resident (who tried to explain to me why local people, herself included, felt they had to spend their meagre money on cigarettes),

We spent less than £100,000 to promote No Smoking Day, 9 March 1988, yet this picture went round the world. I am *not* making a comment on the smell of my feet! The cigarette was made of toilet rolls jammed down a hollow tube and kept threatening to fall to bits *(Syndication International Ltd)*

The team, Department of Health and Social Security, September 1986, at Alexander Fleming House. From left to right: Tony Newton (Minister of State, Health, my immediate boss); EC; Norman Fowler (Secretary of State); John Major (Minister of State, Social Security); Baroness Jean Trumpington (Parliamentary Under Secretary, Lords); Nicholas Lyell (Parliamentary Under Secretary, Social Security) *(Daily Telegraph)*

With Margaret Thatcher at East Midlands Airport during the General Election Campaign, May 1987. A favourite picture *(Rex Features)*

The campaign behind the 'woolly hats' remark. The Department paid for the telephone line which received many thousands of calls, asking for more information. *(Inset)* It was nice to have Cyril Smith's weighty support *(DHSS/Press Association)*

Jeanette Smith, at the Marie Curie Sunnyside Home, in Woolton, Liverpool, October 1988. She died soon after *(Marie Curie Cancer Care)*

Pedalling my message to keep the nation healthy! In the magnificent surroundings of Lancaster House for the launch of the 'Look After Your Heart!' campaign, April 1988 *(Rex Features)*

How not to curtsey — Her Royal Highness the Princess Royal arrives at the London AIDS conference, January 1988. From left: EC; Tim Eggar (Foreign Office); HRH; John Moore (Secretary of State, DHSS). The Princess Royal's speech demonstrated that she knew what she was talking about *(Today News Ltd)*

It doesn't have to be hell to be healthy

Look after your HEART!

The ad that didn't work ('Look After Your Heart!' campaign, April 1987)… and (below) the ad that did, from the pharmaceutical industry *(ABPI/J. Walter Thompson)*

The British die*t*

Right: The daft things I get up to... Launching yet another healthy eating campaign, this time for caterers, at the Pineapple Dance Studios. The flowers were covered in vinegar and tasted quite horrible *(Express Newspapers)*

Left: With Warrant Officer Ash at the Army Catering HQ at Aldershot (16 May, 1988). The food was grand and the soldiers ate vast quantities *(Soldier Magazine)*

The launch of the measles, mumps, rubella (MMR) vaccine at the Queen Elizabeth II Conference Centre, London, October 1988 — kids, bananas, balloons and all. The children were truly marvellous and kept their eyes on the ball, namely the fruit, until it was all over *(Express Newspapers)*

HOW TO PREVENT YOUR SON FROM GETTING THE GIRL NEXT DOOR INTO TROUBLE.

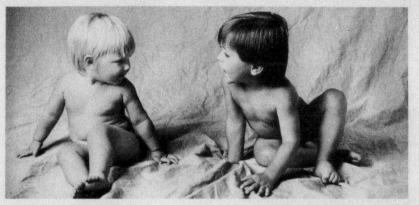

If your son gives Rubella to the woman next door during her pregnancy, the foetus could be damaged.

Blindness, deafness, heart disease and brain damage can result. But this need not happen now. The MMR

vaccination can protect children from Measles, Mumps and Rubella, all of which have serious

complications. Measles can cause inflammation of the brain, convulsions, deafness and blindness.

Mumps can lead to deafness and meningitis. Your child should have the MMR (Measles, Mumps and

Rubella) vaccination at around fifteen months. Four and five year olds can have the

vaccination before they start school, but you can ask your doctor about getting it

done at any time. Local clinics will be only too pleased to give you more information.

Please find out about MMR, for your own child's sake as well as the neighbour's.

MMR
THREE WAY
PROTECTION
FOR YOUR
CHILD

HEALTH EDUCATION AUTHORITY

ISSUED BY THE HEALTH EDUCATION AUTHORITY AND THE DEPARTMENT OF HEALTH.

I didn't see this campaign ad for the MMR vaccine until it was published. Lovely headline and photo, but too much chat to make an impact where it mattered, with the mothers. Still, the overall campaign was a raving success, way beyond our expectations *(Health Education Authority)*

Above: The first meeting of the Ministerial Group on Alcohol Misuse, in the Treasury Boa
Room, November 1987. From left: Michael Forsyth (Scottish Office); Peter Bottomley
(Transport); EC (Health); Francis Maude (DTI); John Wakeham (Chairman, Lord Privy
Seal); Douglas Hogg (Home Office); Patrick Nicholl (Employment); Donald Thompson
(MAFF); Bob Dunn (Education) *(Crown Copyright Reserved)*

Below: Still at it − helping with the first National Drinkwise Day
with local bobbies at Burton-on-Trent, near my home, in June 1989
(Empics)

stood up. 'You must excuse me,' she said, 'I've got to go and feed her.'

'Do it here,' I said, 'I don't mind.'

'No,' she explained, 'they have a room off for people like me who want to feed the babby themselves.'

How odd, I thought, for there were no men around, apart from the doctor. I went up to the desk and spoke to a health visitor. She was the type who, I suppose, would be called one of the old school and I fervently hope that by the time this book comes out she has retired!

'Why are they all bottle-feeding?' I asked.

'Well, that's their choice,' I was told with a shrug – which is of course true, but not the response I was expecting.

'But why don't they breast-feed? At least here.'

The woman bristled and busied herself with her papers. 'It isn't convenient,' she said shortly.

'Why not?' I persisted, getting angry.

'We don't have the facilities for them to breast-feed,' she said, and scuttled away.

She failed, however, to explain what facilities, apart from a chair and a quiet corner, were so necessary. So there we were, in a health-service clinic, and almost every new mother who visited got the picture clearly in her head that the best way to care for her baby, however dire the circumstances, however limited the cash, was to shove a bottle in its mouth, and a dummy after that.

I don't go along, however, with the idea that feeding baby is a public event. Privacy and peace and quiet are essential. Apart from anything else, it all requires some concentration on the part of both participants, at least in the first few weeks. The traditional feminists – for whom, as no doubt the reader is well aware by now, I have very little time – believe that babies should be fed whenever and wherever mother and baby wish, however annoying that may be to others. I was told of the Community Health Council meeting in one of the trendier boroughs in London, where two members were lesbians, one of whom had recently had a baby. The women proceeded – *both* of them – to feed the said infant throughout the council's meeting, passing it backwards and forwards, in an orgy of slurps and pulling up of sweaters. No thank you, I don't fancy that, or advocate it. On the other hand I got angry (again!) at the woeful tale told me by one mother, who had indeed settled down very modestly to feed her baby in a corner of the Natural History Museum (where else?) and was thrown out by security guards. (A letter in the *Independent* of 6 March 1989 suggested the staff there have learned their lesson and are much kinder now, even though women are directed to the Department of Palaeontology, as if we mammals should be stuffed . . .)

In fact, had I carried on in the Department of Health, I had it in mind to encourage public premises such as shops to make facilities available, and to put a sticker saying so on their doors. No one should feel guilty or anxious about caring for their baby in whatever way they choose. It is about time the British learned some lessons from other countries in Europe, where children, including babies and their mothers, are generally made to feel welcome, indeed to be honoured as precious to society as a whole, as they should be.

During 1986 and 1987 the National Childbirth Trust, one of the major charities in the field, started to hassle hard for an increase in its Government grant, with letters to MPs and Peers, planted parliamentary questions and the like. In the autumn of 1987 I sat scratching my head with the officials concerned. 'Aren't we concerned about the drop in breast-feeding?' I asked. 'Couldn't they help us with that? I don't mind giving them public money if we are going to see something for it.' And that was how our breast-feeding initiative was born, in which voluntary organizations are joining with the professionals to encourage women to breast-feed, and to give practical advice and assistance to those women who do. I also roped in the La Leche League and the Association of Breast-feeding Mothers, which had also been receiving small grants from us, on the principle that it was quicker to have the lot together than to have them arguing about who should organize the initiative. At a meeting with all three groups in May 1988 we consolidated all the grants for the next two years, so that a total of £100,000 was available, a big enough sum to run a proper campaign. They undertook to develop local groups, to help with ante-natal clinics, to get into schools, to help support the health visitors and midwives. Then in 1990 we would see whether it was working: that is, whether more mothers were at it, and maybe give them some more money, if progress was being made.

Later I met the manufacturers of baby milks, led by the cheerfully resigned Ron Hendey, and sought their agreement to help fund the campaign further. They said they all believed breast was best, so, ever cheeky, I asked them for £30,000 for the campaign, and got it. I watched out of the Department window as they left the building and walked off down Whitehall. They were shaking their heads, looking a little surprised with themselves, but I hope they all slept with clear consciences that night.

It wasn't all joy and light. Some years earlier, baby-milk manufacturers were accused of promoting expensive milks in very poor parts of the world where clean water supplies and modern hygiene were unheard of, with baby deaths as the unfortunate result. Our Government had agreed, along with many others, to sign the WHO's 1981 declaration on the marketing of baby milks, which was promulgated after this fiasco and designed to avoid a repetition by preventing undue promotion of artificial feeding. We had already in 1983, long before I arrived at the Department, signed an agreement with the milk manufacturers not to promote baby milk, so for some years there had been no publicity photographs of happy smiling babies with their contented mothers, baby milk in hand, in this country. Not that anyone noticed, for the initiative was spoiled by the fact that the bottle and teat manufacturers had been left out, so it was OK to show happy, smiling babies with their mothers clutching a bottle, and as a result many people were not aware of the long-standing ban.

In 1986 the WHO got tough. 'Do something about it,' they said, 'and at the same time make sure that the general rule, that mothers should only learn about artificial feeding methods from trained health professionals, should be effective; and while you are at it, no more free samples of baby milk in hospitals or anywhere else.'

That was a tall order, though I could see their point. The rules, really designed with Third World countries in mind, would do us no harm, though I was only willing to try for an expanded voluntary agreement with the producers concerned, and not for legislation – which the WHO preferred. I did not expect the shower of abusive criticism which resulted from the press, particularly from one magazine in the field, *Mother and Baby*, which seemed to think that I and the WHO were some kind of pocket Hitlers who did not trust the British public – and, of course, their readers – to look at paid advertisements in magazines such as theirs, and make up their own minds. Even intelligent writers such as Barbara Amiel were critical. It did not help that it took the supporters of breast-feeding, some of whom were equally passionate, several weeks to detach themselves from their hungry infants and write angry letters back to the press. When I left the Department the question of the proposed ban was still not resolved. In the end I was not well pleased with that part of the breast-feeding campaign.

Still, somebody must have been listening, for when there was a new Royal baby in the summer of 1988, there was also intense public speculation as to whether Mum would breast-feed or not, far more so than at other Royal births recently. It has to be the family's choice and I refused to make any comment. All mothers – all families – should be free to choose, helped to carry out their choice and not made to feel guilty whichever choice they make, Royals included.

*   *   *

One issue the Women's Health Group considered right at the start, in late 1986, was how we in Whitehall, as a major employer, looked after our staff. Compared with industry the answer often was 'not too well'. I had seen when I had been offered an industrial scholarship the excellent health care offered to employees by BP. During my time as a minister I was in contact with dozens of big companies who felt that health care and screening were an important part of the package they offered their staff. But when I asked what kind of service we gave to Department of Health staff, I was not amused to be given a note which started with eye tests for VDU users and failed to mention heart disease at all.

In fact, like so much else, health policy discussion for employees was virtually confined to whether women employees should have paid time off to go for their cervical smear or whether they had to do it in their own time. The Civil Service will claim that there is now a more enlightened attitude, but if they want to attract and retain staff in the nineties they will have to devote some time and energy to the health of their work-force, or they will find it even harder to persuade good people to work for them.

We did have some success over at the Palace of Westminster, home of both the Commons and the Lords. I was conscious that over 2,000 people work there, including the clerical, kitchen and cleaning staff. While the cervical cancer screening system was being brought in all over the country there were still gaps, and we wanted an extra effort to contact women who had never had a smear, or had not had one for years. Convenience clearly mattered to these women, so I encouraged the Women's National Cancer Control Campaign (WNCCC) in their efforts to raise money for mobile vans in which the testing and advice giving could be done. The Speaker of the House of Commons had already been approached and, to my surprise, when I wrote in my official capacity, told me that the Commons Services Committee had already discussed the question of whether such a service was desirable, had taken some advice, and had said 'no'. I called for their little report and noted with a sigh that they had sought advice from the Civil Service; I'll bet they would have had a different response if they had asked Marks and Spencer's!

We nagged away in a rather desultory fashion, until Lady Ewart-Biggs persuaded the House of Lords that they should go ahead with a mobile screening without the Commons. Don't be surprised – there are a lot more women in the Lords than in the elected house, at least at the moment. The little WNCCC van duly rolled up and seventy-eight women made appointments and had their smear and a breast check done. Of these, nineteen were referred for further advice or testing, though not necessarily for cancer. A frisson of envy went round the Commons. I compared notes with Jo Richardson, the sweet-natured Labour spokesman on women's issues, and in mid-1988 we nagged again; to our delight the answer this time was 'yes'.

Conscientiously I made my appointment, but I was quietly amused when I saw the van the WNCCC had parked at the back of one of the administrative buildings. 'Donated to WNCCC by Britain's Bingo Players' was painted all down one side. I've done some daft things in my ministerial life, but playing bingo with the Bingo Bear – and being a bingo caller at the Top Rank Club for the night for a thousand Kilburn ladies – was one of the better events. I was not alone, for Robert Atkins, the sharp-tongued, laid-back Junior Minister at the Department of Trade, had done the same thing up in Leyland in Lancashire – more quietly than I did – and members of the local rugby clubs had helped in St Helens and Warrington. Still, by supporting licensed Bingo Clubs of Great Britain WNCCC had raised almost £200,000 to buy vans, and we had helped get a message across to their middle-aged customers, who were our target for the cancer screening tests. Evangeline Hunter-Jones, the intrepid chairman of WNCCC, had done something much dafter, a sponsored flight strapped on top of a small biplane flown by her daughter. Would I like to join her? Not on your nelly, I responded! But there the van was, in use for women MPs and all those who work for us. A nice feeling.

*   *   *

Ministers and officials in the Women's Health Group worked very hard on women's health and it was always exhilarating; it was clear that, in John Moore's words when he opened our conference in June 1988, we were 'lifting a veil' on issues that women of all backgrounds, all colours wanted to talk about. Most of all, to my delight, it was clear as time went on that in talking about women's health, ministers had struck a major chord amongst millions of women in this country. They instantly understood what we were getting at, and were very pleased that a coherent and thoughtful approach, which accorded with their own experience and that of their mothers, daughters and friends, was being pursued. These were topics that women talked about among themselves, when the men were elsewhere. My own surprise at the degree of interest aroused was probably testimony to the fact that I had spent nearly all my working life with men. There *is* a different world out there, to which the men will never gain access, just as it is very difficult for any woman, however well-educated, however experienced in the ways of the world, really to understand the values of men. I didn't think so before, but I do now.

The women I met were often shy to start with, then it seemed that they welcomed the encouragement to talk more openly about their fears of cancer, the value of breast-feeding, the loneliness of widowhood, the difficulty of getting a male doctor to understand women's problems, however nice he was, and many other topics. So at functions or dinners I would often be pursued into the Ladies by women guests, who in a flurry of gorgeous dresses and best hair-do's, wanted to tell me their own medical experiences, but not in front of their husbands!

Only rarely did any woman raise a voice in dissent, and then, inevitably, it was on the most difficult occasion of all, my last Question Time in the House of Commons. There was a question on the order paper on women's health, put by a friendly male back-bencher. Up rose the magnificent Dame Jill Knight, MP for Birmingham, Edgbaston since 1966, and Chairman of the Conservative back-bench Health Committee. Handsome, short, greying, splendid in pearls, Jill is a good soul and was kind to me during my years in Birmingham. She asked whether her honourable friend (i.e. me) wasn't also interested in men's health? The answer I gave, of course, was 'yes'; the main targets of the heart disease programme were the men, particularly those under retirement age. It seemed right, however, that we should ask whether that programme was equally appropriate for the rest of us, or whether something else wasn't more suitable. The two groups are not rivals or competitors for health care, but their health needs are different.

It will be apparent by now that I am no traditional feminist. There is no room in my pantheon of gods for militant women who deride men, for those who declare 'Women do it by themselves', or for those who wore stickers on their jackets on Royal Wedding day saying, 'Don't do it Di!' The millions of ordinary women in this country look for permanent and loving relationships and to having children in the time-honoured way, hoping, as women have done for aeons, for a man who is kind, easy to live with and who cares for his family. Many attitudes amongst women are changing and they are becoming much less docile, much more assertive. The women understood what we were trying to do, and I am convinced that they approve and will continue to approve in years to come. Some day we shall have saved women's lives, reduced the pain and misery of illness, diminished the fear of terminal disease and helped women to take better care of themselves and thus of their families. As a woman, I am content with that.

6

Suffer the Little Children

Lord, give to men that are old and rougher
The things that little children suffer,
And let us keep bright and undefiled
The young years of the little child.
John Masefield, 'The Everlasting Mercy'

The ward was cramped, noisy, old. Beds, toys, children, parents, drips, bandages, staff everywhere; tripping over each other, things left lying around on the floor, charts and scientific research papers mixed up with Postman Pat, colouring crayons in a merry but nightmarish jumble with canulas and syringes.

The jovial bearded doctor switched in a second from his kindly avuncular manner with the children to a business-like approach when I appeared. We walked along the corridor to the ward together, trailed by the omnipresent TV cameras, not so much there to record me, for once, but making a *cinéma vérité* series about the life of the hospital, warts and all, shown under the title *Jimmy's* in 1987.

Warts there certainly were, for we were in St James's Hospital, Leeds, the biggest hospital in Europe, with 1,500 beds. Rival to Leeds General Infirmary, Jimmy's had also been created a teaching hospital some years earlier and the two eyed each other across the city. Much of the hospital was old and scruffy. It was built of classic Victorian brick, once boldly red but long-since deeply begrimed by more than a century in the smoky air of Leeds. There were new units, of course, and inevitable plans to rebuild. Replacing that little lot on a cramped city-centre site, without disrupting any of the services, would be tricky by anyone's measure; to do it on a green-field site away from the town would be technically simpler and less expensive in the long run but would raise howls of protest about the 'much-loved building' and its 'perfect location'. So, in true British fashion, they soldiered on, bursting at the seams, with beds in the corridor and sick people waiting patiently in queues for almost every kind of health care.

This ward was typical, they told me. Its name was dry, un-emotional: paediatric oncology. It was an important regional speciality, but I was not prepared for what I was to find there. There were children wherever I looked, and adults. It was hard to tell who was a parent, who a nurse, for the staff did not wear a uniform on children's wards. Even when someone was treating a child, giving an injection or attending to a dressing, it was still impossible to tell, for some parents were so fierce in their love for their child that they would learn the most intricate of procedures and endure the pain they gave their child themselves as the necessary work was done. Some of it was beyond human endurance, I reflected; harder for the parent who understood than for the child who didn't.

Every bed was occupied, with pallid little bodies dozing amongst the noise and general disorder. Other children were sitting on the floor all over the ward. Two little boys with drips attached to their arms played with plastic lorries, only their bald shiny heads telling the tale of leukaemia. In a side ward – just a room off the main ward, really, not insulated from the noise – a couple sat quietly, their child cuddling close to his mother. I sat gently beside her and asked what was the matter with him. Without a word she lifted his head and I saw the tumour growing out of it.

'God in heaven,' I said to the doctor, later. 'What causes that?'

'We don't know,' he said sadly, 'but childhood cancer is rare and seems to be getting rarer. We really don't know all that much about it. Our job is to treat it, and we have quite an expertise in those cancers here.'

He must have seen my face; he continued more cheerfully, matter-of-fact. 'He has a chance these days, you know. It was bigger a few weeks ago.'

He was right, of course. The treatment of children with cancer has made remarkable progress in recent years and is one of the real successes of modern medicine. Once, all such children would die. Now, many of those with leukaemia or with tumours can be treated and some 60 per cent of children who are diagnosed as having cancer survive at least to the five-year mark, which is regarded as the point at which victims may be said to have beaten their disease, at least the current manifestation of it.

It is, perhaps, worth putting on record, as the one who was responsible for the hospital service for children, that almost any treatment which works is available somewhere on the NHS in this country. Only in the most unusual of cases is a treatment only available in another country (typically the USA), for conditions so rare that treatment here is not feasible. The various acts of Parliament which control NHS expenditure do permit the spending of taxpayers' money to send the patient abroad for that treatment. In my time I was involved in two such cases, one a child. Usually the expenditure requires ministerial approval, but it was given gladly and promptly.

That cancer ward haunted me and still does. The staff who work there have remarkable reserves of courage and compassion. If they haven't, they don't last long and without careful management the turnover of staff, particularly nurses, can be very high. The stress level was staggering: it was almost tangible, and hung in the air; we breathed it as we talked. The ward could have done without the television camera, I reflected, and they would have been better off without my visit. But perhaps there would have been criticism if I had skipped their ward. I was glad most of my life was more mundane.

As I left, I knew that I had to take with me something more positive. I asked the doctor whether, despite the fact that the causes of childhood cancer were obscure, there was something that could be done to help these children, some information I could pass on which would make their lives easier.

'Oh yes, that's easy,' said the doctor. 'You do something about measles.'

'Measles?' I asked, astonished.

'Sure,' he said. 'That's the most frustrating part of the whole business. We fix these kids up and they go into remission. We send them home but they are immuno-suppressed because of their drugs. And then they go and catch measles from a brother or sister, and wham! we've lost them. We lost two like that only a few weeks ago; measles is rife in a place like Leeds, but in America it's as rare as cholera. No child in this country should have it and it's a national disgrace. And a killer for children like these.'

That was not my first introduction to the triple vaccine, which tackles measles, mumps and rubella, and which was eventually made available in this country from October 1988, but perhaps it was the most powerful testimony to its importance.

*   *   *

158

Immunisation policy was not, in fact, part of my brief, but for the early part of my time at the Department of Health it was Jean Trumpington's responsibility. The WHO was concerned to improve availability and take-up of vaccines and on World Immunisation Day, 7 March 1987, Jean announced that the new triple vaccine would be brought into general use in this country. Take-up of most vaccines then was poor – from 40 to 70 per cent in most places – not enough to confer general immunity. We announced we would aim for 90 per cent take-up of the major vaccines by 1990.

We have forgotten in Britain the once-dreaded power of childhood infectious diseases. Once every family in the country lived in fear of the killer diseases, especially when there were epidemics. My father came down with tuberculosis when he was nineteen and was sent home from hospital to die. His mother decided he would live, and put him to bed in the attic. She nursed him for many months and slowly he recovered, leaving him with only one lung and a scar two feet long in his side where the tubercular matter had been removed. (He then proceeded to smoke heavily for the rest of his life, commenting only that he should have been dead at twenty so why worry?)

In this country we had also scored a notable success with polio. In 1948, the year of the establishment of the NHS, there were over 20,000 cases of the disease but the real epidemic was to come a year or two later. I lived in a pleasant cul-de-sac in Liverpool. The children in the eight houses there, nearly all products of the post-war baby booms of 1946 and 1949, played together, carefree in a world safer for children than it is now. Gail, who lived opposite, was a bit older; a pretty dark-haired girl. She kept an eye on us and tried to keep us out of mischief. One day during the hot summer she came home with a blinding headache, and was put to bed by her mother. When she woke, she was paralysed and never walked again. She became instead a familiar figure in her wheelchair and I still have a clear memory of our May-time celebrations in that little road, with Gail all dressed up as the May Queen, smiling awkwardly as the sun got into her eyes, flowers in her hair.

In 1987, by contrast, there were only three cases of polio.

Thinking again of the young mother in the Scotswood clinic in Newcastle (as described in the last chapter), I had always taken it for granted that vaccination was a good thing, and I found it difficult to understand the attitude of parents who were against it on principle. My own father was one of them. When I was born, vaccination against smallpox, then still a major world killer, was compulsory and in a sea-port like Liverpool where we lived, it was a most sensible precaution. My father, of blessed memory, didn't agree. He was required, therefore, to explain his objection in court when I was about six weeks old, and he duly did so; my mother was quite disgusted that he could not remember my birth date, but he got his way.

Similarly, some years later when the BCG inoculation against tuberculosis first became available, the wise souls in the Public Health departments in Liverpool, always well in the forefront of the nation in such matters, decided to make it available to Liverpool school-children. I was about fourteen at the time and I was pleased to get a letter at school to take home for my parents to sign. But no, said my father, you're not having that; and so I had to wait until I reached six-teen and did not need his signature, and could have it done quietly myself.

Immunisation was, of course, a different matter if there were any attendant risks as, for example, some years ago with the whooping cough vaccine which was available at the time. It is no good telling some mothers that the danger to their child, unless he is in one of the high-risk groups, is minute. As far as she is concerned, the risk is 100 per cent. Calculations about mischances and figures of the order of millions-to-one are appropriate for governments, but they don't mean much to individual families.

That was one reason why we hesitated about the new MMR (measles, mumps, rubella) vaccine in this country, despite its excellent record elsewhere. Did it work? Increasingly, the answer for MMR was 'yes'; antibodies were found in adults who had been vaccinated as small children, so it looked as if effective, life-long immunity was possible. Was it dangerous? The answer, to our relief, appeared to be 'no'. As an added precaution, and rather than just relying on research from other countries, we tracked in detail the experiences of more than 11,000 children from volunteer families during the early part of 1988. Their mothers recorded how they were for several weeks after the injection and we found even less in the way of side effects than predicted. There was no medical case for holding back any longer.

Of course not all of the MMR vaccine was new. We already offered a measles vaccine but the take-up was poor. We vaccinated teenage girls against rubella; but then pregnant women caught it from little boys. The time was ripe for a change.

We also had an epidemic of measles on our hands. There had been nearly 37,000 notifications in the first eighteen weeks of 1988, compared with 42,000 for the whole of 1987. Measles is a killer. It is particularly unpleasant in adults, as Tony Newton was able to confirm to me when his twenty-year-old daughter came down with a nasty bout, right in the middle of our discussions about whether to go ahead with the new vaccine. In fact, as 1988 wore on, we were hearing, on average, of the death of one child from measles each month, and it was that year's ten dead children who were on my mind as we went into the autumn launch. We could not afford any more lives lost. The third disease, mumps, is also more serious than generally realized and accounts for 1,200 hospital admissions, children and adults, per year. It is linked to encephalitis, meningitis and deafness, and we had never had a vaccine in the United Kingdom against it.

There were two priority groups – children in their second year of life (typically fifteen months old), and children at pre-school entry, when the new vaccine would be given at the same time as boosters for diphtheria, tetanus and polio. Since one jab gave life-long protection it would not in future be necessary to do this second group – the best time to protect the children is when they are very little, long before they start coming into contact with large numbers of other children – but we wanted to do a 'catching-up' exercise which might continue for several years.

The launch of the vaccine was to be on Monday 3 October 1988, at the prestigious new Queen Elizabeth II Conference Centre in Westminster, and it was planned as a Big Event. It was not decided till quite late on which minister should organize it, though I had been angling hard to be involved somehow ever since the first discussions back in 1987. To me this was the heart of effective government work on preventing illness, and I would love to be there. 'You're on', came the word in September 1988 and then the fun began. The Department wanted 'the works' in terms of publicity. We had a budget and so had the Health Education Authority. (I loved their advertisements, headlined 'How to prevent your son from getting the girl next door into trouble', with the picture of an adorable little boy, cheeky look on face.)

I sat down with our advisers and discussed the media event itself. I realized then just how disciplined some civil servants are when faced with a pesky Minister with 'ideas'. It must have taken a lot of effort for the one who had to run the thing to keep saying 'Yes, Minister,' but bless her cotton socks, she did it. Later she told me that I had put thirty years on her life; exaggerating somewhat, I hope.

'I want children, lots of them,' I said. She gulped.

'Children – do you mean it? Real children running around?'

'Of course; it's for them, not for us. It won't be a proper event without the children.'

'Yes, Minister,' she said, sadly, 'but we can't do the inoculations right there, there are rules, insurance and that.'

I charged on: 'And I don't want them given sweets as a reward, that would be the wrong message. I want bananas, and oranges, and lots of mess and peel all over the floor.'

'Bananas? In the Queen Elizabeth Conference Centre?' she queried. 'Oh, dear. Yes, Minister.' She thought for a moment, made a note, then looked at me and sighed. 'Would you like balloons?' she asked, faintly.

'Yes, great idea. Lots of balloons. We're going to have a party, to launch it. We are going to spend public money on the vaccine and we want everyone to know about it.'

'Yes, Minister,' she said.

And it was done. The children were solemn throughout and kept their eyes on the fruit; one little girl picked up an enormous apple and ate it doggedly for forty minutes. I enjoyed myself hugely.

The campaign succeeded beyond our wildest dreams and we were rapidly inundated with demands for the MMR vaccine. The message from the mothers was that they wanted the new jab for their infants right now, please; not in a year or two as we had carefully planned. The nation's doctors were polite but insistent. They could not go on saying 'no' to the customers; please could they have some more, and sharpish?

There was no doubt that we underestimated the demand. We would normally expect there to be some 600,000 children in each age cohort – that is each year's stock of children. Take-up of vaccines in general was then around 70 to 75 per cent, better than it had been but we wanted it higher. For each age group, in the three months from the launch to Christmas, we would have expected to vaccinate around 100,000 children. If the take-up reached its maximum – if no one refused – the figure would have touched 150,000. Now we were after two age groups, not one, so 100 per cent take-up would have been 300,000 doses in three months. We thought we were doing quite well when nearly 300,000 doses had been sent out by the date of the campaign launch, increased to over 660,000 by the end of October. So I was not expecting the barrage of criticism over 'shortages'.

In fact, by 14 November 1988, 800,000 doses had been distributed, and the delivery of one million doses by Christmas 1988 was a remarkable manufacturing feat. We had only one manufacturer, Smith Kline French, to start with; but another came in very quickly and a third by spring 1989. The manufacturers were working flat out for us, and, indeed, diverting supplies on a temporary basis from their customers in other parts of the world. They felt, as we did, that we should catch this tide of enthusiasm and interest as a once-for-all chance to protect the most vulnerable part of the population, our children, against disease.

There is a sequel to this tale. During December, in the Department, there was a lively discussion about taking the campaign further. On 9 January 1989 my successor at the Department of Health, Roger Freeman, announced that as part of the regional health authorities' allocation for 1989–90 a total sum of £7.8 million would be earmarked for MMR purchase. Roger's announcement was excellent news; the money should be enough to buy *another* million doses in the first six months of 1989, and thus vaccinate 2 million children in less than a year since the launch. That's most of the pre-school children in this country done, all in one go, which would be an achievement well ahead of the most wildly optimistic forecasts when we started back in October. On reflection, of all the preventive health matters I was involved in, this launch of the new vaccine left me with the warmest feelings. In years to come when I read *Social Trends* or other weighty government statistical productions, I will turn to the figures of measles infections and deaths, and in a tiny way feel good with myself. I doubt if that civil servant will forget it all in a hurry, either. Others should take the credit, but I am very glad I was involved.

*   *   *

Several other developments came out of that visit to the cancer ward with its strange smells, its little children with no hair. First, we were faced with constant pressure on money and space in wards of this kind, and in other children's wards and specialist teaching hospitals, where the most difficult intensive work was done. The Chief Medical Officer, aware of the problems, already had a group of senior cancer experts offering him advice. They concluded that there was no point in opening a lot more units, for it is the concentrated expertise in a small number of hospitals which is much more likely to save lives, especially for the rarest cancers. The same applies to other uncommon conditions amongst babies and children, such as heart defects or metabolic failures. Also, there is no need to keep the children in hospital, a long way from home, any longer than necessary. So they can now have their chemotherapy and go home – helping to release hospital beds at the same time. The technique is now being used for adults as well. The downside is the wait – at home – for heart or transplant surgery, for children who often look as if they should be in hospital, but are honestly better off on their own sofas.

The pressure on doctors is obvious but they seem to relish it; perhaps they are the sort that thrive on stress. The nursing staff are another matter. Long after the doctor has left for his conference, his research meeting, his supper, they stay with the child. They clean him up, they hold his head, they comfort his mother. The turnover of staff in some units, such as Birmingham Children's Hospital's ITU (Intensive Therapy Unit), was very high indeed and (although they had the money) they could never get enough nurses. In one such unit I found that recruitment was not a problem, but the nurses tended to pack up and leave for easier work within six months, so the unit was always understaffed and unable to cope.

I investigated and found, to my surprise, in the case of the children's intensive care nurses for example, that there was only one training course for them, at Great Ormond Street Hospital in London. That hospital was working flat out trying to provide specialized children's nurses for dozens of hospitals in the whole country. Some of the units had been given substantial sums of extra money to expand their facilities but no one had suggested putting any of it into new courses for nursing staff. The funding arrangements seemed to defeat them – these good people who handled the most powerful cytotoxic drugs every day, who saved lives and saw them slip away week in and week out. So I threw my weight around, nagged everyone I met, threatened Armageddon to idiots who argued. Guided by Ann Poole, the Chief Nursing Officer for England, I met the fourteen Regional Nursing Officers on several occasions and hassled them unmercifully. On one occasion we all met at a hotel near Gatwick Airport. I was a little late, and found that the hotel manager, to be helpful, had laid on a lavish tea for us all in a private room. The tension broke and we all dived with delight into scones with cream and jam, and chocolate eclairs, while the young waiters watched us, amazed.

Gradually new training courses started to emerge, not least in Birmingham, to give a better supply of specialized staff in future. The senior nurses also came to realize that stress management was an important part of their job. It is not enough to leave a young nurse crying in the linen cupboard, while her superior sits at a desk elsewhere drinking coffee. Not all the patients will survive, but if you have cared for them and relieved their pain, you are not a failure. Someone needed – needs – to offer these comforts to every nurse in daily contact with death. That way, they will go on doing the job.

We were also able to offer more support to the families whose stoical acceptance of anguish had been so apparent in Jimmy's. During the discussions in committee on the Health and Medicines Bill in early 1988, we got on to the welfare of children in hospital for some obscure reason. There is a marvellous organization called NAWCH (National Association for the Welfare of Children in Hospital) which celebrated its 25th Anniversary during my time in office. It was led by Jean, Lady Lovell-Davies, one of those tiny, pretty women with a quiet voice, soft skin like a china doll and fair hair, who may look innocent but who get things done. They had presented the department with a 'Charter for Children' saying what was needed.

Once all children were treated at home. Only foundlings and the fatherless found their way into hospitals, where their chances of survival were very slim. After the first war, however, children's hospitals were developed all over the country, often as adjuncts to the new professorial chairs in paediatrics. Parents became regarded as a nuisance, and their visits were discouraged, with the children's tears on parting cited as proof that it 'upset' the child. They were effectively banished for decades. It was not until after the second world war that remarkable efforts were made to demonstrate that the children's disturbance was caused by the *separation*, not by the parting. So grudgingly parents were allowed back on to the wards, but were still regarded as intruders.

The 1971 Department of Health circular was a major step forward – if the presence of parents was essential, they should be encouraged and arrangements made to let them stay overnight. However, the Scots still had no such circular, and increasingly this emphasis on 'essential' as opposed to 'normal' presence was no longer acceptable. So I promised to set the wheels in motion for a new circular to be called 'The Welfare of Children in Hospital', as a tribute to NAWCH, a promise kept on 5 October 1988. If it is implemented, every children's department in hospital should provide facilities to enable the mother and the other members of the family to sustain the normal relationships to which the child is accustomed at home. Hospitals should abolish any rules restricting the visiting of children by their parents, and they should see that any decision to exclude the parents on medical grounds is made only by the consultant in charge. In the

Department's view parents are not 'visitors', therefore they should be encouraged to be with their children at all potentially stressful times. Unlike adult wards, children's wards should accommodate family members who will be present day and night irrespective of the distance of the child's home from the hospital – and perhaps especially if the child is a long way from home.

I also wanted to help when the children were going to die. So we asked that it should happen with some privacy – that there should be a private room available. Equally if the parents wanted to take the child home to die, then every effort should be made to help them do so. That is in the 'Welfare of Children' circular, too. It is already accepted practice to disconnect all the tubes and needles from a dying baby and let the parents cuddle it as it breathes its last. And I also wanted to ensure the recognition of the remarkable group of quiet people, parents who had lost a child and who were available to comfort others, who call themselves The Compassionate Friends. Their first ever government grant, of £55,000, was announced on 15 February 1989.

Most children who go to hospital come out fit and well, others die or remain invalids. Some of these efforts will ensure that they and their parents, and all the staff who care for them, find the whole experience a little less harrowing: it will help them, I hope, to find peace.

*   *   *

The improvements in the survival rate of babies are widely known. Between 1948, when the NHS was founded, and now, the death rate amongst new-born babies has dropped from nearly 39 per 1,000 births to less than 9 per 1,000, and is still falling. Put it another way. In 1948 there were 775,000 births and 18,400 still births (2.4 per cent) whereas in 1987 there were 685,000 births and only 3,400 still births (0.5 per cent). That means that the likelihood of a baby being born dead had fallen by 80 per cent. Perhaps that is the best testimony to the quality of antenatal and maternity care now.

Similarly, the chances of survival of the tiniest low-birthweight babies have improved dramatically. In 1987 there were 45,200 babies born weighing less than 2.5kg (5½lb) of whom *92 per cent* survived. The amount of care and skill that goes into that success is staggering – working at the outer horizons of scientific knowledge, touching the very nature of life itself.

It is quite easy to remember the terms used in this field: 'I', 'N',

'P', in alphabetical order, stand for infant mortality (deaths in the first year); neonatal mortality (first month); and perinatal mortality (first week). They are usually expressed as rates per 1,000 births so that different years, and different parts of the country, can be compared. Most deaths of babies in Western countries occur in the first few days, so perinatal mortality is the significant one for us, and survival rates have been improving for years.

If much of the improvement in the mortality of babies is well known, what is less well known is the sharp drop in the numbers of women dying in childbirth which has accompanied all the improvements for babies. Forty years ago, in 1948, the figures were dreadful: 807 women died in, or soon after, childbirth. Now the figure stands at around forty cases a year – still too many, but a tiny fraction of that terrible toll in the days at the time of the birth of the NHS. Perhaps this is the most significant break with the women of past centuries: for us, childbirth is very likely to be a joyous event for both mother and baby. The wings of death beat more softly now for us than at any time in history.

That raised three very different issues in my ministerial life. The first involved small maternity units; the second, the survival of very sick babies, and the question of abortion; and the third, prevention of handicap in babies. I did not pretend to have the answers to any of these questions, but I did my best.

*   *   *

First, those little maternity units. Very few women have their babies at home now, in itself a remarkable turn around in a generation. It is partly because very few doctors will attend to deliver, although by law a health authority must provide facilities for home confinements – it is not allowed to say 'on your head be it', and to wash its hands of it. The problems of litigation are forcing doctors away from obstetrics altogether and, as a result, more diagnostic work is done, more tests and precautions taken, more caesarian operations performed, and so on, all of which require hospitalization.

I had the utmost sympathy for those mothers who would prefer a 'natural' birth without the high technology, and there is no doubt it does detract from the experience of childbirth and gets in the way. The temptation must be for the midwife to listen to the bleep, not the baby, to look at the monitor, not the mother, and then to wonder why the pregnant lady in the bed gets indignant or distressed. I didn't feel, however, that the answer lay in deliveries in old-fashioned little maternity units with no blood bank, no proper theatre, no anaesthetist on call, no special-care baby cots, and often way out in the country. I had explored this issue before in Birmingham when the health authority first set up a regional neonatal intensive care unit at Birmingham Maternity Hospital. Dr Geoffrey Durbin, the gentle, softly spoken man whom we appointed as our first consultant, had shown me the portable incubator in which sick babies were brought from small maternity units in other towns. It bristled with tubes, plugs, perspex. Curious, I lifted the tiny blanket inside, to reveal a couple of hot-water bottles wrapped up in towels. 'That's the real high-tech system,' I was told. 'That's the one that goes on working when all else fails.'

Most of the little units had closed during the seventies. Those that remained typically had an occupancy below 50 per cent, although they were fully staffed with what were increasingly scarce midwives. What the beds were being used for, we discovered, was 'lying-in'; in other words, the ladies had their babies safely delivered at the high-tech hospital in town, and then were discharged to the little unit and spent the next week lounging around in NHS beds, eating NHS food and using NHS nappies for their babies, whereas every scrap of medical advice is that inactivity is a recipe for thrombosis. My mother, I recalled, had stayed in hospital for a fortnight when I was born. All mothers did, at least those who went to hospital at all. Soon after, she had 'phlebitis' (a clot in the leg) and did not ever make the connection between the two; but those clots can be killers. It may sound cruel to say to a recently-delivered woman that it is a good idea to get up to answer the phone or the door, but she will be fitter quicker and we can spend the money on something else. When I heard that it was common practice at more than one of these little units to admit women in labour, wait to see if problems developed, and then send the poor girl in agony haring thirty miles across country in a bouncing ambulance to the main hospital – and that this was regarded as routine, and a reason for keeping the little units open – I closed them as fast as I could.

I hesitated about home births, too, and for the same reason. Fine if you are low risk. Can be lethal if it goes wrong. And nobody knows which case is which – until it is too late. The corollary, of course, was that we do need to find a happier marriage between the best of modern care and treatment, in big units with all trained staff standing by, and the cosy friendliness of the cottage hospital. That's true for all sorts of patients, including the elderly, and I confess to some affection for the smaller local hospitals, particularly for respite care to help relatives. But when there's even the slightest risk of something going horribly wrong with the new life, then the modern unit is the place to be. Officially the choice is the mother's. In practice, as fewer staff will take risks, virtually all births now are in main hospitals – and I can live with that.

* * *

The second issue came to the forefront during the winters of 1986 and 1987. There was an exceptionally cold spell in the early weeks of 1986. For some reason no one has been able to fathom yet, there was a spate of cot deaths, particularly amongst little boys. The perinatal and infant mortality rates, which had been following a curve steadily downwards, suddenly showed an upward blip for the first time in decades. The numbers were very small, and the downward trend was resumed the following year, but it did set us thinking hard about the causes of deaths of tiny babies.

When you visit a neonatal unit, however, the wonder is that any of these tiny creatures survive at all. A full-term baby is born forty weeks from conception, give or take a few days. When I was young a premature baby was one of eight-months' gestation (thirty-six weeks) and it didn't have much chance. Sometimes seven-month babies managed it, but it was impossible to be less than that and survive, and for years the law had assumed that a limit of twenty-eight weeks for legal termination of pregnancy would give a sufficient gap. By the mid-1980s, it didn't, and a great deal of ministerial time was taken up explaining in painstaking and utterly neutral terms, during debates on Private Members' Bills, how we had effectively, by volun- tary co-operation, secured a ban on abortion beyond twenty-four weeks, and that we would now, as a government, support a change in the law to that level.

I was never obliged to give a personal opinion. I had, however, seen a baby at St James's Hospital in Leeds with a certain twenty- three-week gestation. Looking like a little dark rat (they don't have any body fat at that age, only paper-thin skin through which the dark venous blood is almost visible), eyes shut tight, bandaged against the light, head seemingly too large for body, this little creature had survived ten days already and was wriggling around in its incubator, tubes coming out of every orifice, clinging crossly to life. It was difficult to argue, standing there in wonder and disbelief, that the

169

termination of life at this gestation should continue to be legal.

On the other hand another question was raised and I remember pressing Dr Durbin about it hard in Birmingham. Are we doing anything useful here? Or are we just maintaining life for the sake of it, not knowing what misery and handicap we may be creating or perpetuating? 'We can't really tell,' he 'said gently. 'We will have to monitor them for years, thirty years maybe, until they have had their own children and then we may know.'

One of my constituents, Dr Leonard Arthur, a much-loved consultant at Derby Children's Hospital, had taken the decision that a desperately-ill handicapped baby girl should only be nursed for comfort and that efforts to feed her or revive her further should be abandoned. He was taken to court by the pro-lifers, but acquitted of causing her death. Many parents spoke up for him as the most caring soul of all. I never met him for he died of a brain tumour a year after the case, of a broken heart, many said. Just where stands compassion in all this?

I do not know the answer, and endless prodding of my officials produced nothing further. No one can work without some answers, so I switched some of my attention to the third issue – the prevention of handicap in the first place. Was there anything we could do, I asked, to reduce the scale of the problem? Yes, there was, mostly on rather a small scale.

For example, we should move to eradicate rubella (German measles) from Britain. It can infect pregnant women and damage their babies – over 200 abortions are legally performed every year on such women. That we are trying to do with the triple vaccine I have described earlier.

We should also look harder at screening babies at risk from the inherited blood disorders such as sickle cell anaemia and thalassaemia. In 1988 I got as far as writing to all the health authorities in England to inquire what services they had for these conditions; if the results were not satisfactory I was keen to go further.

Genetic counselling would also help, but it can be expensive and is often only called in after a condition has occurred and a handicapped baby already exists – with the option of termination only in future.

Some of these small changes do work to reduce the numbers of handicapped babies born but it is a long-term business. The Northern Regional Health Authority, alarmed at the high incidence of death and handicap amongst its babies, had instituted England's first regular confidential inquiry into baby deaths some years ago. The figures of outcomes certainly improved, but mainly because early detection led to more abortions. The incidence of handicap didn't budge at all.

I became very interested, and still am, in the research into low-birthweight babies. The women from Bangladesh and Pakistan, particularly, seem to deliver tiny babies which are too often sickly. I actively supported the Asian Mother and Baby campaign – in which women from the same communities, called 'Link Workers', acted as advocates and interpreters to these women, to ensure that they gained better access to the health services of this country – of which many of them were unaware. On several occasions I met Link Workers *en masse*, all dressed up like butterflies in their blue and gold and silver saris and salwar kameez, nose jewellery flashing, bright and beautiful and making me feel very drab in Western dress. Other times, on visits to other parts of the country, I would take the opportunity of meeting local Asian ladies – that usually meant in someone's house, drawing the curtains, throwing the men out, getting out the tea and cakes, and then talking about our menfolk, our children, our homes, and swapping recipes like women all over the world. I think many of them ended up a bit sorry for me, with two daughters only. They told me soothingly to have faith in God and keep trying, I would soon have a son!

Organizations like Birthright, which the Princess of Wales supports, have been beavering around to find other causes of prematurity, handicap and miscarriage, all of which may be related in many cases. Research on the Dutch population during the Occupation, and after, showed that near-starvation in 1944 reduced the numbers of children conceived and born quite dramatically. The level of miscarriage and handicap was also sharply raised. It was possible to pin-point the exact week in which food was brought in: from that point conceptions increased; but the incidence of handicap (measured as the number of cases of neural tube defects – spina bifida and the like) continued at a very high level until *fourteen months* later. That suggested that much of the damage was caused *before* pregnancy, in the ova and sperm of people whose diet was seriously restricted.

Come on, I said to our doctors, is it lack of food in general or any food in particular? But they wouldn't budge from their position that diet had no effect on handicap. All I could get was a grudging admission that a diet completely lacking in foliate minerals – those which come from leafy vegetables – might just be damaging. I feel instinctively that there's more to it than that and the subject really merits further research. We do know that excessive drinking during pregnancy damages the foetus. What isn't clear is whether damage of that kind has already happened *before* conception; it just seems likely.

The only culprit we could put our finger on for sure was the old enemy, the cigarette. Oh, dear, not again! Somewhere in the 400+ chemicals in cigarette smoke lurked some very nasty materials with known effects on the unborn baby. The ISCSH had already referred to the problem in their 1983 report and a warning against smoking in pregnancy was already in use. Their fourth report, in March 1988, said that the links had been demonstrated since 1957.

The mean reduction in the birthweight of babies between those born to maternal smokers and maternal non-smokers ranges between 150g and 250g (rather a lot for those tiny babies) with an increase in perinatal mortality of about 28 per cent. Both the reduction in birthweight and the increase in mortality are directly related to the number of cigarettes regularly smoked in pregnancy. The 3 per cent of women with the greatest cigarette consumption had infants nearly 300g lighter than non-smokers. There was even a small association between lower birthweight and a non-smoking mother breathing in other people's smoke on a regular basis. The report goes on to say: 'Smoking in pregnancy has also been associated with retarded physical and mental development in children.'

So smoking, again, is part of the answer; we don't know why for certain – perhaps the carbon monoxide interferes with the baby's development, perhaps other ingredients reduce hormone levels or damage the functioning of the placenta. Yet amongst women, in the age group at which child bearing is highest, the incidence of smoking is going up, and the number of cigarettes smoked is catching up with traditional male levels.

The cost to the nation of those premature babies, even those which are saved and whole, is huge, at least £100,000 per year per cot. And the cost to us all of one with a disability doesn't bear thinking about. Cigarettes and women don't mix and when they do it is not only the life of the smoker which may be put at risk.

*   *   *

Once, there was a child called Maria Colwell. She was seven when she died in 1973, after a short and terrible life, at the hands of a brutal stepfather, deserted by those charged with protecting her. The media took up the issue of 'baby battering' with alacrity, but ah! it was nothing new, I thought, remembering the bruised face of a school friend long ago. We used to put it down to booze and there was nothing much anyone could do, at least not in the more respectable homes where the blows were received in silence. Much later, as I listened to Esther Rantzen talking so eloquently about the children who phoned her charity 'Childline', I thought of that girl again and realized with a sick feeling that she had suddenly disappeared from school when we were about fourteen, and the rumour had been that she was *pregnant*. We wrote her off then, as a chump. People did; it was usually the girl's fault, wasn't it?

But you couldn't serve long on Birmingham's Social Services Committee, as I did from 1975 till 1982, without realizing that a lot of evil was going on behind closed curtains, in every kind of family, and not just when people were drunk. In the mid-seventies there were over 4,000 children in care (that is, legally the responsibility of social services) in that city alone, with 104 children's homes, including nine residential nurseries. We were spending, I calculated in 1979 – the year I became Chairman – some £15 million annually to keep children in care (particularly in children's homes), and only £400,000 to keep them out, by the use of foster parents, for example. I was always unhappy about parking children in a council-run home. They would never get to see a normal family; never see a gas bill, never have to fit in with everyone else, never see how people can argue and shout at each other without blows, without pulling a knife, and then kiss and make up. A foster home, on the other hand, offered a fair chance of a child having some future model of a normal family, of normal adults who love children. There are lots around like that, and some of them are saintly enough to take in strangers and look after other people's kids.

We saw, as a committee, the reports on the deaths of children in care. After reading inquest reports year in and year out I reckoned I had nothing much to learn about human brutality. One case concerned a baby girl called Clare Haddon. She was born to a fifteen-year-old mother, who was then encouraged by one of our well-meaning social workers to set up home with her boyfriend, a man of twenty-four who was, shall we say, 'known to the authorities'. He had, in fact, been brought up in Birmingham's own children's homes, so there was nothing we didn't know about him, had anyone bothered to check. Within seven weeks the baby was dead. A social worker commenting on the pathologist's report told me drily that the injuries were commensurate with the baby's having been kicked around like a football.

As Chairman of the Social Services Committee I could not dodge that. After long discussions I came to two conclusions. The first was that the Councillors, sitting as the Committee as a whole, had to take responsibility. We could not slough it off by having a special inquiry, by blaming the Government, by engaging Mr Blom-Cooper at enormous public expense to tell us what we already knew. In most of the horrible stories of child murder that have come to light in recent years, there has been no obvious shortage of money. On the contrary, there is often a plethora of publicly-paid staff from a variety of agencies going into the home on behalf of the child, but with a misplaced fear of antagonizing some parents whose belligerence might result in accusations of racism and prejudice.

The second conclusion I came to was that the murderer is not a victim: the child is. And the social worker is not the murderer or the abuser. Social workers won my admiration through those years in Birmingham, for, despite the occasional mistakes, they do their best on behalf of us all in a rotten job. The fact that most children from the most difficult homes grow up in one piece is often due to their efforts, none of which, when successful, attract the least attention. There are other culprits around who deserve a side-swipe of condemnation: the neighbours, those who pass by, those who turn up the television to drown the noise of the banging going on next door. On the other hand it is simply not good enough for professionals, with qualifications and years of training coming out of their ears, to disclaim responsibility. That, surely, is what being a professional is all about? If we *all* slough off the responsibility – parents, neighbours, social workers, health visitors, doctors, teachers – then how come the child died? Somebody must have heard the baby cry. We should not let the children cry in vain.

* * *

Cleveland is the new, 1970s name for the social services area covering Middlesbrough. The tragedy of 'Cleveland' was that it all started as a desire to spot child sexual abuse by a more certain method than any yet available. It got carried away on a wave of fanaticism and professional incompetence of the worst kind; and it made it harder from there on for the public either to believe social workers, or to listen for the faint cries of the children, for fear of getting it wrong. The diagnosis of doctors was also severely questioned and their stupidity in relying on a single mechanistic test in such a complex field of human behaviour was exposed. Virtually no one came out of it with their reputation intact, with the exception of the judge who headed the Cleveland inquiry. During the course of the inquiry Mrs Elizabeth Butler-Sloss was appointed the first woman Lord of Appeal in the country, an elevation richly deserved. She comes from a long-established legal family and her brother, Sir Michael Havers, was briefly Lord Chancellor in 1987. Ministers were keen to have a woman judge on the inquiry when the whole business broke, and she abandoned her family holiday to give us what she thought was just a few weeks to help. In fact, the whole thing took a year exactly, and with the previously published White Paper on changes in child-care law, and the legislation which followed (and which was largely planned before the inquiry, but became essential and urgent after it), ministers were to be personally involved in the affair from 1986 till almost 1990.

There is no place here to tell the full story. It isn't necessary, either, for the Judge's report, written in cool, clear English, tells as much as anyone can be certain of, and Stuart Bell MP's book, *When Salem came to the Boro*, provides the emotional background. Like many MPs on all sides of the house, I hold Stuart in high regard. He is vastly more intelligent and better-educated than the average Labour MP, and honourable and kind-hearted to boot. But I thought he was being a little naive in backing every single parent who came to him to complain, although it was clear that many of them had been deeply wronged, and wrongly accused, by the doctors who had examined their children. However, at least one family he backed to begin with harboured a member with convictions for child sexual abuse, and further convictions were to come. This weakened his case and put him on a collision course with the wilder women members of his own party. (For some of them, I suspected, there were simply no good men, an idea as dangerous as the opposite view I heard in the House of Commons tea-room, that there was no such thing as a deflowered toddler, either.)

During the mid-1980s, encouraged by the Department of Health, many local councils and health authorities had been looking at the way they dealt with what was euphemistically labelled 'NAI' (Non-Accidental Injury), in other words, damage sustained by the hand of another. It often showed up in hospital casualty departments as the child who wouldn't stop crying, or who was unnaturally quiet after a reported fall. Tests often showed broken bones and healed earlier fractures. There were clear procedures for these cases, well known to staff, which put the welfare of the child first, while terrible well-publicized cases such as those of Kimberley Carlile, Jasmine Beckford and Tyra Henry meant that they were always on the look-out for such indications. In 1983 the law had changed to give the social workers full rights to remove the child from home for up to twenty-eight days and parents had little option but to wait for the court hearing.

The scene was set for over-reaction somewhere. If there were spare hospital beds – and changing practice meant that many hospitals had spare beds at night in their children's wards – the kids could just be taken in, there and then, despite the fact that in virtually every other type of illness strenuous efforts are made to keep children out of hospital. I found, to my anger, that the official training video for doctors, which relied heavily on the advice of Leeds Doctors Wynne and Hobbs (who had helped train the doctors at the centre of the Cleveland controversy), perpetuated the notion that it was OK to plonk children – who were still only the subject of *possible* abuse – not in a children's home or with trained foster parents, but in a hospital bed, where they were cared for by nurses, alongside children dying of wasting diseases or being treated for cancer. It was all wrong in my view and at the launch of the video at the Royal Society of Medicine I had a fine old row with Jane Wynne about it.

So the health authorities in the Northern Region had decided, during 1986, to improve their services for children, and on 1 January 1987 a new doctor, a lady from Australia, married, with five children of her own, came to specialize in neonatal care and working with families in need. On paper she looked perfect and there were families who spoke up for her at the inquiry. The *Daily Mail* commented in its leading article on 7 July 1988, the day after publication of the Butler-Sloss report: 'Marietta Higgs is not a bad woman. It cannot be too much stressed that the only evildoers in Cleveland are the small minority of adults within the family who did genuinely subject children to sexual abuse.'

The problem was that she had been introduced to a new technique for detecting sexual abuse, RAD (reflex anal dilatation), which involved examining the anal canal. If it opened up, it was supposed to be a definite sign of previous penetration. The judge, however, concluded that although its presence might arouse suspicion, RAD was also a naturally-occurring phenomenon, and could have other innocent causes such as constipation, or worms.

Had Dr Higgs stuck to her last, the care of the newborn, or had the health authority perhaps checked what work she had devised for herself in her first weeks in the South Tees Health District, the ensuing events would possibly not have occurred. In the week beginning 1 May 1987 some nineteen children had been admitted to hospital in Middlesbrough, referred by Dr Higgs with the diagnosis of sexual abuse. By the end of May it was fifty, and at the end of an eight-week period to mid-June it was nearly 100. From the beginning of the year to the end of April there had been fewer than a dozen such admissions. Dr Higgs and her colleague, Dr Geoffrey Wyatt, were convinced that they were 'only finding what was there' and started looking for the RAD sign in other children who had been brought to the hospital by unsuspecting parents for other reasons. To their horror their child was whisked away, the label 'sexual abuse' slapped on with no more ado, and they were advised to go see a lawyer. That's what you say to criminals, isn't it? Before the whole business was finished even more children – over 200 – were involved.

The hospital wards overflowed with children, many of whom ran around driving the nurses crazy, while furious parents gathered at the ward door and threatened the doctors. The newspapers were filled for months with stories of families whose children had been dragged from them screaming by the doctors, who subjected them themselves, it was said, to painful and humiliating abuse masquerading as medical examination.

By mid-June 1987 parents were refusing to take their children to Middlesbrough General Hospital for fear of losing them altogether and all the local MPs were, quite rightly, making a major fuss. The Minister responsible was Tony Newton and, once again, we had reason to be grateful for his compassion and wisdom. The Chairman of the Northern Regional Health Authority, the redoubtable Professor Bernard Tomlinson, and his recently-appointed Medical Officer, Liam Donaldson, took charge and reported to Tony on 5 July 1987. I sat with Tony as he discussed with officials Bernard's report, the report of our own Inspector of Social Services and the papers which MP, Stuart Bell, himself a qualified lawyer with substantial experience, sent in.

The dry language of officialdom talked of 'interagency difficulties' – ugly rows between the police surgeons and the hospital doctors as to who was right. The police missed at least one case of a little girl who was later shown to be suffering from gonorrhoea. The files are bulky and the stories heart rending. At least one person accused committed suicide. Hidden in the files are cases of genuine abuse, but, as the judge pointed out with reference to more than one child in her report, the doctors didn't make proper notes and made no attempt to take forensic samples. We will probably now never know exactly who was right. What was obvious was that there would have to be a proper inquiry.

The situation was not helped by the fact that the European Court of Human Rights, in a judgement published on 8 July 1987, found against us on five unconnected cases brought by parents who had been denied access to their children. Our entire existing system had been examined and found wanting. Tony made the necessary announcement about the setting-up of the Butler-Sloss inquiry to a sombre House of Commons on the next day, 9 July. I sat next to him feeling sickened and sad.

No sooner was the inquiry set up than things started to happen. The police in Cleveland suddenly found it possible to appoint and train special officers, including women, to deal with this work. A separate building 'in hospital grounds' was provided by the health authority for the children concerned. Virtually all the professionals involved found themselves moved to other work. Money was allocated nationally for training in child abuse – in fact the law had to be changed to make this possible – and guidelines drawn up by the Department of Health for social workers, doctors, and nurses were eventually put out. CSA (child sexual abuse) had arrived in the professional vocabulary.

The Butler-Sloss inquiry sat for seventy-four days, heard 137 witnesses and received 500 statements. Stuart Bell was the final witness on 16 December 1987. The resulting report, which ran to 700 pages of typescript and 200,000 words, was published on 6 July 1988. Of the 121 children diagnosed by Doctors Higgs and Wyatt as cases of child sexual abuse, ninety-eight had been allowed to go home by the date of the report's publication, though some remained wards of court. But long afterwards, caution to the fore, Cleveland Social Services were still finding some thirty children per month who were believed to be victims of CSA – over 300 per year in just one county. Registers kept by the National Society for the Prevention of Cruelty to Children (NSPCC) estimated over 7,000 cases of child sexual abuse in 1987 in England and Wales.

Lord Justice Butler-Sloss's report repays a full reading. The best message to come out of it is the instruction to 'listen to the children' – advice based on the long experience at Great Ormond Street Hospital of Dr Ben-Tovim and his team. Little children don't lie, much. If they describe sexual experiences it is usually because they have had them. If they deny that they have been touched, they are probably telling the truth. Older children – teenagers – may be more manipulative of course. Corroborative and forensic evidence will always be needed in every case. It all demonstrated how wise are the rules of evidence in this country, but it is also good to see that the Home Office will now permit children to give evidence via a video link, so that they do not always have to endure the horrible experience of having to confront their abuser in court.

*   *   *

There was a more positive background to all this. I am a committed admirer of the television personality Esther Rantzen. With her Sunday evening programme, *That's Life*, she has highlighted many a problem with good-humoured and penetrating determination. When she took up the cause of child abuse, we knew something was going to happen. The BBC had carried out a survey on child abuse which suggested that sexual interference was much more common than was once believed. It resulted in a programme she devised called *ChildWatch*, put out on 30 October 1986. Esther and her team felt that what was missing from all the existing statutory and voluntary help was a telephone helpline service for abused children – Childline. She set one up on a wing and a prayer. Norman Fowler promptly provided £50,000 to help; the Prime Minister invited Childline to a Reception at Number 10 on 2 July 1987; and in the autumn of 1988 I was able to put government support for them on a firm footing with a regular grant of £100,000 per year.

The response to Esther's efforts was staggering. There were *56,000 attempted calls to Childline in its first twenty-four hours of operation*. Within eight months (to July 1987) the line had taken 105,000 calls, opened more than 16,000 case records and referred 240 cases to the authorities. Around 8,000 calls were being attempted each day during the summer of 1987. Of course, many of these were repeated attempts to get through, but even in 1989, with much-improved switchboards, at least 1,000 calls were being answered *every day*. By February 1989 nearly 500 cases had been referred to the authorities. There were also many occasions when a child will not give a name, but simply needs to talk, often several times, sometimes only once. I suspected that some of these children were practising, rehearsing, to see whether the strange things that were happening to them were credible to an adult, and to find out which words were needed to explain. Then many of those children would go and tell a sympathetic adult, a teacher perhaps, and events would take their course without Childline knowing anything about it – except that they do get pathetic little anonymous 'thank-you' letters from all over the country. Esther is often accused of going 'over the top'. Why not? It works, often. Not all battles are won by circulars from headquarters.

*   *   *

Nobody got the sack in Cleveland. None of those concerned accepted personal responsibility for what happened. It is exactly 100 years since the first ever Prevention of Cruelty Act of 1889 allowed police to enter a home on suspicion of cruelty to a child. We are still finding new versions of that cruelty.

7

Woopies and Woolly Hats

Grow old along with me!
The best is yet to be,
The last of life, for which the first was made
Robert Browning, 'Rabbi ben Ezra'

There are some old people who seem to glow. Frail, needing to be careful, closer to the next world than to this, they have an ancient wisdom, a slightly ethereal quality which maybe comes through having lived through more, having survived, with the understanding and compassion that survival brings. Dorothy Moriarty is like that. I met her at Help the Aged's London headquarters in St James's Walk. It is a rambling old building, crammed to the ceilings with boxes full of pamphlets, the old brick walls covered in gaudy posters, telephone lines manned by earnest volunteers in their seventies.

We were there to launch the booklet *Take Care of Yourself*, published by Help the Aged, one of the first books written for the old people themselves, instead of for the carers, about what to do for 'the elderly'. It is full of good advice on staying fit and well and coping with problems from holidays to incontinence. Dorothy herself, who was then aged ninety-eight, had written the chapter for what she called 'very senior citizens'. I particularly liked, and read out to the press conference, her section on putting on a brave face:

Do get it into your head that 'old' and 'ugly' are not synonymous. When I was ninety I was asked to a party to meet a local VIP. I put on my best wig, a treasured and well-tended two-piece, a dust of powder, a touch of lipstick, and yes, a whiff of lavender water.

At our introduction he came towards me, hands outstretched and a sudden smile on his face. 'Why, you're beautiful,' he told me.

You see, having been informed of my age, he expected to be confronted by a Witch of Endor, no less. I am not beautiful any more but I do use all the 'props' suitable and helpful in creating at least a pleasant impression on the people around.

Then, when I go to bed I put my dental 'bridge' into a tumbler, my wig on a stand, wash the make-up from my wrinkled face, and hope there will be no night emergency to rob my image of its glamour.

Dorothy had been a nurse and was full of tales of how it was in Miss Nightingale's day. The divine Florence, old martinet that she was, lived on till 1910, scribbling messages in pencil to the world from her sofa. There's one on the wall of the Nightingale Maternity Home in Derby which is now used as a hospice. Dorothy was encouraged by friends to write it all down, too, on a battered old typewriter, and it is being published. She will make a splendid television personality as she heads for 100.

*   *   *

In Western society as we look towards the next century, we face an astonishing phenomenon when, for the first time in our history, there is a large group of elderly people, most of them fit and well, living far beyond retirement age. This country has the second highest proportion of elderly in its population in the world, with only Sweden ahead of us, though other countries, such as Japan, are set to catch up within about twenty-five years. There are almost 10 million retired people already in this kingdom, almost one in five of the population and one in four electors. That overall 10 million figure will not now change very much, but within it the proportion and number of the very old are set to rise hugely in the next decade. On present projections, by the 2001 census there will be some 4.5 million people in this country over seventy-five, a million over eighty-five and half a million over ninety. We know that because they are with us already. Successful campaigns of prevention today will merely increase their number sometime into the *next* century.

The NHS can take some of the credit for this longevity, both by helping people over the risky patches in life, such as being born and giving birth, and by keeping the middle-aged fit and well. The years of austerity during and after the war, when today's pensioners were in their middle years, were helpful also, for that rough-and-ready diet with its rationed sugar and butter produced far less heart disease than the rosier years since. One result is that elderly patients are heavily over-represented in patient numbers. Some 60 per cent of all acute NHS beds – that is, excluding geriatric and most psychiatry beds – are occupied by people over retirement age and they are heavily represented in patient numbers in almost every branch of medicine.

Professor Eileen Murphy, the brainy and attractive Head of Geriatric Medicine at Guy's Hospital in London, told me she regularly teaches the new medical students, taking them on during the first week of their studies if possible. 'Hands up those who are going to be paediatricians?' she will say, and a few hands go up. 'And those who will be obstetricians?' A few more, fewer than there used to be, put off by fear of litigation and dislike of inevitable ghastly working hours. 'Well now, the rest of you will be specializing in care of the elderly,' she will tell them, and then explain, often to a chorus of groans from young men and women who thought they were going to be gastroenterologists or orthopaedic surgeons, that for the rest of their lives the bulk of their patients will be elderly people whose age and social background may well be factors in their care, treatment and recovery.

Tony Favell, the MP for Stockport near Manchester, told me that his local consultant ophthalmologist had done a head-count out of curiosity one week, and found that the average age for eye surgery (mostly cataracts) on his list was over ninety. The vast bulk of those operations, increasingly done under local anaesthetic, will restore both sight and independence for another decade or more. Similarly the majority of the rapidly increasing number of hip replacement operations, over 100,000 per year now, are done on older people. The hefty demand for them is directly linked both to population growth in that susceptible age group, and to the operation's high degree of success in restoring mobility. No more wheelchairs, no more pain, instead tea dances and shopping in ease and comfort once more. If the medical students don't like it, they had better leave now; as the middle-aged follow the young in taking for granted that they will be fit and well, so the shift in medicine towards the upper end of the age spectrum will accelerate.

Longevity not only poses problems for the NHS, but for income maintenance too. Many of today's old people worked before the days of company pensions. A substantial – but shrinking – proportion of them face retirement with only their state pension, and are very dependent on it to maintain their standard of living. There is a generation gap and we should be concerned about the older (mostly female) pensioners. The newer, younger pensioners are much better off, though oddly enough it is the younger pensioners, according to opinion polls, who worry more about money.

For most of the retired population, with or without their own pension, there is, nevertheless, a basic problem. They did not expect to live so long and they did not plan for it. Who, forty years ago, expected to live to ninety? How many of the women in the war-work factories expected that their retiring years would be longer than the years they spent at work? Not many, I'll bet. Yet it was at that time that a fully-funded pension scheme would have had to be created, to give them a high standard of living now, without having to call on their grandchildren to contribute. So the result is that we do not have fully-funded state pensions, but 'pay as you go'. The pensioner today gets his *entitlement* to a state pension from having paid contributions in the past, yet the *money* he receives week by week comes from today's taxpayer. The pensioner will say indignantly that he *has* paid for his pension. But it is his son and grandson who are putting the money in his pocket now. No wonder the savings ratio out of what is left stands at its lowest for many years. All the more reason to encourage today's workers to put good money into their own pension scheme, too. In my view – often expressed – that applies especially to women, whose working life may be shorter than a man's and yet who are likely to live longer. They should not casually depend on their partners for contributions towards a pension. The high divorce rate has put paid to those certainties. Anyway, real equality demands that we pay for our own, girls, and it may cost us far more than we expect.

*   *   *

Is old age a problem? No, I don't look at it that way. It is all very exciting; I am looking forward to being ninety, and actively planning for it – at the moment my ambition when I get there is to be awkward and eat cream cakes. What it doesn't promise, however, is a secure and honoured position in society. It is a slur on all of us that there are so many lonely and neglected old people in Britain today – neglected not so much in terms of money, but simply by being ignored by their families. In a way, it should be getting better. Two decades ago, many of the old people did not have families at all. Two million men died in the first war, so many fiancées lived on alone and childless into old age. The numbers of spinsters left behind are diminishing, but now more than 3 million old ladies, mostly widows, do live alone, and there are more every year. None of us planned it quite like that: but that's how it is.

When once there were few old people, when life expectancy was around forty, and technology did not change as fast as it does now, the old were regarded as a valuable reservoir of information and experience and were accorded a position of some importance. Retirement at sixty-five (or less) is a relatively recent phenomenon. A century ago, three-quarters of the men who survived to sixty-five were still working; now it is around one in ten. But pressure on the work-force will mean that proportion must start to increase again. Then, maybe, we'll stop treating elderly people as though they were all idiots.

In some societies whose demography has not yet caught up with ours, honouring the old is still the case, but not, perhaps, for much longer. I visited the Jaffray Hospital in Erdington, Birmingham, some years ago when I was on the health authority there, and was impressed with the care taken over the discharge of patients who had become infirm following surgery. 'Old Mr Patel won't be any problem,' the Sister remarked. 'He has three sons and two daughters, and they are all willing to have him. He is their revered father, they say, and they are not going to let him stay here.' And so the sweet old man was able to go home to the bosom of his family. But Mr Patel was the only member of his generation in that family still with us. I checked up my own family by contrast. Of the ten children born to my maternal grandparents, eight had survived into middle age, seven into old age, the youngest being sixty-six now. Between them they had only seven children. That will make it very much harder for the children – my generation – to take on the task of caring for them, particularly as some of us will also have to work, to pay taxes and National Insurance contributions, if there are to be the resources to care for them at all.

Some of the politics surrounding old people will probably have to change in the 1990s. All the political parties came in for a fearsome blast from Dr Eric Midwinter and Susan Tester of the Centre for Policy on Ageing in a book *Polls Apart? Older Voters and the 1987 General Election*, published in connection with Channel 4's *Years Ahead* programme. Looking at the way that elderly people were dealt with by manifestoes and party spokesmen, they said:

185

None of the parties seriously addressed the basic issue of older age in our society. Retirement remained, for the drafters of the documents, a kind of postscript to the long working life, to be eked out with welfare in cash and kind, rather than, for most people, a long and novel experience, requiring perhaps new values and sets of opportunities. This 1930s flavour was very apparent.

[It] is clear that, by and large, older people were seen by the politicians as welfare objects, as the recipients of benefits to make good deficiencies. The most vivid instance was probably the Alliance proposal for a double pension at Christmas, a truly awful sample of charitable condescension straight from the pages of *A Christmas Carol*. Most importantly, there were sins of omission. Not one item in any manifesto addressed itself to the central question of how the many millions of older people might, over retirements of twenty or thirty years, lead constructive lives and discover new identities.

Both voters and those who sought the votes were, in essence, agreed – mistakenly so, in the view of many of those closely concerned with the issue of ageing in our society; there was a correspondence in failing, in our opinion, to perceive the more long-term or profound factors of older age.

I agree with that! And none of the political parties should take pensioners' votes or positions for granted. In 1987, excluding 'don't knows', 40 per cent of over-sixties in Channel 4's case studies voted Conservative, compared with 34 per cent Labour and 25 per cent Alliance. (The electorate as a whole voted 42 per cent, 31 per cent and 22 per cent respectively.) Traditionally older people are marginally more Tory, but that may be because rather more women, and more middle-class people (both tending to be Tory), survive than working-class men (who tend to be Labour). 'Labour voters keel over quicker' would be a nasty little headline, but it's true. On the other hand, today's pensioners are not very political and we have seen only glimmers of a 'Grey Panther' movement as in the USA. Perhaps that is set to change, too; many of today's newly-retired voted for the first time in their lives in the Labour landslide of 1945.

We need, in my view, to work hard at four routes for securing for old people respect and comfort, rather than offering only endless welfare. First, we must maintain the productivity of the economy, so that we can go on paying for all those pensions, the NHS and related needs. That will include, in future, asking more of them not to retire at all.

Second, we must develop caring systems that are sparing of scarce manpower and yet maintain human contact, such as warden-service flats and alarm systems – isolation and loneliness are killers. The phone alone is not enough but it is better than no phone. Third, we should encourage the involvement of older people as organizers and carers (which is happening whether anyone plans it or not). We could not, for example, run the political parties without them. Fourth and most important, we need to find ways once again of honouring old people, helping them to feel wanted, not shunned, so that they, too, can look forward to the years ahead with pleasure and anticipation. Dorothy Moriarty and others like her have some of the answers. As I listened to her I resolved to stop talking about 'the elderly' as if they were an alien species instead of our own parents, and our own destiny.

*   *   *

Survival into old age – or any age – raises the question of the quality of life. Who wants to be old and in pain? Who wants to suffer, when death might bring a release? The question always surfaces, in one form or another, when prevention is discussed. People say they would rather keel over suddenly when still active than lose the ability to follow their interests, and become dependent on others. There is a deep-seated serious worry here which applies not only to the long years of retirement but, more poignantly perhaps, to the survival of handicapped children and babies.

Most people will come to their views through religion or conviction from other sources. I have never found it easy to pronounce on such issues, but I felt it was part of my job as Health Minister to ensure at least that very sick people were treated with kindness and not cruelty, so that their outlook on life as they came close to the end was not distorted by needless pain and anguish. In February 1987 I was involved in issuing a government circular on terminal care, the first ever put out by the Department of Health. It had been needed a long time and was urgent because of AIDS. We made it clear in that document (which has the effect of an instruction to the NHS, and followed extensive consultation with the medical profession) that there is a difference between active, curative treatment and palliative terminal care, in which every effort is made to make the patient comfortable. I liked the way families were included: 'The objectives are to control pain and other symptoms; to maintain independence as long as possible; to alleviate isolation, anxiety and fear; to make possible a comfortable, dignified end; and to provide support for the patient's family/close friends both before and after bereavement.'

The hospice movement has rightly divined that when pain is properly controlled and love moves into the sick-room, thoughts of helping people to die are stilled. The circular asked that voluntary agencies such as hospices should be included in planning by the health authorities and their services paid for. The pattern of care should include wise guidance and counselling; it is not enough to fill the patient full of morphine yet still expect him to cope alone with the prospect of meeting his Maker. On the other hand, it is almost beyond belief that, too often still, the painkillers are not available, or are withheld – from dying people – on the grounds that they are addictive, so that we still get death notices in local newspapers reading: 'On Saturday last, after much suffering . . .' I hope the day is not far off when death does not mean suffering, and we can all live each day to the full. Then notices like that will be a thing of the past, and perhaps the demand for euthanasia will recede too.

*   *   *

The acronym 'Woopies' (well-off older people) was not original. It had been around in the circles of those who care for elderly people for some time before I heard it at the November 1986 Annual General Meeting of the British Association for Service to the Elderly (BASE) in Stoke-on-Trent. It recognized, more than any statistics might, that there are now two groups of old people: not quite the haves and have-nots, not quite the younger elderly and the older elderly, and not just the healthier ones as oppose to the less healthy. 'Woopies' cuts across all those categories, and I suppose the reason I like the term is that it conjures up for me the image of a group of people with more leisure and choice than the rest of us, out of the rat race now, with fewer obligations and more freedom, with generally good health and plenty of mental energy, facing several years of well-earned retirement and determined to enjoy themselves.

There was an Opposition day debate on 25 February 1987 on priorities for the elderly and it was my job to close the debate. Not a big parliamentary event – despite the fact that the general election was likely to be called shortly, only five Labour MPs were present for the opening speech by the Labour spokesman Michael Meacher. Nevertheless, I did an enormous amount of reading for it and found myself fascinated by the changes facing old people. A few days later

John Major, then the Social Security Minister, who had opened the debate for us, put out a note via the Conservative Research Department which contained a lot of new material on the ownership of assets. John looks like a young professor, tall and slightly stooped, with greying hair and hiding behind owlish glasses, concealing one of the sharpest financial minds in British politics. To my surprise, he had found out that in 1986, on average, each person sixty-five and over had assets of £24,000. For the homeowners among them (half of all pensioner households) assets then were over £50,000, and must by now be very much higher. Pensioners' net assets are more than 50 per cent higher than non-pensioners' on average, since they tend to have repaid the mortgages and loans of their youth. 'Many of the calculations of concentrations of wealth ignore the fact that many of the wealthiest are also the oldest,' he wrote, 'who are rightly benefiting from their earlier providence.' Woopies indeed.

He pointed out that even in 1985 (the then latest figures), the average married pensioner household had a weekly income over £115, more than double the basic married pension paid for most of that year. The balance of pensioner income comes from SERPS (the State Earnings Related Pension Scheme), from other state benefits such as housing benefit, attendance allowance and the like, from occupational pensions, from earnings from employment and income from savings. Fifteen years ago only one pensioner in three had a works pension; by 1985 it was one in two and rising fast. Back in 1979 the value of SERPS would have been around 95p per week to the newly-retired person. By 1986 it was £16 per week, and now it is over £25 per week. Although the SERPS scheme, because of its expense, has been modified, that will not affect anyone retiring before the year 2000. By then the income from personal pensions, which just about everyone working will have, will be taking up any slack, and far more women will have pensions in their own right. John Major declared, 'We can now anticipate not merely the two-pension family with one state and one occupational pension, but also the four-pension family.'

These figures help demolish some of the unfavourable comparisons which are sometimes made with other European countries. They appear, it is said, to have larger state pensions than we have. It's worth pointing out, for starters, that their funds were built up when their economies were growing much faster than ours, when we seemed to be stuck forever in strikes, when 'The British Disease' meant a low-wage, low-productivity economy. It is only recently that we have shown the rest of Europe how to do it. But there are two other

189

differences which help us to close the gap. First, the large number of personal and occupational pensions which are now a feature of retirement in Britain, with 70 per cent of new pensioners enjoying them. They are less widely found in much of the rest of Europe. Second, it is common in England for women pensioners to claim a state pension not in their own right, but on their husband's contributions. Again, that is rare elsewhere – the wives and widows do far less well. The pensioner household is thus both more secure and rather better off in Britain, and frankly I don't plan to move.

It also means, in the UK as in many other countries, that the proportion of wealthy pensioners will go on increasing throughout this century. Pension funds in this country are already a major force in capital markets. Look at other countries: among those aged over sixty-five in the USA, more than 72 per cent own their house compared with a *lower* figure for the under sixty-fives, while in Japan a recent survey by the Bank of Japan found that people over sixty owned more financial assets than any other age group. Oh yes, and by the early part of the next century, because of declining birth rates in the 1960s and 1970s, close to half the work-force of some countries will be over fifty. Granny power is here to stay; the woopies are only part of it.

*   *   *

During the spring of 1988 I was partly engaged in testing the water for some of the new ideas floating around concerning the funding of health care in this country in future. During Thames Television's *This Week* programme of 24 March 1988, I said: 'I think we should reflect that many elderly people are very fit, and increasingly anxious to maintain their health. They are willing to get involved in insurance schemes, albeit at a slightly more expensive level than when they are working.' And again, later: 'Something like half our pensioners own their own homes and most of them own them outright. They are substantial asset owners.' Prodded by the *Today* newspaper I softened the line slightly, but refused to withdraw it. 'I was merely making the point that widening choices are emerging that are not exclusive to the younger age group. There are all sorts of possibilities and exciting ideas.'

The rules about asset liquidation were, however, complicated. I knew, as does anyone who has served on a social services committee, that since the establishment of the welfare state, anyone entering an old people's council home will have their assets valued and will be expected to pay accordingly. Since the council home is now their permanent residence, the councils were within their rights to insist that the previous home be sold and the cash balance counted as part of the old person's wealth. The residents must then pay up until nearly all their funds have gone. When social security took over these payments, the rules were tightened, and are now quite strict, rightly in my view. It was found, for example, that some people simply left their house empty; its sale then formed part of the estate when they died and went to the beneficiaries of the will or, worse, the family sold it and spent the money on themselves, leaving granny to be looked after in penury by the state.

We had had a case like this in Birmingham when I was chairman of the Social Services Committee, back in the 1970s. A rather wealthy lady had gone a bit senile and no private home would take her. The council had fifty old people's homes in those days and willingly we took her on. Her financial circumstances were assessed – it was months before we got round to it – and then we found that the property had been sold and the assets had vanished. It was when I discovered that her son had bought a yacht with some of the money that I decided this was not on. Despite our asking nicely, he bluntly refused to have anything to do with her. Meanwhile, she was costing the ratepayers (of whom he was not one) more than £50 per week. (It was a long time ago!) We discovered, to our horror, that the only way we could get any money out of him was to declare her a bankrupt, and to ask in court for her assets, which we could claim had been wilfully disposed of, to be returned forthwith. I drew the line at this drastic proposition. Instead I sent one of my larger staff to go and talk to the son, who was a prominent local businessman, just once more. Exactly what was said, I don't know, but the official came back with a broad grin, said that he'd just mentioned my name, the way the local press reported my innermost feelings, and the man had caved in after a bit of bluster! He coughed up half the cost of her care and we all breathed a sigh of relief.

So I knew that not only was it possible to turn a house into payment for care, it was, in fact, the law. This now also covers claims for social security made by the many thousands of people who enter private residential homes. There are lots of complaints from elderly people who feel their savings and assets should be sacrosanct, but no government would ever agree: there has to be a limit. What bothered me then, and still does, was that it was so difficult to do anything else useful with the asset. Only if you gave up your home and went into permanent residential or nursing home care, could you release this money. Jack Jones, the TUC pensioners' leader, said of my efforts,

'It is absolutely outrageous to suggest that elderly people should give up the security of their own homes.' Well, yes, I couldn't agree more, but until the system is reformed it's tricky to do otherwise. If you want to stay put, and pay for a home help, that's much harder. If you want to put in central heating or double glazing or a downstairs loo, that requires some tricky negotiating with a bank or building society. Too many pensioners are in valuable property but struggling to pay the gas bill. Most of the old people don't want to borrow – they feel relieved that they have finished with all that. And (at least before 1988), if you were elderly and you wanted health insurance, the companies would turn up their noses at you.

The professional bodies, claiming to speak for pensioners, over-reacted to my efforts in 1988 on that latter point. Even as late as June 1988 the delightful Sally Greengross, Director of Age Concern, was telling the *Independent* that 'None of the major health insurance companies offers comprehensive cover to new subscribers over sixty-four.' No insurance company will offer blanket cover at any age for pre-existing disease; I couldn't get it to cover my asthma, for example. But I did hope that my chattering in the spring of that year might encourage some of the insurance companies to be more generous and imaginative, and so it proved. In March 1988 Private Patients Plan, which used to refuse comprehensive health cover to new members over sixty-five, announced a change in the rules to allow them to join at premiums ranging from £40 to £61.50 per month. It also introduced a cut-price scheme which provides private cover if there is a wait of more than six weeks for NHS treatment (as there is in many places for hip replacement and cataract operations), with monthly premiums for the 65 to 69 age group starting at £17.05. There are other schemes, too, and no doubt there will be more by 1990. Darling Sally, please note. Discrimination in health insurance has also been splendidly dealt with by the Chancellor in the Budget of March 1989. From April 1990 health insurance for the over sixties will be tax deductible, and the payer claiming the tax relief could be someone else – the son or daughter, perhaps?

But the frozen assets with their frozen inhabitants still bothered me. In Chester on 22 April 1988 I made what became known as 'the woopies speech': 'We are into the age of the "woopy" – the well-off old person – and it is about time we all recognized that fact, planned for our own future, and helped them to enjoy theirs.'

I had described the situation of people who were 'asset rich and income poor' and said, 'I think the situation is crazy . . . It should be just as easy to raise money on a property when the owner is sixty as when he is thirty, and even easier (not harder) when he is eighty.' And so it would be, if the banks and property markets had their heads screwed on. Let me emphasize, I am not talking about selling up and losing the home, but about raising money on it while staying put and retaining ownership and occupancy and control. The borrowing could be some form of term loan, payable eventually out of the proceeds of the house when the owner had died. Again, I knew it could be done, because we had done just this when renovating old property in Birmingham as part of the Urban Renewal programme. There the Council had the discretionary power to give grants up to 90 per cent. The owners had to find the 10 per cent, which was beyond some of them. So we did a nice deal with the Woolwich, who were very helpful, and hey presto! a term loan was available, with a lien on a house which would still be worth more, probably several times over, than the value of the debt when it came to be repaid. Most of the old Brummie pensioners told me cheerfully that you can't take it with you, and were delighted to sign up and have an indoor loo for the first time ever.

One of my nicer colleagues in the house, Bournemouth MP, John Butterfill, an estate agent by trade, knew a lot more about the subject of asset release than I did. He has twice the national average of pensioners on his voting register and many of his constituents were in exactly the difficult position I was highlighting. John sent me a cutting from the *Daily Express* of 27 January 1988 which illustrated the problem. Smart-looking *Express* reader Joan Briggs, aged seventy-seven, who lived in a west London suburb, had a house worth around £100,000. She was photographed, looking delightfully woopy, in her garden. To increase her income she had borrowed £30,000, the maximum the bank would agree, on a home income plan. She took a lump sum of £1,000 and the rest was spent on an annuity, which provided her with just over £70 per week before deductions. But after paying back the interest on the loan, and the tax, her income was halved. That made it seem not worth it really. John was pressing the Treasury to accept the amendment to the Finance Bill he had put down, in which such a loan would qualify for tax relief, and where the interest could be added to the loan and repaid eventually out of the proceeds on the sale of the house. John had collected 233 MPs' signatures to an early-day motion (a form of parliamentary petition), and it was clear that here was an issue that wouldn't go away.

I followed the financial debate with interest, though, as a Minister,

I was not able to sign the motion. Norman Lamont, the Financial Secretary to the Treasury, had the difficult job of pointing out that the real problem was the artificial limit placed on the size of the loan by the banks and building societies. He was right. Watch. When Joan Briggs dies, the financiers will fall over themselves to lend the new purchaser of her house three times as much as Joan was lent, not because the property is worth any more but because he is younger. Their caution is misplaced. There is a huge market of cautious borrowers out there, with equity coming out of their ears, millions of them, just waiting till the financial market drops its silly rules and starts looking after them.

The point about tax relief was answered when the age allowances for pensioners were made much more generous in the 1989 Budget. The Treasury Ministers do listen! So now Joan should have rather more of her income untouched, and I do hope she is enjoying it.

Much of the press discussion of the question of the woopies and their frozen assets was limited to ritual condemnation, which was frankly disappointing. The *Evening Standard* printed a story in their gossip column that my mother had 'years ago remortgaged her semi-detached, bright-blue painted house in Liverpool in exchange for bunce to help her opt out of the NHS'. That was news to my brother and me – as far as we knew, she hadn't needed anything doing to herself for years. The story was completely untrue, but it shows you why many MPs are sympathetic to the idea of right-to-reply legislation; it might just make the press check first. The *Sunday People* protested that old people might prefer to buy a new car or a dream holiday with the money. Maybe, but that suggested, yet again, that health and personal care, however necessary or desirable, were regarded firmly by their readers as the exclusive province of the state with personal possessions and luxuries more important. I sighed about those values and priorities. Age Concern was reported to be 'up in arms' again, apparently forgetting that, along with Help the Aged, they had circulated all MPs in early January 1988, calling attention to the problem themselves, and asking members to sign John Butterfill's motion. It was not the last time they were to offer a knee-jerk criticism of a view very close to some of their own promotional material.

Only Alan Cochrane, in the *Mail on Sunday*, covered himself with glory as far as I was concerned, with headlines like 'It's time our well-off OAPs cashed in on their assets', and full-page articles saying, look at it, it's important and something needs to be done. He had to put up with a tremendous amount of flak and was looking distinctly shell-shocked in the lobby late one afternoon but, bless him, he stuck to his guns. On 1 May 1988 his headline read, 'Not granny bashing but Woopy Lib', and continued:

My view is that Britain's old people are a much put-upon minority, especially those worth a few bob . . . I suspect that a sizeable proportion of those who are 'asset rich but income poor' remain so because their families are content for them to remain so. There are those who don't mind their aged parents living in not-so-genteel poverty, just so long as they leave the house intact, with no debts outstanding, in their will. The last thing they want is for mum and dad to realize some of those assets and actually live decently, never mind enjoying themselves. That would deprive junior of the cash to buy a cottage in the Dordogne, and we can't have that!

An international estate agent told me soon after that more than 40 per cent of the private residential property bought in Spain in 1987 was sold to Brits. Some of them, no doubt, were pensioners, selling up and clearing off to sit in the sun. The others, younger, main home in Bradford or Bristol, may well have chosen Puerto Pollensa instead of the Dordogne. Makes you think.

The weekend after I made the 'woopies' speech I was due to attend a lunch-time buffet in the home of a supporter in the constituency. The weather was fine and sunny so we held it outdoors on the elegant patio. I arrived to find my way barred by two smart-looking elderly gentlemen, moustaches a-bristle, one waving a glass of wine and the other puffing away at a huge cigar and mopping his brow with a silk handkerchief. 'Mornin', Mrs Currie!' they chorused, dancing around, looking just like characters out of *Duck Soup*. I half expected Groucho Marx to come jumping out of the bushes. 'Do you know what we are? Weeeeee're WOOPIES!!!' and they collapsed hooting with laughter in an untidy little heap on a garden bench.

One of the ladies came bustling over, clicking her tongue crossly. 'I told them not to do that,' she said, 'but there's no stopping them. They've been practising for hours, ever since you said it, you know. *They* think it's a compliment,' and dragging her husband by the shoulder she marched him off.

The other gentleman gave me a roguish wink and followed. I looked around at the large gathering, sipping their drinks, sun in their eyes, chattering animatedly. Though most were not wealthy in cash terms, lots of them were woopies, having a grand old time, and good luck to them.

What did I learn? I suppose, if I were doing it again, I would sit down with the voluntary groups, the charities who do work very hard (for all my carping) and who are in contact with thousands of old people, and I would talk the topic through with them first, hoping that when the subject hit the public consciousness they might just agree and give some support. It would be a bit new for them to say 'Yep, the Government's got it right'. They are, after all, pressure groups, and if the Government always got it right their continued existence (funded of course by Government grants) might come into question. But one of these days the woopies will be so dominant we will all have to change our tune.

*   *   *

I had always been interested in the problems of death in winter. Back in Birmingham in the 1970s we used to have a campaign of sorts every winter to try to protect our old people. The year I got involved we called it 'Keep an Eye on Gran', and encouraged all our door-knockers – milkmen, postmen, newsboys – to watch for signs of inactivity in an elderly person's house, and to call the police or emergency services if there was any suspicion that the silence might mean a fall or blackout. We encouraged neighbours and families to be more thoughtful and I made a speech, recalling that famous picture of my youth in the Walker Art Gallery, entitled 'When did you last see your Granny?' The then Director of Social Services, Ron Liddiard, appeared in the local newspapers in a woolly night-cap and clutching a hot-water bottle, to give elderly Brummies sensible advice on coping with the winter. And the only complaints came from the Grandads who wanted to know tartly whether they were to be included or not?

It worked, though. One very bad snowy winter we made huge efforts to keep in touch with the city's large number of old people living alone. At the end of the winter we councillors studied a report. There had been eight known deaths from hypothermia, in all that great city of a million people, and all were known to the authorities, had been offered help and had refused it. You can't force assistance down people's throats. On at least one occasion I had to explain to the local press that we did *not* have the right to cart people off protesting from their own homes, however miserable, if they did not want to move. So I was keen right from the start that the Department

196

of Health should have some sort of winter health campaign for old people.

We were tackling a problem dubbed 'excess winter mortality' (EWM). The difference in mortality between summer and winter, which we note in this country, is small and getting smaller. It is simply not true that vastly more people die in winter any more. Every year in England and Wales we register about 560,000 deaths. In 1987 the difference between deaths in winter and deaths in summer was 25,000. Twenty years earlier it was 60,000 – and life expectancy was lower then, too. In other countries they have excess summer mortality as people keel over in the hot weather. The target was to reduce that differential further, and I hoped it might be possible to make it disappear altogether.

The old Health Education Council had launched a five-year pro-gramme for education on health in old age in September 1984. I'm afraid that although I was a back-bencher and member of the House of Commons Select Committee on Social Services, the event passed me by, though slowly I became aware of bits of it. There was, for a start, the 'Age Well' campaign, all about sensible eating and similar advice. That was run jointly with Age Concern and was launched in July 1985. There was the 'Centre for Health and Retirement Education', which was involved in training health education specialists in the particular problems of the elderly. There was a carers' programme, launched in October 1985 with the Kings Fund, which produced lots of rather good information packs. So there was plenty going on, but it could not be said it agitated the public imagination very much at the time.

Age Concern were one of the voluntary groups active in the campaigns, and I loved 'Celebrating Age', their effort to persuade people that retirement was there to enjoy, which was their main campaign during 1987. We did not neglect the more difficult problems either, in case you think I'm only interested in woopies, and in October 1987 I helped them launch their excellent information leaflets on the management of incontinence. Back in 1970, under the title 'The National Old People's Welfare Council', Age Concern had had a total income for the year of £50,000. In 1987 total income exceeded £10 million, so somebody cares. The organization will celebrate its fiftieth anniversary in 1990. Help the Aged is the other main charity, much of the work of which goes on overseas, but they were very much involved with all these campaigns.

Then there were two other smaller important organizations, both of which treated me to thoroughly enjoyable and thought-provoking afternoons. 'Extend' is the older ladies' branch of the Women's League of Health and Beauty, where they still prance around with scarves to bracing music, gentler and altogether more ladylike than aerobics classes or Jane Fonda (probably less dangerous too). The branch in Long Eaton, Derbyshire, just outside my constituency, were celebrating their 10th anniversary one Saturday afternoon, and they'd like me to come. Other groups would be turning up and it would be quite an event.

They were right! From my seat on the platform with the other local notables, the hall seemed to stretch into the distance, and we could see dozens of pretty scarves waving gently in time to the music as the graceful line tiptoed in. Not a one under sixty, I was told, but without a trace of self-consciousness (why should there be?) the ladies went briskly through their paces. Extend does it gently, but enough to streeeetch the muscles, get that flexibility, reeeach up and again, creak those knees, get the heart going a bit, a warm flush on the cheeks. No, these ladies don't perspire, but the glow was clearly visible from where we were sitting. Then they brought on the oldies, the over-eighties, and the guests were invited down from their perch to join in. They played the music 'Strolling', we all lined up in a crocodile, and we were off.

The idea was to shuffle or step along, depending on how firm you were on your pins, and just rock gently to the rhythm. The pale lady next to me had been hauled out of a wheelchair and clung to me, looking terrified. She was ninety, she told me, and the staff at the nearby old people's home had brought them all along to see. She had not expected to be joining in and found it a bit frightening. Gradually, however, as we shuffled sideways and back, forwards and together, and the other ladies sang along with the music, her confidence grew and her hold on me lessened. We turned, and she was in front of me, my hands on her waist, doing no more than steadying her on her spindly legs. She was singing, in a high little quaver: 'Stro-o-o-ll-innggg! Just stroooooooling, in the light of the mooon abooooooooove!' We turned again, and she was grinning from ear to ear: 'Oooh! Isn't this lovely! I don't eeenvy the rich in their hautomobeeeeles . . .'

The music stopped at last, we were all puffing and blowing and laughing and collapsing in each other's arms. I helped her back into her wheelchair, her face flushed and happy. 'Now did you enjoy that?' I asked.

'Oooh yes,' she answered. 'It beats watching the football on the box any day. Can we come again?'

Once, long ago, I had been involved in increasing the numbers of sheltered housing schemes back in Birmingham. We decided we didn't want too many wardens who were ex-nurses. These were not nursing homes, they were little flats and bungalows for people who might need a bit of help, an eye kept on them, but whose real need often was companionship and the security of knowing there was someone there. One of the wardens we chose was a retired entertainer and his unit was always popular. Whenever I visited, the joint always seemed to be jumping with some lively event going on from morning to night. At another unit, the sad death of a man of eighty-eight occurred and there had to be an inquest. It turned out that the old people were all having a party and he had decided to demonstrate the Can-Can. He had dislocated his hip and died a few days later in hospital of bronchio-pneumonia. His family told me he'd had a wonderful time since moving there, and no, they would not be pressing any complaints.

The other organization was Contact. Their chosen task was to reduce isolation by arranging tea parties. What a good idea, I said: let's have some of their members to tea with us and we'll ask them for ideas and opinions.

This was not long after the Department had moved from the dreadful dump at the Elephant and Castle, called Alexander Fleming House, to the restored splendour of Richmond Terrace, just off White-hall. A government long-since gone had wanted to pull it down, but the conservationists, rightly, kicked up a fuss and by the time we moved in, in January 1988, over £38 million had been spent on it. That's what hand carving costs, and putting lifts into an old building and the like. It was a splendid place. Minister for the Disabled, Nick Scott's room was the old library, lined with carved wooden panelling, which promptly and tragically started to crack and peel in the dry heat. Among the books on his shelves was a false section, bound in bright tooled leather. The titles were all to do with building and engineering, and the 'authors' were the main people who had been involved in the restoration work – the clerk of works and so on. Nice touch, that.

My room was large and plain and not suitable for a tea party, for I like to work at a very big table, with papers spread all over it. It's a bit like playing pelmanism as I, and only I, know where every item is as long as no one moves it! So we booked the main room, above mine, which had been the ballroom or gallery in the grander days gone by. The room is, as it should be, a double cube, all white with gold trimmings, except by the door where finger-marks are turning the door jamb a sticky grey. The furniture is, I suppose, Regency; it looks like Byron's stuff kept still in Newstead Abbey. But don't lean too hard on the beautiful circular table because it is modern and it will *collapse*. Glorious fireplaces, great deep mirrors, elegant windows giving onto the Ministry of Defence, so that we can see the bands massing outside, rehearsing for some state visit next week, shaking the spit out of their trumpets, adjusting their blue cloaks and chatting. And the chandeliers! Real ones, twinkling away, not giving much light, but conferring an air of opulence that most staff in the busiest department in Whitehall hardly notice most of the time.

The elderly people, looking nervous, were already there as I came in. Tea in my own Crown Derby china, sandwiches, cakes – nice juicy ones, cream oozing out – huge strawberries in sticky jammy tarts, *mille-feuille* crumbling on the plate. Make it a real treat, I had told the officials, and they had. And I ate my share, too, waving my arms to emphasize a point and leaving bits all over the new carpet.

They talked a lot of sense and many of their ideas we promptly took on board. One lady pointed out the difficulties that widows, especially, face. The first part of retirement, she said, can be truly wonderful. A good income, travel, comfort and company. 'Then you lose him, and it all goes wrong,' she said. 'Firstly you lose a great big chunk of pension, but your expenses for the house are just the same. More, sometimes, because he used to do the repairs and now I have to get a man in. Then your transport disappears; as I don't drive, the car had to go. Then the tax man treats you as a single person and you can find yourself paying more tax; and most women have left all that, the financial side, to their husbands, so it's very confusing and upsetting.'

That was a message we passed on to colleagues elsewhere, but now I always advise my own constituents to share financial planning from early in married life, and to make a will, so that the survivor is not burdened with impenetrable bureaucracy and red tape as well as worries about the future.

One lady stuck in my mind. She was elegant, carefully dressed and sat bolt upright in her chair. Let's call her Annie. She didn't believe in doctors, they did more harm than good. She had only ever been to a doctor four times in her life. She turned out to be a woman of quite indomitable character, for her real complaint was the state of her housing. She was a council tenant with Brent Council who were always busy crossing swords with the Department and the Government. Annie wrote to me after the tea party asking for some help, and as it happened I was in Brent that evening and asked

Renée Myers, Chairman of Brent and Harrow Family Practitioner Committee and a kind and practical woman, if she would nag the Council and see if anything could be done. I picked the right lady to ask and the two have kept in close touch since.

Not long after I resigned I had a letter from Renée enclosing one to her from Annie:

> I was feeling so alone, miserable, cold and bewildered in my damp draughty flat. The background gas heating was faulty when I moved into the flat and after tradesmen tried to get it in working order again it broke down altogether. The parts needed to put it in working order could not be found so, as my cooker and immersion heater were electric, I had the gas meter removed and the rental charge not having any longer to be paid, I spent the money on buying electric fires. The flooding last July from a burst pipe in the bathroom in the flat above me damaged the heat-and-light heater in my very cold draughty bathroom. The bathroom is in such a bad state I have been forced to have a bath at friends houses which is not very good for an OAP aged ninety-one years and living alone. The flat is lovely in summer and I feel lucky to have it in these days when so many people are homeless.

This is what life is like in London today for some of our old people, the ones who definitely aren't woopies, living under a council elected to care for them, which has plenty of money and, no doubt, plenty of excuses.

The very cold spell in January 1987 gave impetus to the worries about old people, especially those on restricted incomes. A big publicity campaign surrounded the introduction by John Major of a new scheme for exceptionally cold weather payments, and during that year some three-quarters of a million people put in a claim – not all of them elderly – contrasting well with 170,000 in 1985 and under half a million in 1986. There are sensitivities in all this, of course. If there is a government campaign and lots more people come forward, there's the risk that the Opposition might claim it as evidence of considerable unmet need. It seems to me that government, by having such a campaign, is meeting that need and no one should be either mealy-mouthed or embarrassed about it. But concentrating almost exclusively on those needing benefit is to disregard the general improvement in living standards of the many.

The improvements show through in several ways, most of all in that steady fall in excess winter mortality. My target was an ambitious one indeed – to see an eventual end to this phenomenon, to come to a similar position, as in Sweden, where there is virtually no difference, summer or winter, in the number of deaths. It could be done, if we could get people to take seriously the scraps of advice we could give them, and act on them. Hence the emergence of 'woolly hats' in the autumn of 1988.

There was a deeper and quite serious motive behind my advice, which harks back to valuing old people and giving them an honoured place in our society. There we were, bashing away at prevention for the middle-aged, cajoling people to come with us on this new bandwagon. I was beginning to get letters from old people complaining about feeling neglected. They queried particular aspects of the health programmes we were promoting – asking, for example, why there was a limit of sixty-five on the cancer screening systems – but they were really saying, it seemed to me, 'Don't we count? There are ten million of us, but you're only interested in the younger ones. How do *we* stay fit and well, or don't you care about us?' Of course we did, so developing such a campaign was indeed part of caring for them. It was also intended to bring their care back into the mainstream of our approach to health. If we were asking others to change their life-style, we should ask elderly people, too.

Attitudinal research shows there was no particular age at which someone feels they cross over into being old. A Gallup Poll in September 1988 told me that 62 per cent of younger pensioners (aged 64 to 74) regarded their health as 'good' or 'very good' compared to slightly *more* – 63 per cent – of the 75+ group. At the same date, when asked what their priorities were for the NHS, nearly half (46 per cent) of the pensioners surveyed said they wanted it to 'develop and offer ways of preventing illness', with support ranging from 44 per cent among blue-collar workers to 63 per cent among people from a professional or managerial background.

I was often accused of being patronizing of older people, but surely it would be far more patronizing to assume or imply that they were past it, not capable of choice, not interested in change, not able to act on advice. That's the quickest way to write them off, to consign them to the rubbish dump of the unneeded and unheeded, and for me it goes against the grain.

However, sauce for the gosling wasn't sauce for the gander. I might tell a young woman to go jogging and give up the cigarettes as the best way of avoiding early menopause and osteoporosis. Her granny probably didn't smoke anyway and was already suffering from frail bones; energetic exercise would put her in hospital in no time. On the other hand, diet patterns assume an even greater importance as we get older, for the less mobile need fewer calories than the young and being overweight reduces mobility far more for old people. They needed health advice, but it was *different* advice. What should it be?

I asked officials for some basic reading on health in old age, and was introduced to the remarkable work of Professor Bill Keatinge and his team at the London Hospital Medical School. I have never met him, but he was originally Professor of Physiology and is now the Dean of the Medical School. His department became involved in the 1980s doing research on divers in the North Sea, of all things. It had long been known that shipwreck victims are for more likely to die of cold ('exposure') than by drowning: you'll find that observation from the 5th century BC in Herodotus. During the second war it was realized that the majority of the 30,000 men lost by the Royal Navy died in the water rather than by battle injuries, and that without thermal protection they had often died from simple body cooling. The North Sea divers often seemed to make silly mistakes down below which sometimes cost them and colleagues their lives. The research showed that as the body cools something happens to the circulation in the brain and even fit individuals become disorientated, confused and forgetful. Did this help account for EWM perhaps?

I read with fascination Keatinge's Oliver-Sharpey Lecture of 1985, which was published in the more esoteric pages of the medical literature on 4 October 1986 soon after I was appointed, and his study of how elderly residents of two of Anchor Housing Association's centrally-heated sheltered housing schemes fared in the cold snap of January 1986, which was published in the *BMJ* of 20 September 1986.

What was apparent from the research was this: a cold person frequently doesn't feel cold. But their body changes in ways which can be very hazardous and of which they are unaware. Analysis of the EWM deaths in 1978 by Messrs Bull and Morton, in the *Age and Ageing* learned journal, had already shown it was *not* hypothermia which accounts for most of these deaths. Hypothermia causes only about 1 per cent of the excess deaths in winter, and most of those tend to be people who have collapsed of *something else* in cold surroundings and lain a long time before being found. If it wasn't hypothermia, what was it? The answer is that old people were dying in winter of heart attacks, strokes, thrombosis, chest infections, pneumonia.

You can't start experimenting on frail old people, so the London

Hospital took some fit young adults and stood them in cold air for six hours till they were shivering and blue with cold. The results were extraordinary: up went their blood pressure, markedly; the pulse rate slowed; the blood thickened measurably; the cholesterol level rose; the count of the red blood cells and platelets rose sharply. The danger of blood clots was obvious. Here was a sign for us: 'The increases in platelets, red cells, blood viscosity, arterial pressure and plasma cholesterol could clearly all contribute, to different degrees, to the increase in arterial thromboses in cold weather,' they said.

Now, this is a phenomenon for everyone, not just old people. Yet young people recover very quickly and old people don't. Why? Probably because so many older people in Britain already have a weakened heart, already have furred-up arteries, already have raised blood pressure. Under these circumstances getting cold can produce blood clots, which could bring on a heart attack or stroke quite easily. Angina can come on within minutes. Bull and Morton had already demonstrated that deaths from coronary thrombosis reached a peak within twenty-four hours of a cold day. Numbers of deaths from a stroke reach a maximum four days after exposure to cold. And days or weeks later deaths from pneumonia and other chest diseases brought on or exacerbated by tiny clots follow.

Perhaps the habits of some old people didn't help. This is what Keatinge found at Anchor Housing:

Between 0900 and 1600 on 17 January 1986 after overnight frost, the air temperature outside two homes was 2.3–4.4°C; the sublingual (beneath the tongue) temperature of fourteen residents, seven in each home, was 36.5°C, the skin temperature on the back of their hands 30.7°C and the temperature indoors where these fourteen readings were made 22.1°C. Each of the residents had a window open and had set all radiators below maximum. All but one said that they switched off all heating, with windows open, at night. All of the seven who were fit enough made daily excursions outside, walking up to four miles and waiting for buses for up to forty minutes.

As a result, he found that mortality among the fortunate residents of Anchor was identical to mortality among the general population over sixty-five. He went on:

The simplest explanation is that though the quality of life was higher with heated housing, the beneficial effects on mortality of the high indoor temperatures were balanced by the adverse effects of increased exposure to cold outdoors. The results therefore suggest that the traditional tendency of the British to expose themselves to fresh air may be as important as poor heating in causing excess mortality during the winter.

He put it more vigorously to the *Independent* on 18 November 1986: 'Before we had central heating people wore much more similar clothing indoors and out of doors in Britain. People still tend to do the same and put on too few extra clothes when they go out. They don't wrap up well enough because they often don't realize how cold it is until they have been out for half an hour.' And later, in 1988, as I started talking about woolly hats, he made two more observations: 'I sometimes wonder if the free London bus pass didn't kill more old people than the Blitz.' And 'The great British belief that fresh air is good for you should be re-examined when it comes to the elderly.' In *Good Housekeeping* magazine in February 1989 he wondered thoughtfully why, with their far worse winters, there is less hypothermia and no EWM in Scandinavian countries: 'In Scandinavia it gets very dark in winter. In Stockholm, for example, it's just getting light mid-morning and it's getting dark again mid-afternoon, so people aren't so tempted to go walking about.' Di Latham, the *Good Housekeeping* journalist, suddenly got the message: 'Just try stopping your grandfather digging the garden on a sunny, bitter day in March. Try telling your lonely neighbour that it is better to stay indoors than wait for a bus to get her to a WI meeting. If people did constantly drop at our feet in the streets, there would be a massive publicity campaign. But it is still an unnecessary waste of life.'

Now it takes time for the blood changes to cause illness. The heart attack may not happen till the next day, the stroke may not occur till after the weekend. By then the fact of having become very cold, briefly, for an hour or two will have been forgotten entirely. It is complicated medical stuff, this business about platelets and thrombosis, but I hope I understood it and its implications. Don't get cold, don't get chilled, wrap up warm. And it was a great pleasure to get a letter from Professor Keatinge in January 1989 saying quietly: 'The part that I heard of the interview you gave on the *Today* programme about winter mortality presented the facts clearly and was accepted by most people in the field who heard it.'

You don't believe that people do silly things like going out without warm clothes? But look at what happened in the coldest days of January 1987, when more than thirty inches of snow fell even in Kent. In Huddersfield, West Yorkshire, a lady, aged eighty-four, was found dead in her garden. She had gone out in her nightie to feed the birds. Mr Robert Wann, aged seventy-three, died after trying to walk four miles to his cottage in bitter easterly winds and drifting snow one evening. Fife police said: 'It would appear he entered the field to avoid snow drifts on the road and had been overcome by the severe weather conditions.' Not only elderly people suffer in that sort of weather – at least one lorry driver collapsed and died in his cab. In Northern Ireland, an eighteen-year-old youth was treated for severe hypothermia after searchers found him wandering in mountains in County Down. An experienced hill-walker, he had been missing since the previous night. Perhaps the cold had the same effect on the mental state of all these people as it had on divers: they started to do uncharacteristic things, became disorientated and confused, and then collapsed quite quickly.

As early as November 1986 there were discussions about EWM in the Department. It was decided that the best way forward was to invite the Medical Research Council to advise what research might be needed. At that time, remember, we were up to our eyes on AIDS and about to launch LAYH. The experts were interested in EWM, however, and by July 1987 the Chief Medical Officer was meeting the Chief Medical Statistician from the Office of Population and Census Surveys (OPCS) to discuss the apparent sharp fall in EWM the previous winter. The Chief Medical.Officer called a meeting of experts in September 1987.

It was about then that I started reading up on the subject and asking if we couldn't have a sort of 'keep warm in winter' campaign. A background briefing, given to me in July 1987, was sure that the number of these excess deaths had been falling and that this was not solely the product of fewer severe winters or less frequent flu epidemics. It was not then the Department's practice to mount a publicity campaign in the winter on the health aspects of cold weather; instead support was given to such campaigns as: a) 'Your Right to be Warm' – launched in October 1986 by the Health Education Council – aimed at those working with the elderly; b) 'Warmth in Winter' and 'The Winter Warmth Code' – the Health Education Council in association with Age Concern – leaflets, some aimed direct at old people; simple practical advice on clothing, food, insulation, grants and reducing fuel costs; c) 'Keep Warm this Winter' – Help the Aged; for elderly people.

Officials suggested to me that the Chief Medical Officer might wish to propose to ministers that the Department showed more ministerial encouragement. And that was done.

Slowly, therefore, a number of people were coming to the same conclusions. My concern was shared by Nick Scott and Michael Portillo, the Social Security Ministers. None of us felt, now, that it was enough to rely on the voluntary organizations' efforts. By August 1987 ministers had asked officials to work up a campaign covering the whole range of Department of Health and government activity relevant to keeping old people (and others) warm in winter. This campaign was announced by John Moore, as Secretary of State, in September 1987 at the 'Ageing Well' conference of the International Association of Gerontologists. Apart from a brief mention in *The Times*, however, the announcement did not attract attention in the media. (A year later, when the fuss broke over 'woolly hats', John asked me what it was about and was bemused, somewhat, when reminded that he had announced the campaign!)

Other government departments – Energy, Environment, Wales, Scotland and Northern Ireland – were involved, though the latter had their own campaigns, and we kept in close touch with the Fuel Boards as well as the three main voluntary organizations, Help the Aged, Age Concern and Neighbourhood Energy Action who were involved in insulation campaigns. The campaign was launched formally by Nick Scott on 17 November 1987 and was, I believe, quite successful. Television advertisements were prepared and used as fillers – that is, they were used by the ITV companies as public information films to fill gaps in the advertising schedules. That meant air time at low cost and worked well. The costs of the 1987 campaign, around £250,000, came out of the Social Security budget, and the telephone help-line at Help the Aged, which we paid for, received over 10,000 calls. Not bad at all, but I wondered if we could do even better next time round.

*   *   *

The Women's Health Conference in June 1988 had been a great success and we were well pleased at the increased awareness of better health raised by it. So we decided to run a similar conference for the following June (1989), based on Age Concern's 'Celebrating Age' campaign, to take in good health and practical advice to old people, including something useful on avoiding accidents in the home, and the like. We wanted, too, to pick up the fun and pleasure of retirement, and thought of approaching SAGA for a section on holidays, complete with a travel movie maybe. I thought we might also provoke some discussion on the presentation and image of old people in the media, where, in endless soap operas and situation comedies, their brain power was shown to be in inverse ratio to their years; the older and dafter, it always seemed. Why should old people be so often portrayed as subjects for derision? My hope, of course, was that by stimulating debate we might improve matters a bit. I was keen to get away from the idea that old age was a problem to be feared and endured, so for the title of the conference we borrowed the title of Age Concern's 1985–86 Annual Report. Old age, they said, was the time when younger people said, 'you should not be doing this, at your time of life'; and older people said, 'why not, I'm having the time of my life'. So the 'Time of Your Life' conference it was entitled. Sadly it was decided in the spring of 1989 not to proceed with it. I hope time may be found before too long for something of the kind.

The question was how to start increasing awareness of the on-going campaign for winter health, to get the maximum results from our rather modest input. In September 1988 I received an invitation, similar to a dozen received that week, to attend a 'health day' in Reading on the 21st. The twist was that it was to be directed, with the assistance of the local council and age charities, at health in old age. Great! All the health ministers were to be in Bristol the night before for the regular meeting with regional health authority chairmen, so I could stop off at Reading on the way back. By then it had been decided to have another campaign in the winter of 1988–9, called 'Keep Warm Keep Well'. I got clearance from Nick Scott to mention the campaign (for which he had responsibility), and from the Secretary of State and the Prime Minister's office to announce the 'Time of Your Life' conference, and off we went.

Much of the rest of that day is, as they say, history, but it did not quite go with the happy swing I had hoped for, and if the 'woolly hats' business had a harsh edge, it was entirely my own fault. Part of the trouble was that the Reading people thought they were getting a personality to pop in, whereas I wanted a platform for a national campaign, which (despite our efforts in 1987) many people knew very little about. The 'ratpack' of press and TV which by then followed me everywhere didn't help much either.

Like many local authorities, in recent years Reading has invested ratepayers' money in a smart new Council building, all spanking brown brick, architect-designed, with odd-shaped corners. Madam

Mayor, in chain of office, properly turned out, offered tea and biscuits, flower displays in the Mayor's Parlour, a very posh loo, all very hospitable and decorous. Downstairs it wasn't so pleasant. The hall area is a small amphitheatre shape, and it was here that the exhibition was staged, with dozens of stands from local and national bodies. The whole place was packed to the gills, and there was a terrible crush. A small number of hecklers decided to turn up, too. The television lights and the crowd made it hot and sticky and my heart sank. There was a fair bit of pushing and shoving and I was afraid someone was going to get hurt. Anxiety and tension were in the air.

The speech I made was innocuous enough, I thought: the growth in numbers of elderly people; the efforts made by the NHS to keep up and to improve their quality of life; and then our concern about excess winter deaths and Keatinge's studies. I described the forthcoming 'Keep Warm Keep Well' campaign, and mentioned the free telephone line based at Help the Aged. The next bit came straight from every campaign to advise elderly people, back to the year dot: 'We want you all to prepare now – buy the longjohns, find your woolly socks, check your hot-water bottles, knit some gloves and scarves, and get your grandchildren to give you a woolly nightcap, preferably before Christmas – remember you lose a lot of heat on a cold night through your head, ladies included . . .'

'It's either some terrorist organization or Edwina Currie's husband has been sent out to set an example . . .'

Ken Clarke said to me later. 'What happened? Last time I saw you, you were catching a train at Bristol station. Now you're all over the front pages. What's going on?'

'It backfired a bit,' I said lamely.

I had wanted it to come out rather droll; good natured and wise. But it had sounded, especially on the TV news, not fresh and new, but somewhat pompous and arrogant, particularly from a young person and a government minister at that. Many people, and the press, reacted with outrage. There was a terrible made-up picture of me on the front page of the *Daily Mirror*, all wrapped up and looking like the ghost of Christmas past. The cartoonists were much funnier, but many people did not see the joke at all. Large numbers of elderly people wrote to me, saying they didn't need any advice, thank you very much, they had managed through the war, through far greater hardship than I would ever know. Others said they didn't need advice, just more money – but they ignored the fact that the death rate during the winter is not so different for the better-off. The advice was for *everyone*, not just the poorer members of society. Large numbers of people with shaky arthritic hands wrote that they could no longer knit. I felt so sorry for many of them, sitting down alone to pour out their troubles to a complete stranger who could do little to help.

Not long after, however, John Moore was able to announce additional pensions for the very old, and the Budget of spring 1989 has improved the lot of retired people very considerably, so maybe the fuss did some good elsewhere.

I suppose the problem – apart from my generally tactless style – was that this positive approach was rather new. Jollying along the old people was regarded as quite inappropriate. Eric Midwinter was quite right in his criticisms. Politicians, journalists and many of the old people themselves still think of the old as incapable, as needing help, *all* of them, not just some, rather than as perfectly competent people able to act on advice all by themselves. In political terms the old arguments were still strong and were resorted to the moment the word 'old' was mentioned. 'Old' meant 'cold', meant 'benefits', meant inner cities and damp and bad landlords and dripping roofs; 'old' meant Alzheimer's disease, senile dementia, wheelchairs and geriatric beds, not just for an important few but for *everyone*. No one seemed to examine the argument. If one-fifth of all over-eighties were likely to suffer from some form of brain failure – and even that was disputed – that meant that four-fifths were not. What were we supposed to do

– ignore them? If there was some advice we could give to help, we had a responsibility to give it. The fact that the bulk of our old people are not dependent on benefits, that the living standards and incomes both of the average, and of large numbers of elderly, had risen dramatically in recent years, and that this increased prosperity was itself one of the main reasons for their increasing numbers, seemed to have escaped many commentators and many old people themselves. With ten million of them that approach simply would not do anymore. Once again, I was stuck with insider information; I knew the changes were happening but others didn't, and a great deal of time was spent subsequently patiently explaining what we were trying to do.

My job was to look at the generality of old people. Anyone would think that the presence of 'woopies' in our society was some kind of slur, whereas it's a great achievement and one we have been aiming at for decades. Sitting in their centrally-heated owner-occupied homes, surrounded by creature comforts, choosing a holiday from their SAGA brochure or a course from Adult Education, reading newspapers, watching the News, enjoying a glass of something, taking it for granted that they are just as robust as when they were younger – they are the majority. But they were still keeling over with heart attacks in the cold.

*   *   *

The next opportunity to explain and cajole came at Sidmouth in Devon, on 29 October 1988, when I was invited to speak at a day conference organized by the local Conservatives. Sidmouth is beautiful and, as usual, I wished there was time to explore these places instead of seeing them only out of a car or train window. So often they were only names on a file; sometimes the only local facet I had a chance to notice was the change in accent, the only certainty that I have been there at all the little souvenir offered with local pride as the Minister sweeps off for her next important engagement.

The locals were terrific. The hall was large and full, with rows of excited friendly people, most of them older, mostly women, twin sets and pretty scarves, a touch of lipstick, a whiff of perfume – just as Dorothy advised. Several seriously disabled people sat near the side door, sticks arranged like a protective fence around them. The Conservative Party Agent, a bouncy cheerful man who had been in the constituency for twenty-five years, told me the committee had decided not to charge for the event but to make it a treat for party workers and loyal members. Tickets had, however, been changing hands in the town for over a hundred pounds! These were exactly the people I wanted to reach, all over the country; the great army of our citizens retired from paid work, mostly, but not yet retired from life, no sir! not by a long way.

This time I wanted to tie 'Keep Warm Keep Well' in with other government campaigns, emphasizing again the partnership we saw between government action and changing patterns of behaviour on the part of ordinary people, similar to LAYH, for example.

Once, disease and premature death were the results of God's will or bad magic or accident, I said, drawing on my background in economic and social history (I used to teach it). Alexander the Great was dead at thirty-two after conquering most of the known world; he died of a battle wound. Lucrezia Borgia married at fourteen and saw off several husbands; she died of old age at thirty-nine. Death was generally seen as nothing to do with government, except in its role of encouraging peace rather than conflict – and occasionally putting down witches, highwaymen and the like. Then in the 19th century it was realized that the environment had a major part to play in health and disease and that collective action was needed. Edwin Chadwick's water supply was as important to British history in the 19th century as Robert Peel's police or Palmerston's gun boats. (I hoped this bit of the speech might get some notice, but not a scrap.) Government thus did have a major role to play and I for one was not about to deny it. From the Clean Air Act of 1956 through to the tax differentials on lead-free petrol and the Prime Minister's major speech of a few days earlier on the environment, this Government had accepted that responsibility. We were steering a path between the libertarians who said, let them stew in their own juice, their health is no business of Government, and the left who felt it was entirely the Government's business and nothing the individual could do would help.

But we had to move away from the notion that all health was a matter of the Government just building more hospitals, employing more doctors and nurses and spending more money. (There they went again, those goalposts.) 'It is beginning to dawn on us all,' I said, 'how sterile that approach has become, and how incomplete in response to modern needs and illnesses.' Then I did something really rotten and quoted from Age Concern's information pack, 'Winter is on the Way', revised in August 1988:

212

Attitudes to clothing: bodices, long-johns, vests, nightcaps, button-in linings were once common items in everyone's wardrobe. Changes in fashion and the spread of centrally-heated homes and work-places has now rendered these items at best, less common and at worst, slightly laughable. Such attitudes mitigate against sensible dressing for winter. Through publicity and advice Age Concern can help right the balance.

You bet! I hoped this might not only rub it all in a bit, but stop the local Age Concern groups from wittering on about how out-rageous it was to talk about woolly hats. If they had any better ideas I would be glad to hear them, but I was blowed if I was going to take that kind of criticism from them in the face of their own literature.

The good people of South Devon showed they understood. One lady slowly rose to her feet at question time, and to supportive laughter from her neighbours, said good-naturedly, 'I won't tell you my age but it's a good bit more than yours, Mrs Currie. I certainly have no plans to go jogging on the beach. What exercise do you recommend for me to keep myself fit?'

'Well,' I explained, 'it almost doesn't matter what you do as long as you do something; it's whatever you enjoy, even walking regularly will do. Did you know that on average this nation watches nearly thirty hours of television every week? And that pensioners are even worse, with forty hours? We don't get much exercise like that.' I looked at her; she had a country, out-door look about her. 'Do you have a dog?' I asked.

'Yes,' she replied, 'does that help?'

'I believe it does,' I answered; 'they tell me that households with a dog have marginally less heart disease than those without.'

Well, it's true, and they loved it, and we parted friends.

Somebody nationally had to find something to pick at. The RSPCA complained that I should be so wicked as to suggest getting a dog as a cure for heart disease (and perhaps loneliness while you're at it). Didn't I realize pensioners couldn't afford a dog, etc.? I liked, however, the story told to me by Graham Jones, the headmaster of Repton, the public school in my constituency. He had thought this was a great idea, and had asked an elderly relative to look after their rather large dog when they went on holiday. A month later they called to collect the canine granny-sitter. It had all been a great success. The old lady was better than they had ever seen her, bright as a button, slimmer and fitter; yes, she had walked the dog faithfully, it had been marvellous, she was thinking of getting a dog herself now.

In the car on the way home, however, they noticed that the dog was flat out in the back and snoring loudly. The bathroom scales told the sad tale; walkies had been followed by sweeties and double helpings of apple pie, and the dog was now a barrel of flesh on four noticeably shorter legs. 'Perhaps,' Graham said to me quizzically, 'you should put a government health warning on old people. The dog may be good for them, but I don't think they are always very healthy for the dog!'

Meanwhile, my post-bag gradually suggested that many older people did understand exactly what I was getting at, and some of them even appreciated it. One letter from an old lady in Kent was my favourite and I quoted it at meetings from then onwards:

> You are quite right when you advise elderly people to wear extra woolly clothing. Of course, the opposition would pounce on your remarks and say you should give them extra money for extra heating, but that is not the answer.
>
> It is a fact that an elderly person can feel cold in a warm room. I am eighty-nine and the other evening, although my central heating had been on all the afternoon, and in spite of the fact that the temperature gauge in my lounge registered 70°, which should be enough, I still felt cold. I put on an extra cardigan and a warm scarf round my shoulders and I was soon feeling beautifully warm. To do that is far more efficacious than putting up the temperature to some fantastic level, which my friends couldn't stand when they came to visit me. Many of my friends are much younger than I am and they certainly couldn't stand an overheated room of about 80°.
>
> Do not publicize my name, but you can quote my remarks to that silly Labour crowd who criticize *everything* when they are in opposition, and do *nothing* when they are in power. At my age I think I am qualified to give an opinion on this matter. After all, I am speaking from experience. Good luck!

One very senior colleague gave the campaign some unexpected encouragement. A jolly, rotund man, he is often photographed with a glass in one hand and a cigar in the other and is not, on the whole, known for his active personal support of 'healthy life-style' campaigns.

'I can't quite understand what all the fuss about longjohns is about, Edwina,' he said to me one morning. 'My hobby is birdwatching and

I often go crawling around in the Norfolk fens on cold days. I wear longjohns then. If you didn't you'd freeze to death out there – take your whatsits off, that damp cold would. They are a very good idea.' And with that, leaving me agog, he swept on his way.

Who? No, indeed, wild horses . . .

And thus, constant reader, you will understand, I hope, that 'woolly hats and longjohns' was not a gaffe, not after all that work we had put in at the Department of Health. Even as I did the research for this book, encouraging statistics were being published. According to the OPCS Monitor of 31 May 1989, 'the crude death-rate in 1988 was . . . the same as the 1989 rate. This is consistent with the general downward trend in the rate since the mid 1970s.'

'Keep Warm Keep Well' was my main campaign for the winter of 1988–9, hoping we might see favourable mortality data by late spring of 1989, to be followed by the TOYL conference in June 1989. By then, with a fair wind, we should be well on the way to genuine improvements in the health statistics for over sixty-fives. I took it all very seriously. When Neighbourhood Energy Action, one of the charities involved in 'Keep Warm Keep Well', invited me to visit insulation projects I said, 'Fine, can I see what you are doing for my own constituents?' So we all toddled along to Mr and Mrs Young's house in Chellaston in Derby. He hid his cigarettes, she made the tea, the neighbours chatted to the *Sunday Times* like professionals, while I climbed down from a ladder, dusted my hands, and talked to ITN about the problem of salmonella in eggs. A few weeks later Mrs Young, who is the caretaker at the hall where I hold one of my advice bureaux, told me that the workmen had finished, and yes, it was all very nice and her bills were much less and the house more comfortable. 'I suppose you'll have a bit more time for that sort of thing now, won't you?' she added, kindly.

*   *   *

It wasn't just winter's high mortality rate which seized my attention. The White Paper 'Promoting Better Health', published in November 1987, which was to form the background for current changes in the GP service, proposed health checks all year round for elderly people under the general title of 'elderly surveillance'.

We did argue about 'surveillance'. Horrid word! It means in principle keeping an eye on vulnerable people and checking up on them if they haven't appeared at the doctors for some time – making sure

215

no one is missed. In Manchester the three health authorities are all trying different ways of doing such surveillance. The standard checks done are on failing senses and increasing disabilities – sight, hearing, mobility. I wanted surveillance to be more sophisticated – looking out for mental deterioration or self-neglect – but was persuaded that looking for, say, increasing deafness would be a simple and cheap way of picking up potential isolation and disorientation.

Later I also pursued the question of over-prescribing to elderly people. In 1984 the Royal College of Physicians had drawn attention to the excessive number of prescriptions given to elderly people, caused by some doctors' tendency to go on prescribing quite powerful drugs long after the need has gone or when side effects become so dominant that they require treatment too. For example, we give old people diuretics and then wonder why they are incontinent; we give them drugs against high blood pressure and are puzzled why they get dizzy and fall. This problem can and will be tackled by improved 'surveillance' both of the elderly people themselves, and of their doctors' prescribing habits, unpopular with the BMA though that may be.

*   *   *

How old can you go? According to Professor Malcolm Johnson of the Open University, thousands of children born today could live to be 130. He reckons a 'healthier environment, better diet, medical breakthroughs and less smoking and drinking will add up to a ripe old age. And by the year 2050 such life expectancy – nearly double today's – could be commonplace.'

The nation's oldest man, Mr John Evans, lives at Fforestfach near Swansea and made his first visit to London for a three-day trip, guest of British Rail, on Wednesday 27 August 1987, for his 110th birthday. He chatted away on early-morning radio, still a smart cookie, bilingual in English and Welsh. Asked on his way home what he had enjoyed most, he said 'The British Rail breakfast'. Really? 'You see,' he explained carefully, 'I haven't had a proper cooked breakfast like that for thirty-five years. That's when I had a bit of stomach trouble, see, and I went to my doctor. "Eat bran!!" he said, and I have done, ever since. But it isn't as nice, though I suppose it does me good.'

So much for the notion that elderly people can't change, won't change, shouldn't be offered information on how to change. Most people would have written the man off at seventy-five, but his doctor didn't. Similarly the people who help me at my advice bureau on Saturdays are all retired people and they are loving life and enjoying it to the full. Why else would Lily, heading for eighty, make such an effort to be sweet to her man, until they made it to the altar, to the joy and pleasure of us all? Who are we youngsters to say they are too old? Of course they aren't.

My oldest constituent could give Dorothy Moriarty a year or two. Daisy Adams, 109 on 30 June 1989, is a bright bird-like little woman who lived until recently in her own home. She had a bad winter at 105, which put her in hospital. Her GP then insisted that she go into a local old people's home, where she is a bit of a star. She shares a room with another old lady and, if they can't sleep, the two of them sit holding hands and talking far into the night. As a result, she is now much chattier and sharper than she was in her own little house where she had lived for over seventy years. She has all four children living, the youngest being seventy-four. The eldest, Bert, is also my constituent. He used, till recently, to take his mother to fetch her pension in his car every week, with the old lady treated with the greatest respect, sitting bolt upright in the back. Having once followed Bert in his car away from the old people's home, and watched his cheerful disregard for some aspects of the Highway Code, I wondered how he had arrived safely at eighty-eight; still, he has had plenty of practice. Recently he lost a dearly-loved wife. I asked him how he was coping and who was cooking for him, and received the proud answer, 'Meself! I taught meself how to do it,' and he started swapping recipes. Certainly he looked well on it. The family had a hard time of it as children for his father was killed on the Somme. Old Mrs Adams has been drawing a war-widow's pension for nearly seventy-three years.

There will be more like Mrs Adams, and Bert, and Mr Evans, and Lily and Mrs Moriarty, lots more in the next decade and beyond. We will soon have to stop regarding them as curiosities. These are fellow citizens. I hope they are as fit and well and active and respected. A prosperous, peaceful and caring nation can make it so, and can keep it that way.

8

A Day in the Life . . .

Grant that . . . laying aside all private interests, prejudices, and partial affections, the result of all our counsels may be . . . the publick wealth, peace and tranquillity of the Realm
Prayer dating probably from the sixteenth
century, said by MPs at start of day's business

It isn't a glamorous life, not at all. No one believes me, of course. You're up there with the stars, aren't you? You chat to the Prime Minister every day, isn't that right? There's the chauffeur-driven limousine with someone to carry your bags; you don't have to queue up like the rest of us, I've seen you sweeping past, everything ready and waiting the moment you arrive. They even whitewash the pavements before your visit, don't they? No, actually, they don't; and although it would be a lie to say it's never like that, there must be many kinds of lifestyle that are easier (and better paid) than that of a minister, especially a junior minister in a big department as I was.

A more subtle misunderstanding of the job involves the assertion that ministers have real power and can make things happen. Sometimes! Of course the law sets out powers which reside in the Secretary of State and which are devolved to ministers. Use them too often and everyone gets uppity. Persuasion is in the end what works best, backed by the prestige of the job – which is often more effective than any legislation. 'Because I said so' may well carry more weight than quoting chapter and verse of the 1977 National Health Service Act. Many of the areas I was involved in carried no clear legislative backing for ministerial interference anyway. In my experience the councillor-chairman of a major committee in a big local council with a good majority probably has more instant access to power, at least within that council's own geographical area, than many a junior minister, whichever party is in charge, but perhaps rather less influence.

Like most ministers I started, and remain, an ordinary Member of Parliament. That is the hardest and more frustrating job of all. A representative and nought else, an MP cannot make anybody do *anything*, not even the local parish council. There is only the power of the spoken and written word, the former being the stronger, for words spoken in the chamber of the Commons have 'privilege'. That means an MP can say what he likes and can't be sued, which in political life is truly a wonderful protection. There is also what I call the 'megaphone effect'. The MP who stands up and calls a rogue a rotten cheat, who points the finger fearlessly at injustice and cruelty, is not a figment of the imagination but is found in Parliament every day, having a go from both sides of the chamber, and often it works. Similarly the MP who says something nice, a word of praise for example, will find those words treasured evermore in the recipient's heart. The influence of ministers at junior level is not much greater than an ordinary MP's, even though it surprises each junior as he realizes it.

What ministers can do, is command the media. If the minister has something to say to the nation, a press conference is called, and hey presto! in they come, journalists of every nation, of every political persuasion, grudgingly or with gratitude accepting the press hand-outs, the statistics, the minister's view of the world outside and how to cope with it. In a free country with a free press, government statements and views are, on the whole, taken very seriously and, quite properly, then become subject to comment, scrutiny and criticism. Ministers are usually invited to reply, too. The policy during much of my time at the Department of Health was that ministers should accept all sensible bids from the media to put across our point of view. One Secretary of State requested that I submit to him all the bids I turned down. After a week of long lists of silly demands for interviews – on topics including what I eat for breakfast, what I carry in my handbag, what kinds of contraceptive I would recommend and what I use myself, would I please demonstrate breast-feeding (at the age of forty-one!), what my husband thinks of Denis Thatcher and what my children think about everything under the sun – he thankfully relented and agreed I might exercise my own discretion. The net result of all that was Fame – with a 'day in the life' of a minister requiring quite extraordinary stamina, and commitment to our democratic society.

*   *   *

On a typical day, the phone goes at 4.30 a.m., with the world-weary voice of the press officer from the Department, or that nice lad at Conservative Central Office who is never the same one I dealt with the day before, and who therefore needs everything carefully explaining to him all over again.

'We have a spat on, Edwina,' they will say. 'X has got himself on the midnight tapes [the Press Association news] saying such and such. So I've managed to arrange for you to do BBC *Breakfast Time*, and then we'll whisk you away for *TV-AM*, and we can do Radio 4 on the way, and then it's IRN news and then *Kilroy* and then back to the BBC for the *Jimmy Young Show*. Oh yes, and the Secretary of State's called a press conference for 11 a.m., you'll be needed for that, and there may be a statement in the House at 3.30 p.m., and then probably some more for the 5 p.m. and 6 p.m. news, depending on how you get on. I've just had a bid for *Newsnight*, too, for 10.30 p.m. and they always want it live. Got that? There'll be some briefing in the car and it will be at your flat on the dot of 6 o'clock . . .'

That's six o'clock in the morning, and I may only have been in bed, close to the slumbering body of my husband, who hasn't seen me in daylight hours for three days, for a matter of an hour or two. My hair is a mess: better wash it now; no hot water, darn, have to make do with a kettle, better be quiet, everyone else in the house is asleep. There is no decaffeinated coffee in my kitchen. When I need to wake up fast, Café Hag is not what is required.

Performing on breakfast television is a modern form of torture, all the more effective because it feels quite nice at the time. The pain doesn't hit till about twelve hours later, when a dragging exhaustion saps the energy and destroys one's ability from there onwards to talk any sense at all. The only benefit is the professional make-up done by remarkably bright-eyed girls in the bowels of Broadcasting House. They virtually lacquer it on so it stays, firm, smooth, non-creasing, for the rest of the day. I once commented that after early morning TV I looked like Joan Collins. The press missed the joke entirely; she's fourteen years older than me.

Fortunately this time the briefing papers are clear and make sense. I usually asked that each topic be dealt with on a separate page, at the bottom of which is the life-saver, the 'Line to Take': say it often enough and, with a bit of luck, the desired message will start to sink in. The press are only doing their job but there is no doubt that they make any kind of normal life for a public figure in these circumstances almost impossible. The day after I was appointed to the Department of Health in September 1986, I did six interviews before 9 a.m. The day after I resigned, my neighbour counted thirty reporters' cars camped on my lawn, and proceeded gleefully to lead them a merry dance by driving my car all over South Derbyshire (at my request), ending up parking rather ostentatiously in Derby Station car-park. Some of the reporters, I am told, slept in the car-park all night for fear of missing us returning home.

The day does not start early in the morning with breakfast TV. It starts earlier than that – or, rather, the previous parliamentary day has not finished. The chance of ever being in bed before midnight is nil. At least four times a year there is an all-night sitting at the Commons until 9 a.m. the next day, when the MPs ballot for a slot for short debates on subjects of their choice which must have the response of a minister. The list is put up only a few days beforehand. The task of reply goes to the junior ranks, so out goes the dinner party, the evening at the theatre, even the quiet night doing ministerial boxes at home (there are no votes). The hapless minister is required to speak, bright and to the point, at some unbelievable hour the wrong side of dawn. If he's really unlucky, he'll draw both the short and the long straws and be on duty for more than one debate, which seemed to happen to me every time! On more than one occasion I was expecting to be called around 6 a.m. to discuss hospitals in Leicester-shire or community care in South London, and had gone home for a rest. The previous debates collapsed and I was summoned early with a shattering phone call, my private secretary's voice urgent and worried. I raced down Victoria Street and, breathless, up the back stairs to the chamber, to find the minister responsible for answering the previous debate still droning hoarsely on, clinging carefully to the Despatch Box, sagging at the knees, having talked steadily and quite intelligibly for forty minutes to allow me time to get there. As I arrived, he sank gratefully to his seat, murmuring that the Government hoped it had now made its views clear.

Why does Parliament conduct its business like that? During my first Parliament the *average* time the House rose was 12.47 a.m. The ordinary members don't always have to be there all the time, but the whip, the minister and the Speaker (usually a deputy) must be in

221

attendance, however daft the hour and the topic. Wouldn't it be better to have fixed working hours, so that the 650 MPs might have a reasonable home life, might get to the end of a busy session without the bags under their eyes reaching down to their navels? Believe it or not, there *are* fixed hours, settled a century ago when the Fenians' filibustering was making Gladstone's life a misery. We start at 2.30 p.m., which enables colleagues who have other activities on their personal agenda to get them done, and we are supposed to finish at 10 p.m. It requires a decision of the House to continue thereafter, but the chatty eager beavers always agree to more time.

Why not start earlier? That would mean fewer outside engagements. There is an argument for full-time MPs, but those with non-parliamentary interests often talk more sense, for they are closer to the real world than members who spend all their time in Westminster. Ivan Lawrence, the MP for Burton on Trent, is my neighbour and my constituent. He is also a top criminal lawyer and could earn three times or more his parliamentary salary by working at the law full time. Instead, he is there in the House at 8 a.m. looking through his post, before heading off to court for a 10.30 a.m. sitting. He returns in time for the main business of the House at around 4 p.m. and is then there with the rest of us past midnight. He has strong views (which I don't share) against the advisability of fluoridation of water and during the debates on the Fluoridation Bill in 1985 started speaking soon after 4 a.m. one morning and talked steadily, breaking all parliamentary records for a single continuous speech, till around 9 a.m. He then went off to court, won his case, came back and carried on.

There is, quite simply, too much parliamentary business to confine to a nine-to-five day. With the increase in Euro legislation, often taken after 10 p.m., the problem is rapidly getting worse. If we did try to restrict our hours the work would continue, but it would be done by the civil servants, not by the elected representatives, not by the Queen's ministers. In other parliaments with a fixed timetable that is precisely what happens. The papers and drafts which eventually pass into legislation would have only bureaucratic, not democratic, fingerprints on them. At least, doing it our way, the MPs have to take some responsibility for what happens and if any one of them doesn't like it he can call a debate at three in the morning and moan at the hapless minister; and they do.

*   *   *

The life of ministers would become completely impossible if they had to be in Westminster all morning as well as half the night. At least that time is available to get on with some work in the Department before decamping over to the House some time in the afternoon. The mornings, in any case, are useful in Parliament, too, for the discussion of the committee stages of a bill, for example.

A bill can be presented in either the House of Commons or the House of Lords to start with, but it must end up going through both – except money bills which are dealt with in the Commons only, ever since the Lords tried to do something nasty to Lloyd George's budgets in 1910. As a result the Finance Bill has long-drawn-out sessions both in the chamber of the Commons and in committee upstairs. I served on the committee as a back-bencher in 1985. Members of the Finance Bill Committee contribute to a fund for refreshments and go out of the room in ones and twos in the early hours to munch quails' eggs and drink a little malt whisky. When there's an all-night sitting on the Finance Bill the whip buys everyone champagne on the terrace before breakfast. At least, that's how the Tories do it.

There are four stages to a bill in each House: the 'First Reading', when the bill isn't read at all, just printed up and left on the Table in the Chamber; the 'Second Reading', which is a big wide-ranging debate, usually with a whipped vote at the end; the committee stage, which can be a tedious event – merely a delaying tactic by the opposition which eventually leads to a timetabled debate ('guillotine') – or can be a really useful discussion of the issues raised, point by point, with thoughtful amendments offered on both sides. (The best ministers are those who get the Government's carefully thought-out bills through the committee stage intact and on time, without too many hostages for the future in the way of promises to think again, etc.) The fourth stage is the 'Third Reading', when the bill returns from committee and there is some further discussion in the chamber of any amendments. Then off it goes to the Other Place and the whole process starts again.

The main bill on which I served as a minister was the Health and Medicines Bill which, starting in late 1987, took almost a year to pass through all its stages. From January to March 1988 it was in committee, the ministers in charge being Tony Newton, the Minister of State, and myself. Room 6 is lofty but cramped, eminently Victorian, upstairs away from the Commons Chamber. Up on the wall facing me was a large portrait of Joe Chamberlain in morning coat, eyeglass in place, orchid purple in buttonhole. I could swear that the old Birmingham radical winked at me when the going got rough. As people sit outside, waiting to be admitted for the day's proceedings at 10.30 a.m. and 4.30 p.m. twice weekly, they begin to understand the meaning of 'corridors of power'. Bewigged and gowned Queen's Counsel sweep by, trailing papers and briefs bound up in red tape. MPs lounge around in the corridor, drinking coffee, smoking (neither permitted in committee), keeping a wary eye on the clock, for they are only allowed out of the room by the whips for a few minutes so that a quorum is maintained. Journalists, lobbyists, representatives of interested parties mingle, watchful, listening for titbits. One journalist from the *Guardian* intrigues everyone by rushing out of a room, sitting on a vacant bench and typing away into a word processor deck without a screen, so no one can see what he is writing. Maybe that accounts for all the spelling mistakes.

The committee rooms are known by their numbers. Up here, when a vote is called in one of the committees, policemen rush out, doff their helmets and yell 'Di-vi-shun in TWEEELLVE!!!' The startled public scatter, the missing committee members drop the telephone, come running out of the loo. They officially have two minutes to get back into the room, then the doors are locked and a vote call taken, and woe betide the late comer. Once in the 1974 Parliament there were so many committees running at once that one Labour whip, Walter Harrison, had to serve on two at once. The Conservatives contrived to call a vote in both at exactly the same time. Walter voted in the first and hared off down the corridor. The door was closed just as he put his leg inside it. He swears that it is the only time in recorded history that half a vote was accepted.

The committee does not run right through lunch. Ever civilized, it breaks up at 1 p.m. The journalists head for Annie's bar, where nothing is ever on the record and nothing goes unreported either; the members go off downstairs to pie and chips in the cafeteria; the civil servants to sandwiches back at the Department and hurried conferences over the minister's wobble this morning, which the opposition are sure to jump on later, and the ministers more often than not to an official lunch, at which the Prime Minister may be present.

Margaret Thatcher doesn't leave anyone out of the talk and it is well to go armed with a topic you wish to air. On one occasion I teamed up with Colin Moynihan, the sports minister, to tell her about his thinking on the use of drugs in sport. More often than not I would be caught unawares by the sudden emergence of a health topic, since colleagues knew I would be there, minus advisers of course, and I had to think fast about how to win the argument without hurting anyone's feelings, how to make a useful point, and how to please our leader all at the same time. It was hardest when the questions came from her. On one occasion the topic was the allocation of NHS resources around the country. The system since Barbara Castle's day had been known as RAWP, the 'Resource Allocation Working Party'. A fiendishly complicated formula had been devised based on population, particularly the numbers of very old and very young, with mortality statistics as a measure of deprivation. Health regions worked towards targets which meant, roughly, equality of access to hospitals. For some time in the 1980s this had led to relatively low growth of NHS facilities in the South and London, and a huge increase in activity in the Midlands and North. Now they were all close to the target of equality. Should we carry on?

The Prime Minister turned to me with a challenge, asking me to explain how the reallocation of NHS resources to the North of England might be defended to her constituents in Finchley.

She has a powerful blue-eyed look that has turned strong men to stone. You stop whatever else you are doing, and start thinking fast. This lady prefers it straight. She was still looking at me, and so was the whole table.

'Well, Prime Minister,' I replied, 'at least it means that my constituents in Derby are not competing with yours, filling up the same beds at the Royal Free Hospital in Hampstead. They don't have to come down to London. We have our own smart new hospital units in Derby now. Thanks to you. That's how.'

You know you have scored when she nods, satisfied, and turns away to make someone else tremble. Just as she did, however, she gave me a sharp look. She reminded those present that I had been telling all and sundry that it was possible to cut the number of heart attacks. Was that true?

The conversation was taking place during 1987 and I thought about where she had been recently, flying the world, the honoured guest and friend of President Reagan, and having spent an unprecedented eleven and a half hours in secret discussion with Gorbachev. How to convince someone like that in five seconds flat?

'I think so, Prime Minister,' I offered. 'The doctors feel it's possible. They have certainly done it in the USA, very substantially, with a government programme like ours.'

'Really?' she said, interested. Then she floored me completely, saying gaily that she had been taking an interest in blood pressure. Did I know that all the world's leaders had low blood pressure? Was there any reason for that? The mind boggled. Lamely I suggested that maybe those with high blood pressure hadn't stayed the course, had keeled over before they got to the top. Only the low blood pressure people were left. She nodded again. Some weeks later I heard her using a version of my Derby argument in support of RAWP without batting an eyelid, and I breathed a sigh of relief.

* * *

Junior ministers don't, in fact, see much of the Prime Minister. Her dealings are with their superiors, the Cabinet Ministers and perhaps with Ministers of State. There has to be a real row before the junior will be summoned to Number 10, so all my visits there (apart from the last one, made at my request) were pleasant semi-social occasions.

I did find, however, that I needed to see our leader in action every week at the Despatch Box for Prime Minister's Question Time. As a departmental minister, buried in detailed business, it was often hard to know what was happening in other departments, what the current rows and successes might be. Prime Minister's Questions are an instant pot-pourri of the week's issues. If I missed it, I didn't know what was going on, for although every department sends in its own briefing for whatever may come up, the leader answers questions in her own way. Tackling similar questions myself at weekend meetings I could then deftly say that the Prime Minister's view was such and such, knowing that I had heard it first hand, not filtered and filleted by the TV commentary. Hearing tomorrow's news today is the second privilege of MPs. I still love watching from the back of the Speaker's chair, so close I know what perfume she is wearing, so close I can see the felt-tip pen marks all over her notes, three or four colours showing how she has gone over them again and again in briefing meetings that morning; and then seeing this tiny woman (at five-foot-six I tower over her) standing up to a howling mob and making sure she gets her points across. I have always voted for the televising of Parliament. The chamber is not a private club, it belongs to the nation. By the time this book is published I hope millions of people will be sharing the excitement, the fear, the power, of Question Time in the Commons, the greatest gladiatorial contest of them all.

After Questions comes the day's debate. At this point the ministers who are not required will vanish, thankful for a few hours' peace. They may well go off to do visits, and junior ministers especially may find themselves becoming unduly acquainted with the latest British

Rail timetable. Out of curiosity, during the month of September 1988 my office kept count of the invitations – departmental, political and personal – I received. The number came to over 400 and I was able to accept only a handful. In addition we generated suitable events of our own for me to attend, regularly checking the computerized record of hospital building all over the country for key dates such as topping out (putting the last tile on a roof – can be windy up there but the press pictures are lovely) or first use by patients, and I was frequently asked to go to open a new unit. I would try and fit in a Conservative function at the same time. Often I learned more about our work, about attitudes to the NHS, for example, from those coming to tea with me than from all the respected advisers back in Whitehall.

One of the issues which was being raised at the time (1987–8) by right-wingers and fringe groups was whether we needed an NHS at all. Here we are, a wealthy country, they said, with rapid increases in personal income. Why should we not expect people to make their own arrangements for health care as they do in other countries? Why are we all forced to be in the NHS? Frankly, as an asthmatic, I knew the answer to that: because we need it, and mostly we need it when we can't afford it, such as when we are ill, or old, or chronically sick. Too many of us aren't insurable, particularly for those conditions we already suffer from.

The question came up for answer at a Tory tea party in Bristol one sunny afternoon. I enjoyed these events, where cheerful, chubby, silver-haired ladies in their best cardigans tried to persuade me to have another piece of home-made cake, and shyly asked if I would draw the raffle. I had made my little speech, they had all laughed politely at my jokes and now we were on to the nitty-gritty, the bit they all loved, the questions. A young man's hand went up: someone's grandson, maybe; the old lady sitting beside him put down her teacup and blushed with pride.

'Mrs Currie, how do you answer this one? I never use the NHS,' he said, 'so why couldn't I opt out, use the money to buy health insurance and look after myself? Why do I have to go on paying for it?'

He was slim, tanned, nice-looking. Perhaps his grandfather had looked like that fifty years ago.

'Good question, that,' I answered. 'Would you like to stand up and turn around so that everyone can see you?'

Without hesitation he did so, tall and straight and young, and not a care in the world.

'That question,' I continued, 'is always asked by young, fit men – not women, because we expect to use the NHS when we get pregnant and most of us have some glimmer of what having a baby privately would cost, particularly if something went wrong. But there are really two points to make. The first is that you are well; you wouldn't talk that way if you woke up tomorrow with diabetes, or something worse like leukaemia or kidney failure. And the second is that you and I pay not for ourselves alone, but for all those who need to use the Health Service.'

The old ladies were listening intently. I carried on. Softly, softly.

'They are all around you, lots of them in this room. Look at them. *They are looking at you.* Does that answer your question?'

And he started to bluster, but his granny was putting her hand on his arm and nodding, and so were all her friends and fellow Tories, at all the tables, way back to the far corners of the room.

Governments with big majorities are often accused of ignoring the wishes of the electorate. They are sometimes accused of trying to behave like benevolent dictatorships – pushing through measures which they believe to be good for the rest of us. But make no mistake, democracy is never far away. The Tory voters would never approve the dismantling of the National Health Service, and every politician in touch with them knows it.

*   *   *

Even if they do not have privileged access to her, the Prime Minister does support her junior ministers, occasionally in surprising ways. During late 1987 ministers at the DHSS were having a hard time, particularly as the Secretary of State, John Moore, had been taken poorly with pneumonia in November and was not really well again for some time. She came to sit next to me on the front bench in the Commons debate of 21 December 1987, where I was the closing speaker. As Londoners hurried to do their Christmas shopping, we settled in for a typical set-piece debate on the NHS called by the Labour Party. However, the Leader of the Opposition and his front bench were at the movies that night, for the première of Richard Attenborough's film *Cry Freedom*. Their junior spokesman, Harriet Harman, was therefore not well supported on her own benches as she rose to make her closing remarks, and was somewhat pedestrian and predictable. I felt the Prime Minister shifting impatiently beside me.

I glanced at her out of the corner of my eye, waiting for my turn, nervous as hell.

Harriet ran badly over time, leaving me only a few minutes. It was essential that I finish on the dot of ten o'clock, so that the vote could be taken at once, and yet I had hours of debate to respond to. The adrenalin was running; I was on my feet. I chucked my notes away and just laid into the folks opposite. They started to howl, my own side started to cheer; there was so much noise that it didn't matter much what I was saying, as long as I looked on top of it. The microphones would pick most of it up.

'Four minutes more!' hissed the well-known voice at my elbow. 'Keep going!' I looked round, startled. She was clearly enjoying herself. 'Speak to the mike! Two minutes more! Don't stop! . . . One minute! . . . Right – that's it. Well done.' And the vote was called, and we all trooped out to an unexpectedly large majority of over 120.

The whips commented to me afterwards that not everyone had the Prime Minister acting as timekeeper, usually the job of the whip on the front bench. At that beleaguered time, her personal support was very much appreciated. But then, she's like that.

*   *   *

Returning to the Commons in the evening I would sometimes go and eat, sitting with colleagues and friends, listening to their concerns and worries about the NHS in their area, or child care, or the rising number of old people, and we would gossip endlessly about who's up, who's down, who ought to be in next time. When I first entered Parliament I was anxious about how I should go on if I strongly disagreed with the whipped vote on a difficult topic to do with my constituency, or an area on which I had some modest expertise. I needn't have worried. With all of us being constituency MPs it is generally understood that the constituency's views may predominate, so the MP who takes a strong line on behalf of his own people may well be a nuisance to ministers, but wins respect. The MP with an area of expertise, on the other hand, will be cornered in the tea-room by a wise minister and pumped for information, and vice-versa.

I tried to help colleagues with local difficulties and encouraged them to call short debates or ask parliamentary questions on health topics. To the horror of some civil servants I would often discuss with the questioner the reply which would suit his local people best; after all, he was alone up there. Many the MP who has put out a press release saying that he is intending to beard the minister (me) on a matter of great importance; has then brought his cup of tea over to my table and had a brief chat; then gone to the phone and put out another press release to say he has persuaded me to think about it; winning more publicity, and more approval, for his subsequent action and my official reply a week later. It was often difficult for me to explain to my private office that I could not avoid meeting MPs, so it was no good trying to put them off by offering an appointment six weeks hence. That kind of tactic was simply counter-productive, as the said member would then collar me crossly in public (in the voting lobby, anyway) and tell everyone our business. Better to be helpful even if it involved more work, and that way I had a much better feel for MPs' concerns up and down the country.

As legislation wends its way through the parliamentary process, there are long evenings when MPs are required to be there simply to record support. Ministers and the PPSs are dubbed the 'pay-roll vote'; if you don't turn up for an important measure, you may find yourself on the back-benches sharpish. The divisions may be called at unpredictable times, and it is quite a relief to hear that the last vote is *definitely* at 1 a.m. We all find different ways to fill the hours of waiting. Some, of course, go into the Chamber and listen to the debate, but it is unlikely to be sparkling at dead of night, with an empty gallery, the Deputy Speaker half asleep and most members elsewhere, even if the subject is something as exciting as the Scottish rating system.

Others head naturally for the bars and restaurants. The tea-room – cocoa, bacon and tomorrow's newspapers – is for serious conversation, and the smoking room – gin and tonics and Ritz crackers – for gossip. Tomorrow's leaders are, however, to be found in the library, beavering away on next week's speech, glancing surreptitiously at *Private Eye*, which, in the Commons Library, is kept under lock and key by the librarian as everyone keeps nicking it.

I was very lucky to have Tony Newton as my boss for two years at the Department of Health, one of the most thoughtful, compassionate and erudite members of Government. Around 10.30 p.m. I would go down the stairs under the Commons Chamber to Tony's gloomy, smoky room, which for some reason he always kept in half-light, get him to stop working for a bit and just talk, chew the fat, toss around ideas and arguments. One result was a growing closeness of opinion, and I was pleased to find that, as the months wore on, an understanding of each other's thought processes meant we often came independently to the same conclusions. The other result was that it took him even longer to sign his letters, and when colleagues moaned I felt distinctly guilty!

*   *   *

Day by day, whether Parliament is sitting or not, there are, of course, the ministerial boxes. Mine were not red, like the Chancellor's on Budget Day. For a junior minister they are black, with the Queen's crest in gold lettering, heavy (they are made of solid wood covered in leather, no modern materials here) and with grim, secretive security locks opened by big, anonymous brass keys. Most evenings I would expect three or four, packed tight with papers, so tight we broke the clasp on two of them. Feeling alternately virtuous and bad-tempered at the amount they contained, I would toil away in my little room in the Commons late at night, driven both by duty and by curiosity about the contents of the next folder, preferring to get them all done and go home boxless with a clear conscience. It was easiest to tip the boxes out, sort the papers and then work my way through them, initialling, signing, crossing out, rewriting, putting on one side for tomorrow, filling up the boxes again as I went. The door was propped open as usual; all the occupants of the corridor were junior ministers, and friends would lounge in the doorway for a few minutes, swapping news, before going off to plough through their own boxes.

On one occasion David Hunt, the MP for Wirral West, who was then the junior minister at Energy, looked in. 'Busy tonight?' he queried, looking at the heaps all over the floor.

'No, it's always like this!' I told him, and 'Good Lord, I usually only have one,' was his reply, an answer that would be true for many others. But the DHSS had by far the biggest budget of all, and following the split in the Department in July 1988, the social security side is now the biggest, with health second. It would be more surprising if the boxes were empty.

So what was in them? First, lots of letters to sign. At the DHSS they were called 'yellow-jackets', for obvious reasons, and boy! did I dread them. Ministers reply to all letters from MPs, peers and one or two other VIPs but not usually to members of the public, who will get a missive (saying the same) signed by a civil servant instead. If you wanted a reply signed by me, you had to write to your own MP first. Lots did. In a typical week, when Parliament was sitting, when I'd made a speech, when the Department of Health was in the news,

231

I would expect to sign over 300 such letters. The text is put up by civil servants, of course, but as with speeches it was essential to put one's own gloss on it. More than once I have simply written 'I don't agree with this; not signing it, sorry,' on some pompous absurdity or politically unattractive submission. Juniors do most of the letters inevitably. During election campaigns the task is taken on by the minister in the House of Lords. Jean Trumpington did this job from May to June 1987 for all her DHSS colleagues and clocked up 5,000 letters in three weeks, signing 500 in a day several times. In a normal year I must have signed 10,000, with the junior minister on the social security side responsible for about the same number. I asked that, wherever possible, letters should be short and crisp enough to fit on a single sheet. It took several seconds less to top and tail each one, and could save an hour or two every week.

The box also contained parliamentary questions (with dark green jackets) for a written answer in the next day or so. My policy was to be as helpful as possible to MPs, and not fob them off with bland answers, but that all meant more hassle for the civil servants, working under pressure to get the answers ready on time. If we went beyond the deadline set by the MP a very public apology, along the lines of 'I will reply to the Hon. Member as soon as possible', has to be printed there in *Hansard*. The shame of it! So they got their answers fast, and to my mind it is a brilliant system for digging out information, a remarkable part of our democracy.

I didn't always feel so kindly. In the autumn of 1988 David Hinch-cliffe, who was Walter Harrison's successor for the Wakefield seat, was demanding to know when the Department would publish the guidelines on cook-chill catering for NHS caterers. I had only seen the proposal draft in the late summer and – not being a rubber stamp – wanted changes. It would go out when I was satisfied and not before, certainly not at the bidding of Mr Hinchcliffe, whose manner is cheerful and whose appearance close to that of a garden gnome (without the woolly hat), but whose politics are somewhat to the left of Fidel Castro.

From the General Election in June 1987 to October 1988 he had asked 115 questions on health, and had kept me up late for a rather bad-tempered adjournment debate. So when on 14 November 1988 he asked why the new guidelines had not yet been published, I answered in *Hansard* at column 478, 'Because they are not yet ready.' On 28 November he persisted: 'Why . . . are they not ready?' and my reply was 'Because we need more time. They will be published when they are ready.' Not put off, on 1 December he asked why more time was needed. Oh, take a running jump, I thought and gave him at last a ministerial reply; I referred him back to my answer at column 478 without further comment. 'Because they are not ready,' was the answer. And that, bluntly, was that.

The House of Commons computer tells me that during the months I was a Minister I dealt with just under 3,000 parliamentary questions, mostly written. They can only be asked when Parliament is sitting so that works out at around 150–200 per month; usually twenty-five to forty per working day, and a full hour's work several nights a week.

The red-jackets would contain the minutes of Cabinet and Cabinet committee meetings, in dry, cool, elegant language, 'SECRET' stamped on many a page. The light-green-jackets were invitations with the departmental view attached: 'We do not consider that this Health Day in Little Puddlecombe, despite its proximity to the Minister's home, merits the Minister's attendance. She might prefer to tour the hospitals down in X; the train journey from London only takes three hours . . .' The jumbled heap at the bottom would be copies of correspondence, or departmental papers, or briefings for tomorrow, or an outline for a speech next week, or Thursday night's debate, or press bids, or requests (yet again) for a healthy recipe or a limerick or something to auction for charity. (From September 1988 onwards the latter problem was neatly solved as we cheerfully passed on the woolly hats sent to us in very large numbers by irate pensioners.)

And the several buff folders would be constituency papers, brought over by my long-suffering secretary from the House of Commons. Oh yes, we were still MPs, most of us. Ministers who have constituencies to look after don't stop and can't hand over the work to someone else: it just has to be fitted in somehow. Being a minister sometimes helps constituents, of course, but I had a spectre in mind. My predecessor in South Derbyshire was the ebullient George Brown, in the days when it was called Belper. He was a very important man indeed in the 1964–1970 Labour Government – Cabinet Minister, Foreign Secretary and Deputy Leader. But he failed somehow to secure his home port before setting sail and in the 1970 General Election, after twenty-five years, they threw him out. That's how we do it in a free country.

The computer also tells me that for 1986–8, there were fifty-eight adjournment debates, four Consolidated Fund (late night) debates and twenty-six other debates in my name. That meant I could be sure of speaking at the Despatch Box at least once a week: more than most ministers. I never got blasé about it. It was always exciting, always an honour, always scary. The House of Commons Chamber is quite small and you can see the whites of the Opposition's eyes. Every single debate requires a carefully-prepared speech, cleared with all concerned, as statements by Ministers in the House are instantly Government policy. Awesome responsibility for the speaker and you are never allowed to forget it.

Many of my days ended with me doing my bit answering an adjournment debate. These short debates take place at the end of the business of the night on the formal motion 'That this house do now adjourn'. They occur five times a week, late – at least 10 p.m. – after business Monday to Thursday, and at close of business, 2.30 p.m., on Friday, which means standing room only on the train going home from St Pancras, even in first class. The debate can only take half an hour, the MP who has raised the subject will not normally be interrupted (everyone else has gone home), and the minister must answer. The record, of over 100 adjournment debates, is held by Sir George Young, who had my job from 1979 to 1981 and then moved to the Department of the Environment till 1986. But it took him five years to get to the ton, whereas I found myself at the half-century by 27 May 1988, some twenty-one months into my term of office. That'll teach me to encourage friends to use the technique to get a ministerial answer. Still, it is one of the best ways for an ordinary MP to raise an issue, guaranteeing coverage at least locally, often nationally, and commanding a ministerial reply. I said once that it is an honour to attend at the Despatch Box to answer, even at 2 a.m., and I meant it.

During recess, ministerial work does not stop. It just ends a bit earlier each evening. The minister can guarantee attendance at an official dinner instead of worrying about rushing away to catch the 10 p.m. vote. The boxes will be taken home in the ministerial car and collected first thing in the morning. It was never very clear to me when my government driver slept! On Bank Holidays, on Christmas Day, even at the height of the holiday season, each department has a minister on duty. So while MPs may travel far on important fact-finding tours to the Bahamas and the Far East, while the rest of the nation queues grumbling at Gatwick and Luton for the delayed package tour flight, you may rest assured that somewhere in London, steaming gently in a non-air-conditioned office, the minister who drew the short straw is cursing the weather and doing his boxes. Makes one feel almost sorry for them.

Why do ministers do it? Isn't a backbencher's life easier? If you can't take the heat, you can always leave the kitchen. But the door to the Government kitchen is shut tight to a non-minister. Occasionally, there are chinks of light around it and a little information filters out, a crumb from the kitchen table for which he is duly grateful. Seeing how the cake is made, taking part in the baking, is a greater privilege, against which the occasional long night, the child's missed birthday party, the wedding attended by everyone else in the family but not by its most famous member, can seem insignificant. Power carries its own adrenalin, its own satisfaction, its own secrets.

*   *   *

The end of the proceedings in the Commons is heralded by the remark, 'Who goes home?' called out by the policemen and door-keepers, a reminder of days long before in previous centuries when the streets were as unsafe as now. Then, footpads lurked and members went in groups for their own safety. Now they stand forlornly at the Members' entrance, sheltering from the rain, waiting for a taxi while ministers sweep by, blind and cosseted, in their official cars. On one occasion, however, the cry 'Who goes home?' had a particular poignance for me. It was easily the strangest episode in all my time at the Department of Health.

The weather was cold, deep down cold, cold enough to freeze the breath in the air, to make walking outdoors arduous, unpleasant, cold enough to turn diesel fuel to sludge, to fill the mountain passes with deep snow, to bring traffic to a despairing blue-nosed standstill. Temperatures of $-20°$ were being recorded, with daytime levels rising only to $10°$. The weathermen looked gleeful and the farmers gloomy as they rescued dying lambs from snow drifts. It was January 1987.

Ministers in the DHSS met for Monday 'prayers' on 19 January in the usual way. The talk was of cold-weather payments, temperature trigger points, staff managing to get to hospitals, home helps battling in to work against all the odds. The discussion, with civil servants present, was detailed and urgent. Just as we broke up at lunchtime, Norman Fowler turned to me. 'I'm worried about people sleeping rough in London and other places, Edwina,' he said. 'Can you go out quietly and get something done? You know the ropes from your Birmingham days. Just make sure that for want of somewhere to go for shelter, nobody freezes to the pavement.'

I was wearing my best suit, a green and black woollen concoction bought in the post-Christmas sales, dressing up a bit to speak in a

235

debate later in the Commons. I felt singularly ill-equipped for such a mission. 'You want me to go out, with the Salvation Army and the others, and bring people into shelter?'

'Yes,' he said. 'Just do whatever is necessary. Make sure you succeed.'

That was a tall order. Nobody really knew how many people were sleeping rough even in London. The pressure group Shelter (which doesn't shelter anybody, just moans about the problems) talked about 100,000 homeless. The police told me about 700, and that we needed to create additional hostel places fast, as the good ones were filling up rapidly with people who usually braved the elements. I called together the officials concerned, who turned out to be a lively crew of capable and steadfast women. Contact had already been made with the main charities, which functioned under the umbrella of 'Crisis at Christmas'. They had only just packed up after feeding the down-and-outs turkey and mince pies for the festivities but were already appealing for funds, helpers and locations for shelter. A meeting was fixed for the following morning.

Setting up temporary hostels, in church halls for example, was not difficult, but keeping them going for what could be several weeks needed competence as well as compassion. And it needed cash – or, at least, the firm promise of payment. Out of an underspent budget deep in the heart of the DHSS we found £100,000. This would be available, I decided, to pay the legitimate bills of approved organizations for providing shelter and care. If the cold spell went on a long time we would need more – but in those less likely circumstances we would be facing other big national problems anyway and our night shelters' needs would be tiny by comparison. I was anxious about what the organizations would spend the money on, so we did not give it to them as grants, but paid their invoices. I saw many that came in for mattresses, for blankets and sleeping-bags, for food, for hiring vans, for rent for halls and accommodation all over London and other major cities.

I needed to know the scale of the problem. My debate on speech therapists' pay was scheduled for 11.45 p.m. I raced through it, my mind working furiously on that matter elsewhere, the bodies on the frozen pavements. Outside it was snowing again, big, soft, cold flakes, clinging to the ministers' cars waiting in Speaker's Courtyard. We finished at 12.12 a.m. It was very late, very quiet, and getting colder by the minute. My private office had arranged for one of the civil servants and myself to go to various hostels run by the Salvation Army and St

Mungo's, to the Bondway House in Vauxhall, and to the Whitechapel Mission and various churches to see what was already happening. Then I could go out in the van with the volunteers who would check on regular haunts and try to persuade people to come indoors.

The van was unheated, freezing. A dirty old blanket covered the passenger seat. There had been no time to change so I snuggled into my coat and pulled a head scarf over my ears. I was supposed to be incognito but one old tramp recognized me later on and tried amicably enough to start a political discussion. With no police, no security, it was not safe and we moved on quickly. The van was filled with cheerful young people in jeans and anoraks who were giving up their time, without comment or criticism, to help; during the day they were city workers and students. Crammed in with them were bread baskets and plastic cups and huge urns steaming with soup, misting up the windows.

'What sort is it?' I asked, and they all laughed, poking each other, disclaiming responsibility.

'Sort of vegetable,' they said. 'That bit is cabbage, isn't it? You can try some later.'

The man in charge, driving, was older, rougher, harder, thinner, a full-time social worker for one of the hostels. He had seen and heard everything. His soft voice, matter of fact, sad, not judging, describing, was my guide in the fearful darkness that night, as we set off on the soup run.

The first part was easy, checking on doorways and the brightly-lit entrances to the tube stations. It had been suggested that the station platforms would be a good place to sleep but London Transport had not been happy because of the live rails, and because they could not keep an eye on everyone. The old hands agreed. Best to stay around the entrance, they said, the police don't bother you but they make sure you're not rolled over either.

'Who would do that?' I asked in astonishment.

'Oh, you'd be surprised, some strange people in London, looking for drugs or liquor like, it's not safe where you can't be seen.'

We had picked up a young man, ready to come back to a hostel for the night. 'Too f'ing cold out there tonight,' he said, his strong Glaswegian accent making his short comments guttural, grating. He was twenty-four and had come to London looking for work, had slept rough for four years. He was clean and presentable.

'Why do you sleep out?' I asked him.

'It's convenient and easy once you know how,' he explained.

'There's a – you know – hierarchy out there, who gets the best spots like. Mostly if you have a job, say early morning cleaning, you sleep nearby. That's why some of them won't come in, even on a night like this, they are scared of losing their pitch.'

'Are they all like you?' I asked him later.

'No, there's all sorts out there. The older ones, some of them, have been sleeping out for ages. They'll go into a hostel say, once a week, have a bath and get a change of clothes, then go out again till the clothes are all falling to bits, then they do it again. Some came out of the army and couldn't settle. Some left mental hospital years ago and never managed to cope anywhere. They all have a routine, day by day. The young ones mostly don't stick it.'

The driver joined in: 'Often the older men have gone downhill after a marriage breaks up, or the wife dies. You hear some sad tales out there. A lot have been in prison and prefer it now out of doors. Usually drink is involved somewhere along the line. Often the reason they are on the streets is they never behave in the hostels, disturbing everyone, and get thrown out. I don't blame the hostels: we all have to be very strict or things fall apart very quickly.'

We found ourselves in Whitechapel, the long road stretching away, sky purple as the snow fell, street lights twinkling, all sound deadened. Up a back alley was the mission, now being used for a hundred sleeping men. More clustered around the entrance, clutching mugs of cocoa and munching hunks of white bread. I had seen many sights in my time in Birmingham and Liverpool, but nothing like this. The air inside the hall was warm, steamy, a bit smelly. The bodies in sleeping bags and on mattresses, toe to toe, moved restlessly, muttering. A man with white stubble and an unlined face was curled up in a corner, sleeping almost in a sitting position, mouth open, head back, snoring loudly. The mission people giggled. 'If he goes on like this he'll have the neighbours complaining,' they whispered, 'and then we could have trouble: we're only a day centre, not supposed to have anyone sleeping, no facilities, see.'

One more visit in this extraordinary night, to Lincoln's Inn Fields. My twenty-four-year-old guide made me look carefully, and there, in the bandstand, were the cardboard boxes and newspapers and the shuffling grunting noises of human beings.

'Who sleeps here?' I asked him.

'They are the crazy ones,' he said. 'See how dark it is? Not safe. Lots of drugs there. No one with any sense would sleep there – Holborn Tube Station's a much better place.'

It was like being in the litter-strewn wilderness of some mad science fiction film. We offered bread and soup. Some was accepted, grumbling, it wasn't hot now. We offered shelter, but the dark figures turned away. We left them there.

Over the next few days, the voluntary organizations and the DHSS's own units created over 900 additional places for people sleeping rough in London. In other cities there was similar action, though it was only needed on a much smaller scale. By the end of the week churches had sleeping bags all over the pews and had discovered the incompatibility of anti-social clients and Matins at 8 a.m. The good churchgoers of St James's in Piccadilly decided in the end that they could not cope with carousing during the Creed and snoring bodies at noon, and regretfully withdrew. Nevertheless, I was not satisfied till all the night shelters were reporting vacancies. They reckoned they had acquired about 700 additional clients, so the police were right. Some were still sleeping rough, but that was their right in a free country. Some complained that they could not get any rest with so many do-gooders waking them up to feed them soup and offer them a bed! But we knew who was still out, and where. We knew they were safe and relatively warm. We knew they could come in if they wanted to. Nobody would freeze to the pavement for want of a bed: nobody did.

I went out again the following week but the weather was easing off. We spent most of the money and used the remainder to help the volunteers plan for such eventualities in future. Solving the problem of the cardboard city is clearly not just a matter of money or of mattresses, though. It is far more complex than that. There used to be more hostels, and Shelter moaned about their standards. I had seen the Rowton Hotel in Birmingham years ago before it closed and was appalled that men then paid £7 a week for a cubby-hole, so small I could touch both walls with my arms outstretched. Make the shelter better, more elaborate, more organized, and the sleepers won't come. Try and improve their lives, offer them hope and the love of God, and they turn away with a sneer. Create a night shelter, very basic, no rules, everyone welcome drunk or sober, and local residents complain until it is closed down. Leave them in a warm corner, under an archway, let them be in peace; they will pull the blanket up to their chins and go to sleep, while someone will write yet another article about the callousness of the modern world.

That day ended close to dawn, with me very silent. The adjournment debate on speech therapy seemed a million years ago. During that brief discussion I had touched on the hours worked by NHS therapists – then only thirty-three per week, which accounted for their lower pay. Archy Kirkwood, the Scots Democrat MP, had demanded to know how many hours Ministers work.

'More than thirty-three,' I had told him.

'Not all of them!' was the reply.

My clothes were stained and would have to go to the cleaners. My feet were so cold I could not feel them. The smell of wet cabbage and carrot clung to my hair. I was desperate for a hot bath and a warm bed. As I put the key wearily into the lock on the door of the flat, the phone was ringing.

It was *TV-AM* . . .

9

The Thatcher Revolution

Methinks I see in my mind a noble and puissant nation rousing herself like a strong man after sleep

Milton, *Areopagitica*

What happened?

What happened, indeed?

By 1988, it seemed, we had moved the goalposts with a vengeance. Prevention of disease and the promotion of good health, through changes in life-style and an increased acceptance of personal responsibility, had become a major part of the activities of the Department of Health. With a few exceptions our campaigns had won the confidence of the public, and the ready agreement of many health professionals. Most of what we were doing met with thorough-going public approval, and they shared the jokes and the fun, too.

Up and down the country, health authorities and local councils held 'Health Days', weighing local notables and measuring their blood pressure in public, and sent out free sheets extolling the virtues of wholemeal bread. 'Low fat' became an advertising slogan guaranteed to increase sales, while rapidly increasing quantities of low-alcohol beer and lager poured down thirsty British throats and breweries brought out new brands every week. Persistent smokers were bodily removed from planes to the cheers of the other passengers, while a popular soap opera, giving careful thought to the messages it sent to 20 million viewers every week, kept a bowl of fruit on the table and showed an alcoholic, not as the traditional old lush, but as the wreck of an attractive young woman. Your health is your business, they were all saying. You can do something abut it. 'Yes, we agree,' said the people. 'Tell us how.'

241

At various stages in 1988 I was involved in publicly-funded campaigns on heart disease, drink-driving, anti-smoking, donor cards for transplants, immunisation, Europe against Cancer, 'Keep Warm Keep Well' for the elderly, and a few others beside. We were encouraging women to take up their invitations for cancer smear tests, and explaining the breast cancer screening programme and why they couldn't all have their test at once. We were promoting every kind of 'healthy' foodstuff from rice to apples to fruit juice to pasta, even, on one unforgettable occasion, marigolds (ugh!). I seemed to be on television all the time and any press library cuttings file on me must be inches thick. Too much? I don't doubt it.

By the summer of 1988 I was, to my complete surprise, well known indeed. *The Economist* commissioned an opinion poll to establish who among the leading figures of government was known to the public. My picture was in there for comparison and they found I was the best known after the Prime Minister, after less than two years in post. That was all very embarrassing, and must have annoyed many far worthier people. I had not set out to become famous and I don't recommend it. The lack of privacy it brings is not only a darned nuisance, but can diminish one's ability to do a job well, perennially surrounded by the ratpack of press men and TV cameras.

When I had sat down on 18 September 1986 to write 'Moving the Goalposts', I had had several motives, not all of them conscious then. The most ambitious was also the most transparent: to do whatever I could, along with other colleagues who also felt the same way, to use my office at the Department of Health to improve the health of the nation. There was, and is, a limit to what hospitals and doctors can do for us. The increase in modern diseases, the main ones at least – including heart disease and lung cancer – had a lot to do with the way each of us lived, day by day.

That objective was both worthy and serious, and appreciated very quickly by the vast majority of ordinary people, at whom most of our efforts were to be directed. Even those who made no attempt to change their habits approved of us for trying. I knew it was likely to be a popular mission, for I had seen details of opinion polls, some commissioned by the Department before I arrived, which had asked what people wanted for and from the NHS. It needs more money, they all said, as they always said, and then various other items were mentioned: no waiting lists; better information; make it easier to change doctors; and the like – all of which we tried to improve. But there at the bottom of the list had loomed one request, mentioned more than most others: more prevention, please, they said, more advice on how to stay well, and 70 per cent wanted that. So I knew that politically it would be a Good Thing.

For me, personally, if I could handle it well, then prevention would do my position no harm and might do it some good. Other ministerial colleagues had made headway on topics of interest which had been lying around, waiting to be tackled with some energy and conviction: David Mellor on drugs, David Trippier on small businesses, Kenneth Baker on the need for information technology which the rest of us know as computers. It is also much more fun in politics to get one's teeth into a subject, to become knowledgeable about it, and thereby to influence effectively the political decisions in that field, thus trying to bridge the huge divide between the non-political experts (to whom the answers are always obvious) and the politicians seeking short-term gain (who may not understand the first thing about the subject).

I had some long-term objectives in the back of my mind, too. Other countries had shown that heart disease, for example, could be reduced by deliberate action over a decade or so. By determined action we could cut the number of deaths from cervical and breast cancer. The MMR programme should mean that measles would disappear. Excess winter mortality should fall away. If we could persuade young women to stop smoking we might see further falls in the perinatal mortality rates, and so on. All this without compulsion, without legislation. I happen to believe that the British electorate is one of the best-informed and most thoughtful in the world. They vote on substance, not rhetoric. They might just approve of what we were up to in the short run, but in the longer run we could show them more concrete evidence that our brand of partnership between public and state worked. We could claim now that we cared, and we could hope to prove it, some of it at least, by 1991 or 1992 at the next general election – but even more so the election after that. Ambition!

There were other considerations, too. Sooner or later, someone else was going to twig that people wanted to take a greater interest in practical aspects of good health, and the subject might get taken up by one of the other parties. The Labour Party was lumbering slowly towards greater sophistication and might just stumble over this issue, though I reckoned the overweight men in smoke-filled rooms at Walworth Road and Transport House might have trouble selling it to their executive committees. Philosophically they might also have difficulty taking the line that some causes of ill-health might lie partly with the individual, when they were hammering away at the notion that it was all the Government's fault. The middle parties were already a bit sympathetic but they had no solid base amongst the millions of working people whence the two main parties draw their support, so I wasn't bothered about them. With the notable exception of Cyril Smith, their members were already beansprout eaters, as their party conferences in small towns showed, and, anyway, there was a long tradition of us pinching their ideas (including some from David Owen's book *Our NHS*) rather than the other way round. But there was a vacuum there, a public and political need that was not being filled, and, in all innocence, before anyone else tried to seize the high ground, I set out to take it.

What was apparent very quickly was that we had hit some kind of bedrock, some very basic issues with profound meaning for millions of people. They already knew that much disease could be avoided. Only a few moments thought, chatting in a pub at Sunday lunch-time, could bring out mention of illnesses long since disappeared through a combination of competent action on the part of governments, and the co-operation of the public won through leadership. There was thus a long tradition of partnership between government and the electorate on issues of this kind. What was new was the range of topics. Who would ever have thought that heart disease was preventable? You got a bad heart from stress and overwork, didn't you? Wasn't it all caused by unemployment? What do you mean, my breakfast might have something to do with it? How can sausages cause angina? No, I'm not kidding you, I'm not having you on. I'm sorry, is my cigarette bothering you? Yes, it is, relieved to be able to say so at last. Isn't a good diet lots of meat and protein then, like we used to be taught? Come on, have the juices off this beef, it's lovely, and a few more roast potatoes and buttered carrots; there's apple pie and cream for afters. What do you mean, can you have a salad and some fruit? Now then, Minister, have a drink, and another. Orange juice? Oh, I don't know, I'll see if we have got some . . .

People from all walks of life would sidle up to me at functions, pull shyly at my sleeve and tell me they had given up smoking, lost two stone, thrown out the frying pan and stopped eating pastry, bought a dog and started taking exercise. On a visit to Pollockpark in Glasgow, then one of the poorest areas in Europe, a fat woman leaned out of the top floor of a tenement building as I went past and yelled something obscene about chips. 'The message is getting across even here,' grinned Scottish Office officials happily, as we walked past.

There were undoubtedly rapid changes of behaviour already under way in some areas, food purchasing for the home, for example. Elsewhere, attitudes were changing, as the drunk driver became a pariah, with the smoking traveller not far behind. Condemnation of bad behaviour took the place of condoning it. There appeared for the first time a readiness to attribute many of the ills of society, from football hooliganism to rape, to excess alcohol. We were not really aware of these shifts in 1986 but there is no doubt the bandwagon had already begun to move. All I did, if anything, was to give that bandwagon a hefty big shove. It felt at times as if I was being carried off in the slipstream of something I didn't start and couldn't stop – and did not want to stop or slow down, for all this progress on health is, to me, a great personal pleasure which I hope will continue.

Prevention fitted with my own philosophy, that the state was not and should not be all-powerful, that personal responsibility should come first. It seemed to fit with the growing sophistication of many of the electorate, too: at last we were offering people something they could do themselves. After our resounding success in the 1987 election, and my huge post-bag throughout 1988, it began to dawn on me that maybe this was all part of the Thatcher revolution.

Back in 1975 when Margaret Thatcher was elected Leader of the Conservative Party, I was not in the least surprised. The mess of 1974 had shown that new solutions to the nation's problems were needed, and there was a restlessness abroad, a feeling that we had all been let down by yesterday's men half-heartedly touting yesterday's ideas. That feeling grew through the next five years, particularly after James Callaghan became Prime Minister; he did not seem to have much of a clue about solving the problems of strikes, low productivity and the general sense of mediocrity. Indeed, on more than one occasion he did not even seem to be aware that there was a problem. Soon after the 1975 leadership election I was elected councillor for the Northfield ward in South Birmingham, with nearly thirty of the city's hundreds of tower blocks and where over half the voters were council tenants. The following year Conservatives won control of the City Council, and we had a whale of a time for the next few years. The parliamentary constituency, also called Northfield, was then a pretty safe (10,000 majority) Labour seat, held by Ray Carter, who was a junior minister. That meant we seldom saw him; a lesson I tried not to forget in my own constituency a decade later. On election day in 1979 not even the policemen at the polling stations recognized him, and to our wild and incredulous delight, at nearly 4 a.m., after two recounts, it was announced that Jocelyn Cadbury had won the seat for us with a tiny majority. Council elections were on the same day and I was returned as councillor for a second term. And Margaret Thatcher became Prime Minister.

I had therefore followed the political debates of the time with great interest, and agreed with Sir Keith Joseph that we should abandon the collectivist consensus. Government could not create jobs, government should not intervene on incomes. We should see the unions not as a central and desirable part of the collectivist state but as monopoly suppliers of labour, to be dealt with accordingly. We did *not* have to accept socialist solutions. He felt that we should instead try to identify the 'common ground', the place where the real lives and aspirations of most people were in practice acted out. Heady stuff, and genuinely exciting for Birmingham's youngest councillor, fresh from winning scholarships to university which took her a long, long way from home. You'll find the development of the philosophy all discussed in a slightly disdainful way in Hugo Young's book *One of Us*, published for the tenth anniversary of the 1979 election. I attended the 1975 party conference, my first ever, and heard Margaret Thatcher say great things: 'Britain and socialism are not the same thing . . . let me give you my vision: a man's right to work as he will, to spend what he earns, to own property, to have the state as servant and not as master; these are the British inheritance. These are the essence of a free country . . .' Oh, yes, I could fight for that. Delegates stood and cheered her to the echo. And there on the doorsteps, the voters agreed with us.

We thought that we had won the 1979 election because of the winter of discontent. The new Prime Minister pointed out, with some satisfaction, that the gap in votes cast between the two major parties was over two million, the biggest difference since 1935. We thought, at the time, that we won the 1983 election because of the Falklands, and certainly, canvassing yet again on the doorsteps of Birmingham and then South Derbyshire, the strength and determination of the leadership during the conflict was repeatedly mentioned with approval. Michael Foot, the Labour leader in 1983, was more shrewd, and was reported to have said that Labour lost the election because of all the new front doors gracing the recently-purchased houses on the council estates. When we won the 1987 election, three in a row, unprecedented in recent British political history, with the gap between the leading parties heading for four million, it began to dawn on us that something special had been happening under our noses.

The research showed us that the Conservatives were drawing heavy support from better-off people, the ABs of advertising jargon, and with increasing national prosperity there were lots more of them, living in their suburbs and little country towns. But among the skilled and semi-skilled working class, the C1s and C2s, Thatcherism – often in its rawest form – had an increasingly solid base. Come election time, only a third of trade unionists voted Labour now and the membership of the old unions was dropping fast. Let the intellectuals turn their noses up at selling council houses, at shares for the masses, at personal pensions, at compulsory ballots against strikes. The masses bought their homes, paid into the new pension scheme, put the share certificates in a tin box under the bed and voted to go to work.

I was seeing it happen in my own South Derbyshire constituency. In 1984 the local pitmen voted by a huge majority to stay at work and defy Arthur Scargill, and then they put up with a year's misery as pickets found their way to Cadley Hill colliery. Even the NUM leadership realized how quickly they were turning off their own people, for they took away the Yorkshire pickets, whose taunts had aroused such fury, replacing them with gentler men from South Wales. All summer in 1984 the chaps from the Rhondda stood on the bridge near my home which overlooked the railway line to Willington power station, and watched resignedly as the train drivers took the coal wagons in, waving their union cards, and more besides, as they did so. By late August the Welshmen were sitting under the bridge fishing in the canal and the Prime Minister was set to win the next election.

The pit has closed now. Management at other dying pits nearby is inundated with demands from the men to be able to take early retirement and their redundancy money, and they will be closing ahead of schedule. The power stations will soon be in the hands of the people and the only questions I was asked by that industry's workers during the 1987 election campaign were: When would we be privatizing? What would happen to the pension fund and how many shares would they be getting, like?

In ten years my typical constituent has moved a long, long way, too. In the early 1980s he would have worked underground, controlled by his union, led by the demagogue who once stood for election carrying the banner of the Young Communist League. He would have come home dirty on a bike to a house he did not own. His idea

247

of a night out would have been darts in the local on a Saturday night, and his idea of a holiday was a week in Skegness. He expected that his son would leave school at the earliest opportunity and follow him down the pit. And he took it for granted that everybody round here votes Labour.

Now he works somewhere else, cleaner, safer, better paid, where he isn't obliged to be a member of a union. Perhaps he is even in his own small business, went in with the brother-in-law. He drives home in a smart car with a foreign name, to the house with a garage and gas central-heating he bought a couple of years ago; nice, that. His idea of a night out is £50 for a meal for the family in the Carvery in town, and he takes two weeks holiday with everyone else in Marbella. He's using his British Telecom shares as collateral for the loan for the double glazing. His son is at college and wants to design cars for Toyota; the lad went ski-ing this year with his pals. And nobody takes their votes for granted any more.

Where's the proof? The travel agent in Swadlincote recognized it before I did. He took over the local slag heap, applied for a grant and built a dry ski-school on it complete with après-ski facilities and good-looking ski instructors. It's always busy and he has extended it twice so far, and now sells his expertise to others wanting to do the same.

I watched my constituents getting interested in their health, too. As the shop-floor worker suddenly realized that he could go for a supervisor's job, he started going to the hairdresser and cut down on the potatoes. They don't approve of smoking at work, so he cut that down, too, and eventually stopped; saved himself a lot of money. His mate had a bit of a heart attack and he thought, that could have been me, stuck at a desk all day now, so he joined the running club and next year he might just have a go at the half marathon in Derby, just for a lark, mind, would you sponsor me? The wife was worried about her figure so off she goes to an aerobics class, and now she insists that I eat that Flora stuff: you pleased with me, Mrs Currie? And he sips his Tennants LA and we laugh about it all, this silly business of looking after yourself, but, yes, he does feel a lot better and fitter these days and he is glad he's made the effort and thinks more people should.

Once they have secured their homes and their future, once they feel more prosperous, once, indeed, they take that prosperity for granted, the ordinary people of this country can think far more than ever they used to about other issues. 'Life-style' issues, they have been dubbed.

None of my efforts would have worked had unemployment been increasing, had industry been collapsing. 'Look after your heart!' would have sounded cruel and fatuous when people were trying desperately to look after their jobs. You don't need more money in your pocket to eat wisely for health, but you do need the time and mental energy to pursue these new ideas, and enough faith in the future to make it seem worthwhile. It has long been the case that the better-educated members of British society have adopted the latest fads with alacrity, while the rest of us, more cautious, more ignorant (yes!) take time to be convinced. But it is the essence of the Thatcher revolution that people were ready to take more responsibility in a host of ways. Taking up the health life-style messages rang a sound bell for many, many people – particularly once they realized I was serious, that I meant it all, that I tried quite hard to do it myself and I wasn't going to give up easily. It fitted with the increasing interest in the environment, also once thought of as the dotty doubtings of freaks, but now mainstream politics and winning votes. It manifests itself in angry feelings on law and order, a sense of outrage that homes are violated, old people roughed up, housewives raped, the city centre not a nice place to go at night. It helps explain the increasing assertiveness of women, making up nearly half the work-force, and more than half the electorate, bringing their own pay-packets into the home, cheesed off at being patronized at work by men thicker than they are. (But that, perhaps, is a subject for another book.)

I would argue, therefore, that my only contribution was – in the words of Theodore Roosevelt – to say what everyone was thinking but a bit louder. I didn't *know* they were all thinking that! But the interest was swiftly shown to be there, favourable, approving, amused and slightly mocking, and it persists still.

If my analysis is right, then the life-style issues are important for the British voter, and are likely to be so increasingly. We will need a new agenda for the next election to take us into the nineties. The Conservatives can't go on fighting on the same basis as they did ten years ago, selling council houses and taming the unions; we have done all that. There's still some way to go to counteract the damage done by 'loony left' councils, but the community charge and the unified business rate will help. There's a limit to the amount of privatization, for as we pass old industries back to their shareholders, there's not much left now. The electorate, in any case, draws a line when it comes to the NHS: leave that, they say, more or less as it is, generously funded out of taxation, we will pay. We can't keep fighting on the basis of how awful Labour Governments used to be, either – most people can't remember; show half the electorate a photo of Harold Wilson and they would say, who's that?

The issues are changing, in my view, but they have more to do now with the quality of life, related to the degree of control exercised over the lives of an individual, of a family, and who has that control and to what uses it is put. The consumer counts here, with a vengeance. Government is seen increasingly as standards setter and standards enforcer – for a much higher-quality environment. That's why, sooner or later, there was going to be a row about salmonella.

Mine is not an original argument. Very little I ever got involved in, as a minister, was original. But I hope it is a realistic and accurate assessment of the next stage of the Thatcher revolution. And I hope these efforts, to build part of the health revolution into the life-styles of ordinary men and women in this country, will put votes into the ballot boxes in future. I shouldn't be in the least surprised if they do.

10

Endgame

. . . Yet the first bringer of unwelcome news
Hath but a losing Office . . .

Henry IV, Part II

Birmingham Children's Hospital is the main children's unit for the West Midlands. Like many other provincial hospitals, it does quite remarkable work with desperately sick children in very tatty facilities, built before the first world war in the centre of the city. A chronic absence of maintenance over many years, and the longing to remove the hospital in its entirety to the suburban site of the Queen Elizabeth Medical Centre, have exacerbated the hospital's problems. Long planned, the move is now scheduled for the nineties. Perhaps. This visit, however, took place long before, in the seventies.

The members of the grandly named 'Birmingham Area Health Authority (Teaching)' were to discuss the Children's Hospital at their monthly meeting that afternoon, so some of us had accepted the Administrator's invitation to come and see for ourselves. We stood now, hot and sweating, in the kitchen from which thousands of meals a week were sent upstairs, as they prepared our lunch. My heart sank. It was not very reassuring, I thought, as I looked at the staff in their grubby uniforms and food-streaked aprons, at the strange-smelling puddles on the floor, at the unwashed equipment, the cracked tiles, and the untidy crockery piled high near the broken dishwasher. The place was stifling, cramped, dirty. The staff looked bowed down with work and there was a distinct feeling of failure to cope.

The management were explaining, waving their arms, wringing their hands, as my colleagues listened attentively. Quietly I moved

251

away round a corner. Two of the male staff were standing watching us and were startled as I appeared. A sympathetic approach seemed best. 'Is it always like this?' I asked. 'Bit of a mess, isn't it?'

'Oh yes,' they agreed, 'very difficult to work here.'

I moved over to a huge mixer, still half full of an anonymous cream-coloured mixture. There were dollops all over the floor. 'What's this?' I asked.

'That's the mousse,' they said. 'It's for the kids' tea. Comes in a big sack. We mix it up in that, and then it goes in little dishes and up to the wards.'

'And what,' I asked further, fighting down my retching stomach and reaching for the utterly filthy tea-towel, stiff with dried mixture and dark with oil from elsewhere on the machine, draped over the side of the big bowl, 'what is this for?'

'Well, it's a tea-towel,' one of them helpfully replied. 'We use it to wipe it all down, see. Keep everything clean.'

'I understand. Can I borrow it?'

'Sure, you go ahead. And make sure you vote for our pay rise this afternoon.' They grinned, as I carefully put the disgusting piece of cloth in a plastic bag which they cheerfully provided.

It reeked right through the meeting under the table, producing one or two odd looks from fellow members. At last we came to the item on the agenda, and after listening to some of the others pooh-poohing the idea of spending any money on the kitchens – after all, we did have crown immunity, we couldn't be sued – I produced it with a flourish.

The offending object was by now so stiff it stood in a tent shape on the table without support and in the warmth of the committee room its stink was unavoidable. 'We need,' I roundly declared, 'two things – we've got to make that kitchen easier to clean, and then we've got to insist that they clean it and keep it that way – otherwise the standards represented by this object will persist.' The tactic worked; the authority voted £20,000 to start off, to repair the floor. The union claimed it was the fault of management and the management claimed it was the fault of the union. The tea-towel went in the bin.

That was a very long time ago but I never found reason to change my approach to the subject. The events at Stanley Royd Hospital, Wakefield, in 1984 brought back to me the tea-towel that could stand up by itself. Anyone who has any doubt what an outbreak of food poisoning is really like should read the report of the Committee of Inquiry published in January 1986.

Over the period of a warm August Bank Holiday weekend, the report says, a food poisoning outbreak took place at the hospital. It was probably caused by raw chicken contaminating meat which had already been cooked, sliced and left out on trays for serving cold some hours later. There was nothing unusual in such behaviour in that kitchen, or in other practices which might have been designed to promote the spread of infectious disease. Refrigerators did not work, their doors wedged open; food was left in a store-room through which hot water and steam pipes passed; there were cockroaches everywhere; raw and cooked food were regularly mixed up; the drains overflowed because they were blocked with lost cutlery and were never cleared, and gave off so offensive an odour that no one would go near them; cleaning practices, almost unbelievably primitive, included washing down the floors with jets of water which splashed all over the food preparation tables, and the regular wiping of these surfaces with squeegee mops which had previously been used on the floor.

The kitchen staff did not become ill. Apparently they ate the chicken, well cooked, and went home. Then the nightmare began. Over that weekend and subsequently, many of the patients who had eaten the Saturday evening meal, most of them old and frail, suffered terribly. On the morning of the Sunday, the first patient succumbed at about 7 a.m. By 9.15 a.m. some thirty-six patients in eight wards were affected; by 6.45 p.m. seventy patients, and by 9.15 p.m. ninety-four patients. At 11.35 p.m. the first death occurred. By the Tuesday 240 patients were ill. The report said: 'Conditions on a severely afflicted ward . . . will be appreciated as defying description.' The outbreak was not brought under proper control for more than a week. In the end 355 patients were affected by salmonellosis, and a further 106 staff. Inquests established that nineteen deaths were caused by the ingestion of contaminated food at the hospital. Only nineteen dead; it could have been far worse. It needn't, of course, have happened at all.

Later, as a minister, I visited Stanley Royd Hospital and was shown round the kitchens. No blocked drains this time and a floor so clean you could have eaten off it. And a plan to spend £1 million to install a cook-chill system, in which food cooked on Monday would be kept in a fridge – properly controlled this time – until it was needed sometime before the following Friday. The food would lose 18 per cent of its vitamin C every day it was in store, of course, so it would be necessary to give the patients a vitamin supplement as well. And it would have to be reheated quickly and not kept warm for any length of time, which turned out to be rather a problem as the electrical wiring of most of the old blocks at the hospital would not take the additional equipment. Cook–chill is safe, I was repeatedly assured, and I don't doubt it. Provided, of course, that all the sensible regulations are carefully observed.

It was with some pleasure, therefore, that one of the first things I agreed to do as a minister in the autumn of 1986 was to help put through part of the Government's response to the Stanley Royd tragedy. The Government decided to accept the amendment proposed by the House of Lords that the NHS (Amendment) Act should remove crown immunity from health authorities. Absolutely right. Of course, there were worries about the possible cost of capital works needed to get the kitchens and serveries up to scratch, but in my view the health authorities should have been doing this already and it simply wasn't worth their while taking any risks, with so many vulnerable people in their care. Maybe it would mean not decorating the doctors' dining-room this year, or tarmacking their car-park. The language of priorities mattered more.

One more incident may help to illustrate my own background to such events. On 1 April 1982 I became the Chairman of the Central Birmingham Health Authority, while continuing as a City Councillor. A widespread outbreak of *Salmonella napoli* infection occurred in the Midlands and elsewhere during the next few months. In all, some 245 cases were confirmed by the laboratories, fifty-one people ended up in hospital, sixteen of them seriously ill with bacteraemia (blood poisoning), and the infection was traced to imported chocolate bars. On 23 July 1982 the Department of Health issued a public warning and four-fifths of the consignment of 3 million chocolate bars were recalled and destroyed. The outbreak quickly came to an end.

For all these reasons I was probably the worst person to get involved in any dispute over food safety. All my experience was in one direction. If there was illness you found the source. Often circumstantial evidence was all that was available, for in food poisoning cases people have usually eaten the only other evidence. A food vehicle is identified with any kind of certainty in only 20 per cent of cases of food poisoning. Having, either for sure, or with the strong balance of probabilities, identified the cause of the problem, you warned people about it and insisted on its being removed. End of problem – for the time being. But eternal vigilance was the key, particularly as the bugs modified themselves frequently and always seemed one step ahead of us. Fortunately good hygienic practices could protect producers and consumers, whatever the little nasty might be next time.

* * *

In the summer of 1988 it was apparent that we did have a little nasty on our hand, and it was growing rapidly. It was called *Salmonella enteritidis* phage type 4 (PT4) and it offered two new variants on other salmonellas. First it seemed to cause a particularly unpleasant illness and I was advised that its virulence, especially in vulnerable individuals, was worrying. Second, like other salmonellas, it was found in chicken, but it was being isolated more and more often from a very common food, eggs, and, more important, instead of being caused just by poor handling was being found *inside* the eggs. There was evidence that it had adapted to living symbiotically with the adult hen – in other words, it had learned to live with its host without killing it, or even making it ill (except chicks, which would die).

The chart overleaf is taken from the evidence of the Public Health Laboratory Service to the Select Committee on Agriculture, which inquired into the problem and reported on 1 March 1989. It demonstrates very clearly what was happening.

During the summer of 1988 officials told me that the number of all cases of food poisoning was rising rapidly (it is a notifiable disease). The number in which this kind of salmonella was being isolated appeared to account for the increase. The figures accepted by the Select Committee, for example (pages 6 and 17 of vol.II of their report), show that six years earlier, in 1982, out of a total of 12,322 proven cases of all types of salmonella in humans in England and Wales, there were some 1,101 cases of *S.enteritidis*, which accounted thus for less than 10 per cent. Of these, 413 cases – about 3 per cent – were PT4. In the first ten months of 1988, the year in question, the total was 23,038 cases of which 10,544 were for *S.enteritidis* PT4 alone, almost half the total, and close to the *total* only a short time before. The evidence of the Public Health Laboratory Service to the Select Committee says: 'In 1988 to the end of October there were about twice as many isolations of *S.enteritidis* PT4 as in the same period for 1987. In summary, *S.enteritidis* PT4 now dominates the epidemiological picture.'

Remember, too, these were the cases where someone was sick

S. enteritidis
1981 – 88

Humans, England and Wales

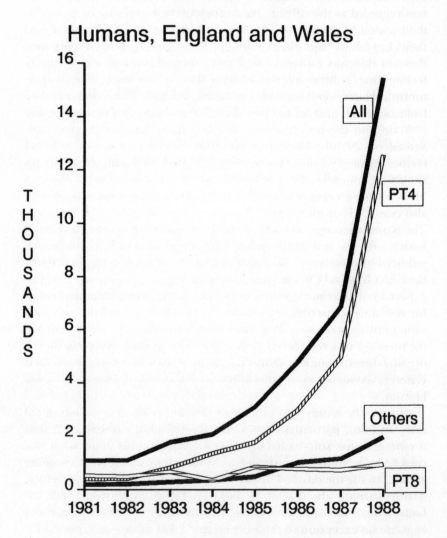

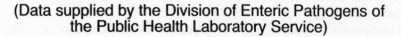

(Data supplied by the Division of Enteric Pathogens of
the Public Health Laboratory Service)

enough to call in the doctor or attend the hospital or even be admitted as a patient; these were not cases of mild indigestion. And this was just England and Wales, though something similar was happening in Scotland. They did, however, include cases where a catered event spread the illness amongst a large number of people, as, for example, the Mansion House banquet in which a savoury dessert, flash grilled, was regarded as the culprit, and a reception at the House of Lords for the London Magistrates Association which laid low large numbers of their Lordships and their distinguished guests. At first everyone thought this was rather comical and I would guess that there was a feeling that a little over-indulgence lay at the root of the upset tummies; but several members of their Lordships' House told me they had really been quite ill and it was a thoroughly unpleasant experience.

Acting on the best information we had available at the time, we agreed on 29 July 1988 to warn NHS catering managers that 'all recipes currently using raw shell eggs and which involve no cooking should be amended to specify the use of pasteurized egg' and that 'those nursing practices which entail the use of raw shell eggs should also cease'. (That meant not using eggs for pressure sores and ulcers.) The same message was offered on 2 September to environmental health officers and local authorities, all of whom were asked to publicize the message. We went further on Friday 26 August when the Chief Medical Officer issued a general public health warning: 'The expert advice to the Department of Health is that it would be prudent for consumers, particularly those who are more vulnerable, to avoid eating raw eggs or uncooked foods made from them.' On 5 September the message was reinforced by being sent to some thirty-six different organizations, ranging from the British Hotels, Restaurants and Caterers Association to the WRVS, the Army and the Cheshire Homes.

At first, the worry was just about raw and cracked eggs, but in the early autumn, particularly following a number of cases from Wales, it emerged that soft-boiled eggs, or even scrambled eggs, were not cooked long enough to kill the bug, which needed at least one minute at 80°C to die the death. On 21 November, therefore, another public health warning about cooking eggs thoroughly went out: 'For the housewife, it is clearly always safest to cook any food thoroughly and eggs are no exception to this general rule.' The advice to caterers was repeated: 'In the catering context . . . we would advise caterers to use pasteurized liquid egg.' That is five warnings by the end of November. The Select Committee felt that 'some earlier warning to the public could and should have been given'. Really? Frankly I think that comment is nonsense, particularly in view of subsequent denials that there was a problem at all when the warning *was* given loud and clear.

By the end of November we were getting reports from the laboratories of 500 salmonella cases per week where we could be certain of the type of bug and *S.enteritidis* PT4 accounted for the bulk of the numbers, as the chart shows. It was found in both chicken and eggs. There was no huge increase in the amount of children being sold. There was no sudden change, as far as we knew, in the cooking habits of the British housewife. But whatever the cause, it was on the increase with a vengeance. At that time we knew of over 20,000 cases of infection during the year so far, which must mean far more in the country as a whole – it was suggested to me that there had probably been around a quarter of a million. Within those totals we had knowledge of more than 1,000 cases where the same bug had been isolated from the food eaten *and* had been found in the eggs, or products containing eggs.

If it was indeed in eggs, any eggs, that was desperately serious. One of our commonest foods, they are widely used in a raw or undercooked state, and are often the first solid food fed to vulnerable people, to invalids and small babies. We did not want people to stop eating eggs altogether; we wanted people to cook them properly and not use them raw. I felt a real sense of outrage that autumn as we had to announce that they should stop eating soft-boiled or runny eggs – a health warning, it should be repeated, which is strongly endorsed yet again by the Select Committee and is still extant.

In the United States in late August the Department of Agriculture introduced a scheme to eradicate *S.enteritidis* from laying flocks, using inspection, testing and slaughter. By late 1988 I had discussed the matter with officials and was aware that my opposite number at MAFF, the excellent Richard Ryder, had been trying to persuade the egg industry to take the matter seriously, but was meeting with little success. The issue was emerging into the media and a number of the better-informed writers and programmes were highlighting it, including Derek Cooper's well-informed *The Food Programme* on BBC Radio 4. For weeks my office had been fending off demands for a comment or remark from me from all over the country, from local radio and television stations which had picked up their local Environmental Health Officer's warnings. But I referred them to the Chief Medical Officer's two statements. I knew I was going to have to talk about it sooner or later – and there was no reason not to after the issue of public warnings – but if I was going to raise the profile of this important topic it was not going to be on a radio phone-in in Norwich, but properly, nationally.

So when ITN asked if I would comment on the decision by Plymouth Health Authority, as always one of the most clued-up health authorities, to switch from shell eggs to pasteurized eggs as we had suggested, I said 'yes'. It was time to reinforce the message that they were doing what we had advised *five months ago*, and to ensure that the public were rather more aware of the health warnings already issued, in the weeks running up to Christmas.

It was a freezing cold day, Saturday 3 December 1988. Our breath hung in the misty Derbyshire air. We were on the outskirts of Derby, in a little council estate in Chellaston where the 'Keep Warm Keep Well' campaign had been insulating the homes of pensioner constituents. Outside, a young man cleaned his car, radio blaring. And the short interview went precisely like this.

'Rolling, everyone happy? Mrs Currie, what's your reaction then to this lead taken by Plymouth, not to have shell eggs in hospitals?'

'I understand that the Plymouth Health Authority have decided, taking some local advice, that they will not use shell eggs in the hospital catering service, they will use pasteurized liquid egg, which is of course still real egg, for all their catering and that seems to be quite a sensible thing to do.'

'How strong is your concern about salmonella in eggs at the moment?'

'Well, I think people have got to take a balanced view of this. Something like 30 million eggs a year are sold in this country and we have only a handful of outbreaks. Most of the ones that we've had, have involved caterers using lots of shell eggs, perhaps not always handling them quite as they should do. But the advice we have always been giving to caterers, and to people who are looking after large numbers of people, particularly vulnerable people, is that they should use pasteurized liquid egg, which seems to be sensible advice.'

'You say "vulnerable people". Is that why it is particularly important for hospitals to be careful?'

'I suppose we in the Health Department are very sensitive because of the sort of incidents we've had in the past. The people we look after are already sick, and may not have quite the resistance to disease and the robustness that other people might have. This particular strain of salmonella is quite nasty.'

'Do you want other hospitals to follow the lead taken by Plymouth?'

'I think what Plymouth have done is take local advice and look at the source of eggs available, and make sure they have a ready supply of pasteurized liquid egg which is of course still egg – it still comes from our farmers. They have taken their own decision. Now we won't stop them and if other health authorities follow suit, we would hope that they have simply taken good advice and followed it.'

'The Ministry of Agriculture have been quoted as saying that the warnings about eggs are alarmist. Would you go along with that?'

'We work very closely with the Ministry of Agriculture. In fact the Department of Health with their acceptance has issued two warnings about eggs this summer. We have to issue these warnings; we would be failing in our duty if we didn't. But they are quite right to point out that millions of eggs are being eaten – this week – with no harm at all, and people simply have to be sensible.'

'What about the general public, what can they do?'

'*We do warn people now, that most of the egg production in this country, sadly, is now infected with salmonella. If, however, they have used a good source of eggs, a good shop that they know, and they are content, then there seems no reason to stop. But we would advise strongly against using raw egg: mayonnaise, dressings, bloody Marys, that sort of thing. They are not a good idea any more.* Light cooking probably helps a bit, but thorough cooking, for example in a cake, would be perfectly all right.'

'Can the Department of Health do more, do you think, to cut down the risk in the future?'

'We are working very closely with the Ministry of Agriculture in this country and in other countries, to try and see what can be done to eradicate this very nasty salmonella strain. I think it is a great tragedy; I have constituents who are in this business and I think it is a tragedy that this strain has been allowed to get into our chickens and our eggs so that we have to keep warning people. Do be careful; always cook food thoroughly; don't let chicken stay pink, for example, defrost it properly; and if you're using eggs, make sure you know where they come from and that you are being sensible about the handling of them.'

'Finally, can I just recap on one more question; which is, what advice are you giving to other health authorities in the country?'

'The health notices that we have issued have gone to everyone concerned, and we hope that our health authorities would think about their supply and their use of egg; stop using raw egg entirely, it is not safe, and think about using pasteurized liquid egg instead, which is readily available to caterers for most of their cooking.'

'Thank you very much.'

The words italicized are those used by ITN for the evening news. The interviewer clearly did not think I had said anything special, as his questioning shows. I did not deliberately choose inflammatory words and, indeed, was very surprised to see the transcript several days later. I was convinced until then that I had carefully qualified the comments by saying 'We do warn people, we are afraid that, etc. . . .' and had otherwise stuck to the approved script. We did not know then, and we do not know as I write, what proportion of laying flocks are affected by disease. It certainly isn't 'most' and the vaguer word 'much' would have covered me. Given the information available to us at the time, though, the proportion did not seem negligible either. My words, however, could be set alongside the Welsh Public Health Laboratory Service article in the *Lancet* of the day before, which said: '*S.enteritidis* has been cultured in the UK from bulk liquid egg, dead laying hens, and from ovaries and oviducts of dead birds. In the USA and the UK vertical transmission of *S.enteritidis* is regarded as a new and important public health problem. The consequence for the public is that all eggs, including intact clean eggs, should be regarded as possibly infected.'

*　　*　　*

All politicians, all public speakers, occasionally fail to make their meaning absolutely clear. We all get careless sometimes. But if you live by the word and stand by the word, you die by the word. It was emphatically *not* my intention to damage the egg industry but to protect public health, which was my job. Consumption of eggs had been declining for years, and had dropped (according to the Select Committee) by about 10 per cent already, following the previous warnings. The industry did not collapse because of my words; it was already in trouble, at least in part because of the worries expressed by many others that there might be something lurking in the eggs – or at least in some of them, with no way for the consumer to tell which. The difference the interview made was that afterwards *everyone* knew about it.

Why didn't I correct myself at the first opportunity and change the words? As is now apparent, there were several reasons. First, it wouldn't have mattered what I said – once I had raised the profile of the issue, it was up and running. If I had simply read out the official warning, with a look of concern on my face, it would have had much the same effect. And there was no doubt in my mind that once the subject was in the public domain there was going to be a flaming row; that had been very obvious for some time. The laboratories had been screaming at us for months and – according to evidence I had not seen on 3 December – were already worried about deaths. Deaths? Oh, yes. In the words of the Select Committee: 'In the first ten months of 1988 there were 120 cases of bacteraemia due to *S.enteritidis* reported by laboratories to the Public Health Laboratory Service. Some of these patients were known to have other serious illnesses. Twenty-six of the 120 have died, twenty-three of whom were infected with *S.enteritidis* PT4. These figures, too, must give cause for concern.' The Committee adds, '. . . although they represent only 0.2 per cent of the total cases.' These are people, mind, not chickens.

So I was not too surprised at the rapid rise in interest, and saw no reason to back off. The argument in any case, as it turned out in the first few days, was not at all about 'much' or 'most' but about *'any'*. Long after the event I would watch egg producers on breakfast television deny that there was *any* infection in *any* eggs at all. It was all the fault of poor handling in the kitchen, they said. How did the salmonella get there in the first place? Ah yes, I thought, my Derbyshire housewife constituents go out into the garden, scoop up a peck of dirt and dish that up with the eggs and bacon. And if it isn't the eggs, how come we have so many cases where the laboratories are certain they are the problem, and so many diverse examples where the culprit is believed to be undercooked or raw eggs: home-made ice cream, mousse, scotch eggs (bound with egg white), egg sandwiches, mayonnaise, lemon meringue pie (with gently cooked meringue) and so on through a very long list? To back off would have permitted the total denial to predominate, and the public health risk to continue, so that was my second reason for staying quiet.

I didn't mind the personal criticism, though some of it was nasty, because, as Kenneth Clarke, my boss, put it to me, 'If you read the weather report, Edwina, you'd get blamed for the storms.' I was used to it; it was part of the job, though very wearing; and on nearly all the other issues for which there had been some personal criticism, as I have tried to describe in this book, there had also eventually been some vindication. Call it arrogance if you like, but on this issue both I and the officials at the Department of Health were genuinely worried. What I had in the back of my mind was that if the rapid increase in infection continued unabated, a hot summer ahead could really land us with a lot of seriously ill people, many of them needing hospital care, all over the country. I did not feel that we should wait for it to happen. Good government anticipates problems rather than simply acting in their wake.

'On second thoughts, Edwina, I'll just have toast.'

Much of the reduction in egg purchase in the next few days was, in any case, due to the spate of commentaries and articles, many no doubt already in preparation, which opened up a heated debate on possible sources of infection. My huge post-bag contained large numbers of these articles, particularly one, entitled 'Are we handing it to germs on a plate?' by Phyllida Barstow in the *Daily Telegraph* of Tuesday 6 December, which opened:

> Government warnings against eating lightly cooked eggs or less than thoroughly defrosted poultry because large numbers of intensively reared chickens, turkeys and probably ducks have been infected with a virulent strain of salmonella, highlights the question of whether it is desirable or safe to feed animals and birds intended for human consumption with the remains of their fellows.
>
> Any species which indulges in cannibalism traditionally is considered unclean, but battery hens fed on pellets containing broiler

waste and processed feathers have the grim choice of eating what is put in front of them or starving . . .

Whaaa . . . aat?

I did not know that animal and bird feeding stuffs contained ground-up remains, and, of course, did not need to know. My concern was not the health of poultry. Information of this kind, by now rapidly disseminated and widely discussed, produced a cry of horror and fury from large numbers of people who were disgusted at what they read. It seemed to them prima facie dangerous. To feed any creature material which is biologically identical, particularly if that material may be the poorly-sterilized waste of others which may have harboured, or even died from, a systemic infection, must be asking for trouble. According to the Select Committee report – and forgive me for constantly referring to it, but it is there for all to see – in paragraphs 57 and 61, in 1988 12 per cent of all domestically produced animal protein feed-stuff samples tested, and 38 per cent of the imported batches tested, turned out to be contaminated with salmonella. Mr Foxcroft, of the UK Renderers' Association, said in evidence, 'We do not think there is anything wrong with the product'. Nevertheless, he took the 'political' decision to stop recycling poultry waste for laying hens in this way within a matter of weeks. In the debate (one of many) in the House of Commons on 7 March 1989, the Chairman of the Select Committee, nice man that he is, said: 'While it is true that it [poultry feed-stuff] can be infected with salmonella, there is no evidence that that was the cause of any outbreaks, nor indeed would any ordinary person be particularly repelled by the substance, which is simply brown coloured powder, except possibly by its rather rich smell.'

There were other reasons, too, for not trying to correct a particular word or words. The third was that, to my intense irritation, for many days the debate was about something I did not say anyway, namely 'most eggs'. I knew that was wrong; the most pessimistic survey I had seen, in suspect flocks, suggested one egg in a thousand. Still a lot of eggs, but having once earned my living teaching statistics, I knew that wasn't 'most eggs' by any stretch of the imagination. I tried to put this right behind the scenes and by the following week most of the press had corrected it, but it was too late by then.

And I could not put it right in public, anyway, even when it was apparent that the public was over-reacting wildly (I never said, 'Don't buy eggs' either, but that's what happened). The fourth reason was, as everyone now knows, because my boss had instructed me on the Monday morning, 5 December, not to say anything and not to accept any request for a comment from the media. I rather misunderstood his instruction and took it to mean only for that day, but he made himself clearer on the Tuesday in a kindly way – there was never any row between us – and we retained a joint determination to protect the public health. It was an instruction I could not ignore and did not disobey. Perhaps colleagues thought it was just another Edwina spat, and if we all kept our heads down it would go away. But it didn't, and ten days later, with writs flying around, I handed in my resignation.

The *Sun* wrote up the story of my February 1989 appearance at the Select Committee in an hilarious way, pointing out that as a last resort, if I continued to defy them, I might be sent to the Tower. I would have gone to the scaffold before I told anyone that the reason I said nothing, and did not attempt to put right any misapprehension, was because I had been told not to. I would have taken the blame for the handling of the issue because personal responsibility was part of the job. I was really very surprised indeed, therefore, when, in the middle of my evidence to the Select Committee, having been kept waiting for the best part of an hour and not having been able to hear the evidence of the two Cabinet Ministers who preceded me, I was told that Kenneth Clarke had explained to the world his ban and the circumstances. That was very good of him and resulted in his taking a lot of criticism in the Select Committee's report. Had he said nothing I would not have done so either, then or at any time since.

As for the Committee – shall I describe the day I gave evidence? The splendid room off Richard III's Westminster Hall, where Henry VIII played tennis with Anne Boleyn and Charles I was condemned to death? Tragic ghosts lurk in that room. Shall I give you my personal picture of the chairman, knowledgeable about farming, anxious face furrowed with effort, or Labour's clever little health spokesman sitting up high, leprechaun-like, right behind him, chuckling into his little red beard? No photos may be taken in that room, no TV, then. It was, however, packed to the rafters with reporters from all over the world, friends and others, some of whom had queued since 8.30 a.m. that morning for half a seat. The BBC alone sent seven reporters, I was told afterwards. The *Daily Telegraph* published a drawing done at the time showing all the Committee members, faces bland and smiling. They did not look like that from where I was sitting, on a chair in the centre, the only open space in that whole hot packed room.

I did *not* want to be there. I had asked the Committee to permit me not to attend, saying I had no more information to give them than they had gleaned already from others – doctors, scientists, businessmen, ministers. That was true. I was there because I liked the chairman, who is a Conservative colleague, and also a former minister. I wanted to save us both further hassle. It had come to something when I could not even hold my advice bureau in the depths of Derbyshire without half a dozen reporters queuing up with my constituents and pestering them for their views.

The Select Committee Report was published three weeks later. Some of its conclusions are quoted in this chapter. The verbatim account of evidence given by every single witness including myself accompanies the report. It was no good their asking for secrets: I had none to offer. It was no good their seeking a scapegoat; this lady is not a sacrifice.

It does, however, seem such a pity that a Committee which so castigated my ministerial colleagues for being 'extraordinarily sluggish', that offered 'severe criticism . . . that a public health problem in eggs was required before they saw fit to act', that points an accusing finger at 'ineffective policing . . . not a satisfactory excuse for failing to protect the consumer', and so on, should have failed itself for so long, despite repeated official health warnings, to notice the problem of salmonella in eggs. Until, of course, on 3 December I used the words with which they were kind enough to open their important report.

*   *   *

Perhaps the whole horrible experience of salmonellosis food poisoning suffered by some people can best be described in the words of one lady from Manchester who wrote to me after the whole affair had died down:

> Before the birth of my children, aged seven and five, I worked in the catering trade for a total of fifteen years, as a confectioner and as a cook. As you will realize, within this time I have used a great many eggs and never before had I come across a case of salmonella due to them.
>
> However this was to change on 28 November 1988 when I received a phone call from the school both my sons attend. I was informed that my younger son had 'fallen' during morning

assembly and had banged his head, and it was thought he might have had a 'fit'. Fortunately one of my sisters had called the same morning and was able to drive me to school to collect him, on to the doctors and from there to the local hospital, by which time the child had started to be violently sick. After a thorough examination I was assured there was no physical damage and that it was very unlikely he had had a fit. The fact was he had actually fainted and I was advised this could be the onset of a virus infection, mumps, measles etc.

By the same evening my older son had also started to be ill. From that day I had the awful experience of nursing two very sick children day and night over two weeks. Until this time I had never seen anyone hallucinating and although I am a mature and sensible mother, I was very frightened indeed. They obviously had severe stomach pains and the vomiting alone took over a week to bring under control, the passing of blood with chronic diarrhoea was even worse and took over a fortnight to clear. They were both being treated for a 'tummy bug' and I am aware that the treatment for salmonella was the same. No one wanted to know when I suggested it could be food poisoning. Eventually samples were taken on 8 December and it was proved that both children had the salmonella virus present in eggs, which just happened to be the last thing I had cooked for them the day before the illness started. I had inadvertently poisoned my own children.

Through this they had both missed what to small children is the best part of the school year – the build up to Christmas – visit to the pantomime, school concert, Christmas party, etc. I even had to postpone my younger son's fifth birthday party from 21 December to 8 January as no children were allowed in the house and both boys couldn't go out. The fact is, we were prisoners in our own home for nearly a month.

I do not consider myself a 'crank', just an ordinary Mum . . . I consider myself lucky to have been able to nurse my children in my own home. Younger, smaller children would have been hospitalized. My experience was both traumatic and very tiring, but at least we were able to stay together. I can only hope cases like this will soon become a thing of the past . . .

The door which had once opened wide to government had now shut tight. It is never pleasant to give up, to walk away; for that is what a resignation is. This chapter, and this book, will end with the exchange of letters between myself and the Prime Minister, which I hope will also summarize the work I tried to do in my time in the Department of Health. The idea for the book came out of the letters, for I felt they were a balanced and appreciative summary. The press coverage the weekend after my resignation, however, to my dismay had dwelt endlessly on 'gaffes', and failed to mention any of that more worthwhile work, particularly on women's health, which will save, I hope, so many lives and so much pain and anguish in years to come. This lot, I decided in the dark hours of the night, this lot I have to put on record. I served under three Secretaries of State at the Department of Health, all with their own strengths, all different; I saw a revolution taking shape in health care and in interest in good health, and as I grow older I will benefit from it all, along with millions of my fellow citizens. The ministers now at the Department of Health are good and competent. They have the interests of the nation's health, and its health service, at heart. I have every confidence in them.

As for me, like Izaak Walton – whose words you will find on the title page – who spent a great deal of his time enjoying the rivers and dales of Derbyshire, I thank God for the two blessings; good health is only the second blessing, and a good conscience is the first.

*   *   *

Edwina Currie to Margaret Thatcher:

When I asked to see you this morning I told you that, having considered the matter very carefully, I had concluded that I should offer my resignation from the government. I think that in all the circumstances this is the best course.

It has been both a privilege and a pleasure to be a Minister in the Department of Health under your leadership. Your immensely successful efforts to improve the economy have made possible record funding for the NHS, producing standards of care for all our people, especially women, unrivalled in the world. Greater prosperity has also made people far more interested in the promotion and preservation of good health, a movement in which I am proud to have played a part.

You first appointed me as Parliamentary Private Secretary to Sir Keith (now Lord) Joseph at the Department of Education and Science. Since then, I have served as a Minister under three

Secretaries of State – Norman Fowler, John Moore and Kenneth Clarke – and would like to put on record my admiration for all of them, and appreciation of their help and guidance.

Finally, my thanks to you personally, for your encouragement, for your wisdom and courage, and for all you are doing for our country. I remain a firm and committed supporter of the Conservative Party and this government and look forward to further successes in the years to come.

Margaret Thatcher to Edwina Currie:

I have received your letter today with great personal sadness. It has, I know, been a very difficult time and I fully understand your reasons for resigning.

We shall miss the great energy and enthusiasm you have brought to all your work both for the government and for the party in the country. No one could have worked harder or more loyally, not only for your own department but in support of government policy as a whole.

At the Department of Health, you have made a tremendous contribution, among other things, in making all of us realize that better health is not just the responsibility of doctors and nurses but that so much depends on the way we look after ourselves and our families.

In the country you have been tireless in promoting our cause. Locally, you helped to achieve notable successes in Derbyshire where most recently we won control of Derby City Council.

I know that you will remain a staunch supporter for everything we are trying to do. We shall continue to work together for what we both believe in.

Chronology of Events
Mentioned in this Book

10 September 1986	EC appointed Parliamentary Under-Secretary of State for Health
20 September 1986	Keatinge's study of the elderly residents of two housing schemes during the cold spell of January 1986, published in the *BMJ*
24 September 1986	Visit to Newcastle
6 October 1986	Granada 'World in Action' follow-up to Newcastle speech
7–10 October 1986	Conservative Party Conference
25 October 1986	*BMJ* article on declining heart disease in Finland
28 October 1986	Health Education Council launches 'Your Right to be Warm' aimed at those working with the elderly
30 October 1986	Esther Rantzen's TV programme 'Childwatch' on child sexual abuse
30 October 1986	'Childline' set up
4 November 1986	Sub-committee known as H(A) set up under the chairmanship of Lord Whitelaw to tackle the AIDS problem
7 November 1986	Crown Immunity for hospital kitchens removed
18 November 1986	EC attends her first meeting of a Ministerial Group on the Misuse of Drugs (MGMD)

271

21 November 1986	First House of Commons AIDS debate
26 November 1986	Sir Donald Acheson reports 500 known cases of AIDS and an estimated 25,000 people infected with the HIV virus
28 November 1986	Sir Patrick Forrest's report on breast cancer screening received by government
9 December 1986	Women's National Cancer Control Campaign lunch
11 December 1986	James Anderton, Chief Constable of Greater Manchester, makes a controversial speech at an AIDS seminar in Manchester
End December 1986	610 cases of AIDS in the UK, of which 293 had died
1 January 1987	Dr Marietta Higgs starts work in Middlesbrough
From 12 January 1987	23 million government AIDS leaflets delivered to households throughout Britain
19 January 1987	EC visits 'down and outs' in London (*see* Chapter 8)
19 January 1987	Andrew Irving Associates warns MGMD about increased use of cocaine, drug cocktails and under-age drinking
3 February 1987	'Iceberg' AIDS advertisement appears on television for the first time
25 February 1987	Opposition day debate on the government's priorities for the elderly
25 February 1987	Norman Fowler announces breast-screening programme and the extension of cervical cancer screening to young women
27 February 1987	'First AIDS' television programme transmitted by LWT
27 February 1987	First Department of Health circular on terminal care issued

Chronology of Events Mentioned in this Book

7 March 1987	World Immunization Day: Baroness Trumpington, Parliamentary Secretary at DHSS, announces the introduction of a new triple vaccine
12 March 1987	'No Smoking Day' described as the most cost-effective health promotion campaign in the world
13 March 1987	Independent Scientific Committee on Smoking and Health (Froggatt Committee) Interim Statement on passive smoking
16 March 1987	MAFF bulletin reports on National Food Survey for the last quarter of 1986 showing the consumption of low cholesterol and 'healthy' foods up, and high cholesterol and 'unhealthy' foods down
Spring 1987	Ministers considering third annual drugs advertising campaign. Drugs and AIDS campaigns merged – both run by the advertising agency TBWA
22 April 1987	£2.5 million LAYH Campaign launched by Norman Fowler
28 April 1987	David Ashby MP sponsors exhibition and demonstration of cholesterol testing in Upper Waiting Hall, House of Commons
1 May 1987	Within one week, 19 children admitted to Marietta Higgs' hospital in Middlesbrough and diagnosed as being sexually abused
Mid-1987	About 3 in every 100 men and 2 in every 100 women attending sexually transmitted disease clinics found to be HIV positive
7 June 1987	General Election. Conservatives returned with a majority of 101. In the reshuffle following the General Election, John Moore becomes Secretary of State, DHSS
June 1987	In eight weeks from 1 May, nearly 100 children admitted to hospital in Middlesbrough and diagnosed as victims of sexual abuse

273

2 July 1987	Prime Minister invited 'Childline' to a reception at 10 Downing Street
8 July 1987	European Court of Human Rights found against the Department of Health over parental access to children in care
9 July 1987	Inquiry into child sexual abuse in Cleveland announced (Butler-Sloss Inquiry)
15 July 1987	Speech launching first summer drinking campaign with Peter Bottomley, Parliamentary Under-Secretary, Department of Transport
2 September 1987	John Moore launches 'Don't Inject AIDS' (anti-drugs/AIDS) campaign
15 September 1987	John Moore announces campaign on keeping the elderly warm throughout the winter months
17 September 1987	EC visits Scandinavia
18 September 1987	Douglas Hurd announces the formation of Ministerial Group on Alcohol Misuse (MGAM)
23 October 1987	Debate on prevention of disease and promotion of good health, House of Commons
23 October 1987	HEA takes over public education on AIDS
3 November 1987	First meeting of MGAM (Wakeham Committee)
17 November 1987	Launch of first government campaign directed at helping the elderly keep warm in winter
25 November 1987	White Paper 'Promoting Better Health' published
16 December 1987	Stuart Bell was final witness to the Butler-Sloss Inquiry which had sat for 74 days
End December 1987	1227 cases of AIDS in the UK, of which 697 had died
January 1988– March 1988	Health and Medicine Bill in Committee

Chronology of Events Mentioned in this Book

26 January 1988	Princess Royal opens first WHO summit conference on AIDS in London
January 1988	Committee on the Safety of Medicines: Bulletin on tranquillizers
9 March 1988	No Smoking Day
10 March 1988	Dr Anna McCormick, of Public Health Laboratory Service, reports that deaths from AIDS amongst young men were really twice as high as reported
15 March 1988	Chancellor abolishes the minimum duty charge on beer in his Spring Budget
23 March 1988	Independent Committee on Smoking and Health, 4th Report (Froggatt Committee) on passive smoking published with government response
24 March 1988	EC appears on 'This Week' programme, commenting on increasing affluence of some pensioners
26 March 1988	Private Patients Plan announces change in rules to allow comprehensive health cover for over 65s
29 March 1988	Advisory Council on the Misuse of Drugs publishes report on AIDS and drug misusers, saying that AIDS is a bigger health risk than drugs
31 March 1988	Interview given by EC for the May 1988 issue of *Family Circle* makes national headlines with the comment 'Don't screw around and don't smoke.'
22 April 1988	EC makes 'woopies' speech
2 May 1988	Richard Peto speaks to private seminar at the Department of Health on cholesterol and its role in heart disease
18 May 1988	All District Health Authorities in England have computerized cervical cancer screening systems

10 June 1988	Debate on Women's Health, House of Commons, in which EC announces £100,000 grant for breastfeeding campaign
22 June 1988	DHSS Conference on Women's Health, House of Commons
6 July 1988	Publication of Butler–Sloss report on child sexual abuse in Cleveland
23 July 1988	Government reshuffle: DHSS split in two. Kenneth Clarke becomes Secretary of State for Health. David Mellor appointed Minister of State
27 July 1988	OPCS five-yearly report on breastfeeding reports breastfeeding becoming less popular
29 July 1988	Government warning to NHS about the use of raw shell eggs
26 August 1988	Chief Medical Officer issues general public health warning about the consumption of raw eggs
15 September 1988	Announcement that Childline awarded regular grant of £100,000 per year
20 September 1988	Meeting of Breast Care and Mastectomy Association; EC speech on consent forms
21 September 1988	Health Day in Reading at which EC makes 'woolly hats' speech
26 September 1988	New code issued for advertising of alcohol
3 October 1988	Launch of triple vaccine for measles, mumps and rubella
5 October 1988	Draft DHSS circular 'The Welfare of Children in hospital' published
11–14 October 1988	Conservative Party Conference
3 November 1988	Visit to Bethlem Royal Hospital, London
9 November 1988	EC announces £70,000 grant for telephone helpline for tranquillizer victims

Chronology of Events Mentioned in this Book

14 November 1988	800,000 doses of triple vaccine have been distributed
End November 1988	Over 500 salmonella cases per week reported to laboratories
2 December 1988	Welsh Public Health Laboratory Service report in *The Lancet* on *S. enteritidis*
3 December 1988	Salmonella interview with ITN
16 December 1988	EC resigns
End December 1988	1982 cases of AIDS in the UK, of which 1059 have died
8 February 1989	EC gives evidence to Select Committee on Agriculture
1 March 1989	Select Committee on Agriculture report published

Index